3

WITHDRAWN

THE JUDGE

THE JUDGE

PATRICK DEVLIN
Fellow of the British Academy

Oxford New York Toronto Melbourne

OXFORD UNIVERSITY PRESS

1979

Oxford University Press, Walton Street, Oxford OX2 6DP

OXFORD LONDON GLASGOW
NEW YORK TORONTO MELBOURNE WELLINGTON
KUALA LUMPUR SINGAPORE JAKARTA HONG KONG TOKYO
DELHI BOMBAY CALCUTTA MADRAS KARACHI
NAIROBI DAR ES SALAAM CAPE TOWN

© *Patrick Devlin 1979*

British Library Cataloguing in Publication Data

Devlin, Patrick Arthur, *Baron Devlin*
    The judge
    1. Judges—England
    I. Title
    347'.42'014   KD7285   78-41201
    ISBN 0-19-215949-6

*Printed in Great Britain by
Butler & Tanner Ltd., Frome and London*

Preface

INVITATIONS to deliver half a dozen lectures or addresses within what is for me a short space of time, 1975 to 1978, have stimulated me to put together some thoughts on different aspects of the same subject, the English Judge. More accurately described, they are thoughts on different facets of a single aspect, which is the place of the judge in the political life of the country. What part does he play in the government[1] of it? What service does he give to the community? This is an aspect of the judicial function which at points comes closer to the study of political science than to the study of law. So I have tried to avoid—or at the least to explain—legal technicalities.

The first chapter contains the lecture which started off this line of thought. Should judges be lawmakers, law reformers, and even social reformers? In the exercise of their craft they must be handymen, but I do not think that they should aim higher. It is their job to apply the law and they must try to make it fit; but new suits and new fashions should be designed by legislators. In this respect English judges seem to differ from American.[2]

What is in the first chapter is an exact reproduction.[3] From then on I begin, conscious of a theme and unwilling to restrict its expression to the customary hour in the lecture-room, to expand on what was orally delivered, sometimes with thoughts whose formulation time forbade and sometimes with additions to give continuity with other lectures, completed

[1] I do not mean 'government' in the narrow sense of the executive; likewise, I use the word 'political' in its broadest sense.

[2] I have since taken these thoughts a little further in an article on Professor Berger's *Government by Judiciary*, a critical study of the Warren Court, and Professor Griffith's *Politics of the English Judiciary*; see 'Judges, Government and Politics', *Modern Law Review*, Sept. 1978.

[3] It has already been printed as 'Judges and Lawmakers' in the *Modern Law Review*, Jan. 1976.

or yet to come. Sometimes I have frankly digressed, hoping that my readers will be interested generally in the workings of the judiciary whether or not they come under the chapter heading.

Digressions are most frequent in the second chapter, which begins by asking whether judges should be penologists and answers that they should not. I affirm that justice means retribution and nothing else. Vindictiveness is the emotional outflow of retribution and justice has no concern with that. But it is concerned with the measurement of deserts. The point was put lucidly and simply by the Vicar of Longton in Lancashire in a letter to *The Times*, from which with his permission I quote.

Firstly, far from pretending that retribution should have no place in our penal system, Mr Levin should recognize that it is logically impossible to remove it. If it were removed, all punishment would be rendered unjust. What could be more immoral than to inflict imprisonment on a criminal for the sake of deterring others if he does not *deserve* it? Or would it be justified to subject him to a compulsory attempt at reform which includes a denial of liberty unless, again, he *deserves* it?[1]

Reform and rehabilitation, where they are possible, are tasks for penologists. I seek a line whereby justice and penology may be practically divided, each at work within its own province, instead of being assimilated. To make a judge a penologist would be to make him an expert in a subject other than the law. Thus I am led on to consider the function of the English judge as the non-expert, the non-specialist, the expounder of the common sense, the substitute for the jury.

The second part of this chapter considers the limitations of a working paper. Am I wrong in thinking that the working party was invented by Sir Stafford Cripps as a thoroughly modern, almost proletarian, roll-up-your-shirtsleeves alternative to the starchy meditations of the Royal Commission? As an instrument for effecting improvements to a running machine it is excellent. But its place is in the workshop, not in the designing-room. It is a most unsuitable instrument of planning for institutional change, which is what would be meant by the training of judges in penology (or in anything else) as the Paper recommends. An examination of what the Paper overlooks illustrates the character of the English judge.

In particular, what effect would the special training of judges have on the relationship of the Bench with the Bar? Would it not be bound to produce the inquisitorial judge? This leads to the third chapter, which considers the English judge in his traditional place as the president of or arbiter at the trial. In this chapter I compare the adversary and the inquisitorial systems and describe the pressures which are already pushing our procedures

[1] The Revd. A. M. Roff in *The Times*, 24 Dec. 1977.

towards the latter: sheer cost in the case of civil procedure and in the case
of criminal the weakness of our pre-trial processes, at present under examination by a Royal Commission. I say 'already' because we have yet to
meet the attractions of the European system.

The fourth chapter tackles a question which nags at the conscience of
every judge and, indeed, of every practising lawyer. To what extent does
the law prevent the judge from doing justice in the individual case? This
is the conflict between justice according to law and the aequum et bonum.
I explore the unadvertised entries through which the aequum et bonum can,
if it bears itself humbly, walk into the legal process. But I do not, I hope,
exaggerate the differences between the two and I come back, especially in
the last lecture, to the need for the law.

The fifth chapter is on the judge and the jury. It seems to me, though
inevitably the most technical, to be also the most topical. For a long time
in our constitutional life we have been trying to find all the practical answers
to the question of how best to govern with the consent of the governed,
and some of them still elude us. Recently in our industrial life we have begun
to look for the answer to the question of how to manage with the consent
of the managed. We could benefit from a comparative study of the solutions
found for both these problems in the evolution of the jury. While in politics
we entrust power to the governors under remote control by the governed,
in criminal justice we entrust power to the jury under the close control of
the judge. The judge manages the trial; to a considerable extent he manages
the jury too; but the sovereign power of acquittal resides in the jury.

The practical results on trial by jury of the House of Lords decision in
Stonehouse v. *D.P.P.* in 1977 are negligible, a curious tailpiece to the fanciful
career of Mr. Stonehouse. Its theoretical results are of great significance,
ending a border warfare that had gone on for years over the boundaries of
the jury's power. It takes me back to the root of the sovereign power of
acquittal and to the extraordinary doctrine that the jury have the power,
but not the right, to override the law. How did this come about, in what
way can it be supposed to make legal sense, how does it work in practice?
This is the first part of the chapter.

The second part discusses a decision of the House of Lords given four
years earlier, *Stafford* v. *D.P.P.* Its consequence is the startling one that
men and women can now be kept in prison for serious crime otherwise than
upon the verdict of a jury. The way in which this has been brought about
is too complicated to be summarized here. It is a way that is open only in
the rare cases in which a verdict has been affected by the discovery of fresh
evidence. Notwithstanding that Parliament in 1964 provided for this situa-

tion by empowering the judges to order a new trial by jury, they have preferred in effect to conduct the new trial themselves. This is a major constitutional change which the law lords held to have been dictated to them
by a change of wording made in 1966 to a section of the original Criminal
Appeal Act of 1907. If it were the habit of their lordships sitting judicially
to glance at what they had said when sitting legislatively, none of them could
have supposed that in 1966 any substantial change was intended. But it is
not their habit and, strictly, it is not permitted. Because cases of fresh evidence are rare and because the abortive jury trial leaves behind it the husk
of a verdict to distract attention from what is really happening, the new doctrine has apparently caused no alarm. It does not, however, offer a durable
solution to the problems created by fresh evidence and has in particular led
to an unhappy result in the case of the murder of the Luton subpostmaster,
R. v. Cooper and McMahon, which has now been five times before the Court
of Appeal.

I do not know of any English judge who is against trial by jury, but I
know of some who like to keep its wings clipped. This no doubt is why
the perceptive Blackstone warned future generations, not so much against
open attacks on the jury, as against sappings and underminings and precedents begun in trifles. By those whose horizons are limited, trifles are easily
confused with technicalities.

It is not as a fence against great incursions upon our liberties, against
marches with bands playing and flags flying, that a bill of rights is so urgently
needed; it is to warn off strayers. The way to a temporary or partial sacrifice
of individual liberties, or even to a fundamental change in them, must not
be for ever blocked. But I would set across it a rock that administrators
could not squeeze past or judges unaided roll aside. It would be a rock that
only an explosive could move; and I would have the explosives kept in a
safe of which a Parliament, acting by convention as a true Parliament of
the nation and not as a pack whipped by the executive which itself may
be lashed by its tail, would hold the key.

The sixth lecture was occasioned by a dictum of Lord Chief Justice
Widgery which surprised me. He referred in 1976 to case law as fettering.
If it is treated with servility it can be fettering, but I do not think that our
system exalts servility. I compare the place of case law in the English system
with its place under some Continental systems and I enumerate the purposes
which I think it ought to serve. Should its grip on English law be relaxed:
did Lord Widgery mean more than this? There are other dicta of his—not-
ably his exhortation to appellate judges to go by the 'general feel' of the
case rather than by the evidence—which suggest that the aequum et bonum

may be destined to make deeper inroads into the criminal law than I should like to see.

If it does so, it will be because in 1966 the words 'unsafe or unsatisfactory' in relation to a conviction were substituted in the Criminal Appeal Act for 'unreasonable or cannot be supported having regard to the evidence'. It can happen in history—in legal history as well as in any other—that common-place words are inflated with the spirit of the hour and swollen into high significance. A change of phrase, which seemed negligible in 1966, has become symbolic of a change of attitude which may enable the judges of criminal appeals to push the jury's verdict into the background and get down themselves to the business of doing justice unshackled by precedents. Would this be a good thing?

Contents

I

The Judge as Lawmaker

IN recent years a number of pens have been put to paper to criticize the English judiciary for its torpidity. What is needed today, it is said, is a dynamic, or at least an activist, judiciary, ready and willing to develop the law to fit the changing times. The sloth of the British judges is contrasted with the zest of the American. Certainly no one who reads of the doings of the Warren Court in a book such as that by Professor Cox[1] can fail to be struck by its boldness. Professor Jaffe in his book *English and American Judges as Lawmakers*[2] compares in an attractive and balanced way the two judicial attitudes and gives his reasons for preferring the American.

Behind some of these ideas there seems to me to lurk an assumption too easily made that judging and lawmaking are much the same thing, that a good judge ought to be a good lawmaker, that the two activities call for the same qualities. I question this assumption and must therefore begin by distinguishing between judging and lawmaking.

First, lawmaking. I am not one of those who believe that the only function of law is to preserve the status quo. Rather I should say that law is the gate-keeper of the status quo. There is always a host of new ideas galloping around the outskirts of a society's thought. All of them seek admission but each must first win its spurs; the law at first resists, but will submit to a conqueror and become his servant. In a changing society (and free societies that are composed of two or more generations are always changing because it is their nature to do so) the law acts as a valve. New policies must gather strength before they can force an entry; when they are admitted and absorbed into the consensus, the legal system should expand to hold them, as also it should contract to squeeze out old policies which have lost the consensus they once obtained.

[1] Archibald Cox, *The Warren Court*, Harvard University Press, Cambridge, Mass., 1968.
[2] Clarendon Press, Oxford, 1969.

I have now used three words which are frequently employed in discussions of this sort—*consensus, activist, dynamic*. I must give each of them a sharper definition.

Alistair Cooke has written: 'When the people in power can neither keep the consent of the governed nor keep *down* the dissent of the governed, then there will be a blow-up.'[1] Adopting this aphorism one may say that the consensus in a community consists of those ideas which its members as a whole like or, if they dislike, will submit to—what is for one reason or another acceptable. By activist lawmaking I mean the business of keeping pace with change in the consensus. Dynamic or creative lawmaking is the use of the law to generate change in the consensus. A law that tried to impose an alien idea upon a free society would come to grief. But in a free society the progress of a new idea from the attraction of some sympathy to the support of an active minority, thence to the acquiescence of the majority, and finally to a consensus, is usually very slow. Since all men are not the ardent and enlightened beings that reformers would like them to be, a touch of the whip to hasten laggards can have a good result. Reformers are always anxious to try it and recently we have seen it used in this country with varying achievements. It is generally agreed that there was no consensus, probably not even a bare majority, for the abolition of capital punishment or the reformation of the laws against homosexuality. Nevertheless both changes were made and are now accepted; the latter change has surely helped to promote a more tolerant attitude to homosexuals. The law has likewise been used cautiously in the field of race relations with, I believe, some success; and not so cautiously in the field of industrial relations without success. To be successful the exercise has to be nicely judged; the *vis inertiae* must be calculated and hostility assessed in terms of the power to resist actively or passively; the ability to make this nice judgement belongs to the art of politics.

Of course I am not saying that there should be no legislation without consensus, nor am I concerned to offer an opinion about the wisdom of dynamic lawmaking. On the one hand it is said that government should offer leadership to a nation; on the other hand it is certain that a series of political misjudgements in the use of the law would diminish respect for it. My question is not about dynamic lawmaking but about whether the judiciary should be employed in it. It would seem to require a surer political touch than a judge is likely to have. Nevertheless there are demands for a creative judiciary to operate upon subjects which governments shirk. It is argued, for

---

[1] Alistair Cooke, *America*, B.B.C., London, 1973, p. 122.

example, that judges made the law of homicide and so ought to be ready to give a lead on such aspects of it as euthanasia and abortion.

So much for the moment on the lawmaker. What is the function of the judge? Professor Jaffe has a phrase for it—'the disinterested application of known law'.[1] He would put it perhaps as the minimal function. I should rank it as greater than that. It is at any rate what 90% or more of English judges—and I dare say also of all judges of all nationalities—are engaged in for 90% of their working lives. The social service which the judge renders to the community is the removal of a sense of injustice. To perform this service the essential quality which he needs is impartiality and next after that the appearance of impartiality. I put impartiality before the appearance of it simply because without the reality the appearance would not endure. In truth, within the context of service to the community the appearance is the more important of the two. The judge who gives the right judgment while appearing not to do so may be thrice blessed in heaven, but on earth he is no use at all.

A judge must be a very arrogant man (and so probably a bad judge) if he supposes that even on questions of fact he is always right. In a high percentage of cases he is, otherwise he would lose credibility. But there is an appreciable number in which, confronted with two conflicting stories and little else, he has to base his decision, mainly if not entirely, on his impression of the witnesses. In difficult cases he cannot be right every time; certainly he will not convince the losing party that he is right. The object of the process is not, however, to force the contender to submit to superior reasoning. It is to provide a civilized method of settling disputes. It is, as I have said, to remove a sense of injustice.

It is not the bare fact of physical injury or the loss of property that arouses a sense of injustice in a man—this may happen accidentally—it is the feeling that he has been wronged by another whom he cannot challenge or to whom he is forced to submit. It is the affront to his dignity which, if it is left unrelieved, will lead to disorder and, if others like him are similarly wronged, to social unrest. The most primitive means of relief—trial by battle or by ordeal or the duel—are better than none. In the world of nations, if I may venture on the parallel, we have in the twentieth century done away with trial by battle without substituting anything for it. By trial by battle in this context I mean the nineteenth-century concept of fighting between combatants only and in accordance with the Hague Conventions and the other laws of war. Since nuclear massacres are beyond the reach of most aggrieved per-

---

[1] Jaffe, op. cit., p. 13.

sons, they resort to terrorism—hijacking, kidnapping, and the plastic bomb.
We ought never to forget that judges and juries are the institutions which
secure us from comparable disorders within the nation and that their value
to the community is to be measured by the extent to which they do this
and not by the extent to which their judgments and verdicts are pleasing
to the critical eye.

Dr. Johnson observed that 'authority from personal respect has much
weight with most people, and often more than reasoning'.[1] Respect for office
is not so great as it was but respect for the person remains, which is why
in all walks of life so many inarticulate people are influential. A judgment
must be weighty, but weight, especially in questions of fact, is not given
solely by soundness of reasoning. It is the virtue of the English system that
from first to last the judge is exposed to the parties; they do not read the
judgment: they see and hear it being made and given.

This is why impartiality and the appearance of it are the supreme judicial
virtues. It is the verdict that matters, and if it is incorrupt, it is acceptable.
To be incorrupt it must bear the stamp of a fair trial. The judge who does
not appear impartial is as useless to the process as an umpire who allows
the trial by battle to be fouled or an augurer who tampers with the
entrails.

In the course of their work judges quite often dissociate themselves from
the law. They would like to decide otherwise, they hint, but the law does
not permit. They emphasize that it is as binding upon them as it is upon
litigants. If a judge leaves the law and makes his own decisions, even if in
substance they are just, he loses the protection of the law and sacrifices the
appearance of impartiality which is given by adherence to the law. He
expresses himself personally to the dissatisfied litigant and exposes himself
to criticism. But if the stroke is inflicted by the law, it leaves no sense of
individual injustice; the losing party is not a victim who has been singled
out; it is the same for everybody, he says. And how many a defeated litigant
has salved his wounds with the thought that the law is an ass!

So I am not distressed by the fact that at least nine-tenths of the judiciary
spends its life submerged in the disinterested application of known law. Indeed, to say that one-tenth rises above the waterline that is marked by notice
in the legal journals would probably be an exaggeration. The House of Lords
most of its time. But the Court of Appeal spends more than half its time
on the important task of reviewing on the written record the more difficult
decisions of fact. There is an occasional emergence of a judge of the High

[1] James Boswell, *The Life of Samuel Johnson*, J. M. Dent & Co., Everyman edition, London,
1906, Vol. I, p. 615.

Court. Circuit and county courts work in the depths where even the rays of the *Modern Law Review* penetrate only in a refracted glow.

The disinterested application of the law calls for many virtues, such as balance, patience, courtesy, andd detachment, which leave little room for the ardour of the creative reformer. I do not mean that there should be a demarcation or that judges should down tools whenever they meet a defect in the law. I shall consider later to what extent in such a situation a judge should be activist. But I am quite convinced that there should be no judicial dynamics.

So much for the nature and function of the judge. I return to the lawmaker and consider what, if anything, judges and lawmakers have in common.

The lawmaker takes an idea or a policy and turns it into law. For this he needs the ability to formulate, and a judge in common with any other trained lawyer should have that. Is the judge any different in this respect from a professor or a parliamentary draftsman? Yes, because he has experience of the administration of the law. So has the barrister and the solicitor, but it is an advantage to see it working from the Bench. So there is no reason why, given the policy, a judge should not be a good activist lawmaker. The question, to which I shall return, is whether he should be the complete lawmaker or whether he would not do better work in committee, pooling his judicial experience with the social, commercial, and administrative experience of others.

Let me repeat the distinction, since it may be one which is fresh, between activist and dynamic lawmaking. In activist lawmaking the idea is taken from the consensus and demands at most sympathy from the lawmaker. In dynamic lawmaking the idea is created outside the consensus and, before it is formulated, it has to be propagated. This needs more than sympathy: it needs enthusiasm. Enthusiasm is not and cannot be a judicial virtue. It means taking sides and, if a judge takes sides on such issues as homosexuality and capital punishment, he loses the appearance of impartiality and quite possibly, impartiality itself. In mercy-killing, for example, Professor Jaffe considers[1] that the judge might, after consulting the common ethic, allow the defence. But if one judge allows the defence, there will be others, perhaps many others, who will not. And those who outrun the consensus will not keep in line. Thus the law will suffer a serious loss of clarity and coherence.

All this seems to me so obvious that rather than elaborate upon it, I prefer to search for an explanation of how it can be that wise men apparently think

[1] Jaffe, op. cit., p. 13.

differently. I think it must be because the wise men and I do not start from
the same point. We do not take the same view of the function of the judge.
This is why I have stated my view at some length; and because it is important
I shall come back to it now by way of an examination of three factors which
I think have misled critics into devising too exalted a function for the English
judge and then blaming him for not discharging it. The first factor is the
historic role of the judiciary as lawmaker. The second is the shining example
of the Supreme Court of the United States. The third is a confusion between
social and personal justice.

As to the first, there is no doubt that historically judges did make law,
at least in the sense of formulating it. Even now when they are against innovation, they have never formally abrogated their powers; their attitude
is: 'We could if we would but we think it better not.' Most commentators
therefore start from the assumption that English judges *are* lawmakers and
that the real question is whether they should not make law with more verve
than they do. But as a matter of history did the English judges of the golden
age make law? They decided cases which in the commentaries and textbooks
were worked up into principles. The judges, as Lord Wright once put it
in an unexpectedly picturesque phrase, proceeded 'from case to case, like
the ancient Mediterranean mariners, hugging the coast from point to point
and avoiding the dangers of the open sea of system and science'.[1] Or as
Dr. Johnson, if I may quote him again, put it the other way round: 'The
more precedents there are, the less occasion is there for law; that is to say,
the less occasion is there for investigating principles.'[2] The golden age was
an age of precedent. Its judges were not rationalizers and, except in the devising of procedures, they were not innovators. They translated into law the
customs and the steady morality of their times. They did not design a new
machine capable of speeding ahead; they struggled with the aid of fictions
and bits of procedural string to keep the machine on the road. The appellate
courts were still in their infancy.

Today more is expected of the judges, at least of the appellate courts.
Lord Wright was himself one of the proponents of the modern appellate
judgment which surveys the whole field and seeks to order all that lies within
it. But at the same time as judgments are expanding, the sources seeking
to contribute to the formation of the law are multiplying. The golden age
was not an age of sociology. Judges extracted the law from below the surface
by primitive means. Today there are numerous mines being worked by
sociologists, by professional and trade bodies, and by those who are only

[1] The Study of Law' (1938) 54 L.Q.R. 185 at p. 186.
[2] Boswell, op. cit., Vol. I, p. 416.

half derisively called 'do-gooders', and the surface bubbles with ideas of what the law should be.

I come now to the second factor. There is no doubt that the Supreme Court has been dynamic. In three fields—racial desegregation, voting rights, and reform of criminal procedure—it has legislated where consensus was non-existent or at least doubtful. The distribution of legislative power between the Congress and the fifty States is such that national legislation on these subjects would be almost impossible to secure. The famous desegregation decision of 1954[1] helped to avert a destructive explosion. The Supreme Court has almost from its inception been an organ of government. Professor Cox endorses as up to date de Tocqueville's observation that hardly a political question arises in the United States that is not converted into a legal question and taken to the courts for decision.[2] Consequently the Supreme Court, a Council of Wise Men as it is sometimes called, is and has to be as much political as judicial in its character. Few of its members come to it with judicial experience and many of them have political experience; the political beliefs and philosophy of the candidate are always highly relevant.

The Supreme Court like the vines of France is not for transplantation. The soil and climate in which it flourishes are not those of Britain; the hands that tend it have now like the Bordeaux vignerons acquired unique skills. Moreover, it needs two things which Britain has not got: first, a Constitution as a source of life; second, a legislative vacuum for it to fill. In a unitary as distinct from a federal state there is no such vacuum.

I shall not presume to assess the value of the Supreme Court to the United States. But it is surely wise to remember that there have in the past been periods of slump, that the Court may now be coming to the end of a progressive boom, and that for the boom years there may yet be a price to be paid. Professor Cox has written:

The gains of decisions advancing social justice are evident when they are rendered; any costs in the erosion of the power of law to command consent are postponed until the loss accumulates.[3]

It must be remembered too that institutions can just as easily be reactionary as progressive and that half a century ago the progressives were preaching the doctrine of judicial restraint. Indeed, Justice Frankfurter, for whom principles did not blow hot and cold, never lost his attachment to judicial restraint. But usually enthusiasm for an institution coincides with enthusiasm for what it is doing. I have yet to meet an American who says of the

[1] *Brown* v. *Board of Education*, 357 U.S. 483.
[2] Op. cit., p. 1.   [3] ib., p. 23.

Supreme Court, 'I disapprove of what you say, but I will defend to the death your right to say it.'

The third factor I have mentioned, the confusion between social and personal justice, is caused by an ambiguity in the use of the word 'justice'. We do not have different words for what, to use legal terminology, I might call justice *in rem* and justice *in personam*. We can use the word to mean social justice and then we say that a law is just if it conforms to some social principle, such as that all men are equal; this is justice *in rem*. We use it also to mean justice *in personam*, that is, between parties to a dispute. Personal justice in a community is dependent on the existence of laws and its exercise consists in the just administration of them. Social justice is above the law; it is the body of principles with which the law should conform. Social justice guides the lawmaker: the law guides the judge. Judges are not concerned with social justice, or rather they need not be more concerned with it than a good citizen should be; they are not professionally concerned. It might be dangerous if they were. They might not administer the law fairly if they were constantly questioning its justice or agitating their minds about its improvement.

A confusion between social and personal justice must be one of the reasons why judges are supposed to be natural lawmakers. It can only be some confusion of thought that leads intelligent progressives to imagine that the British judiciary could ever be made a pliable instrument of social reform according to their ideas. There are progressives who, like moths outside a lighted window, are irresistibly attracted by what they see within as the vast unused potentiality of judicial lawmaking. They would surmount the obstacle of a reactionary judiciary by reconstructing it, diluting the alleged potency of its public-school spirit, and imposing some regimen, as yet unprescribed in detail, upon the daily lives of judges which would result in their becoming less remote. I do not believe that measures of this sort would make a pennyworth of difference. Let the practice of the law be opened up by all means and let the judiciary be composed of the best that the practice of the law can produce. You will find, I am sure, that judges will still be of the same type whether they come from major or from minor public schools, grammar schools, or comprehensives, and whether they like to spend their leisure in a library or in a club. They will all be the type of men—there will be exceptions of course, but the type—who do not seriously question the status quo, men whose ambition it is to serve the law and not to be its master. You can see this already at the university where students in the law faculties all over the world are nearly always on the right while those in sociology are on the left. Lawyers are not naturally interested in social reform, any more than policemen are or soldiers. Without policemen society would be threatened from within, and without soldiers from without. Judges too are necessary to society, especially in a time of social change. For change, in the measure of its beneficence to the many, causes hardship and displacement to the few. It is essential to the stability of society that those whom change hurts should be able to count on even-handed justice calmly dispensed, not driven forward by the agents of change.

It is this even-handedness which is the chief characteristic of the British judiciary and it is almost beyond price. If it has to be paid for in impersonality and remoteness, the bargain is still a good one. It is British justice rather than English or Scots law that has been the gift of British lawyers to the world. You cannot visit the countries of the Commonwealth without realizing that. Those who brought the gift to these countries were the second-best, for naturally the best stayed at home; their social contribution to the countries in which they served was nil; they were, if you like, the judicial blimps. But it is the handiwork of the blimps that has survived. In our own country the reputation of the judiciary for independence and impartiality is a national asset of such richness that one government after another tries to plunder it. This is a danger about which the judiciary itself has been too easy-going. To break up the asset so as to ease the parturition of judicial creativity, an embryo with a doubtful future, would be a calamity. The asset which I would deny to governments I would deny also to social reformers.

I have now made it plain that I am firmly opposed to judicial creativity or dynamism as I have defined it, that is, of judicial operations in advance of the consensus. The limit of the consensus is not a line that is clearly marked, but I can make certain what would otherwise be uncertain by saying that a judge who is in any doubt about the support of the consensus should not advance at all. This, however, leaves open quite a large field for judicial activity. In determining its extent it is necessary to distinguish between common law and statute law. This is because the requirement of consensus affects differently the two types of law. The public is not interested in the common law as a whole. When it becomes interested in any particular section of it, it calls for a statute; the rest it leaves to the judges. The consensus is expressed in a general warrant for judicial lawmaking. This warrant is an informal and rather negative one, amounting to a willingness to let the judges get on with their traditional work on two conditions—first, that they do it in the traditional way, i.e. in accordance with precedent, and second, that parliamentary interference should be regarded as unobjectionable.

In relation to statute law, by contrast, there can be no general warrant authorizing the judges to do anything except interpret and apply. Beyond that the support of the consensus depends on the subject-matter of each particular statute. When the consensus behind the purpose of a statute is clear and strong, a judge could perhaps risk—later on I shall stress the risk— going beyond interpretation towards development. But remember that to be effective a statute does not need to have consensus; it could be extremely controversial. Then a judge must be very cautious about any extension of the written word and may have to decide the case 'in typical English judicial fashion', as Professor Jaffe remarked[1] of the decision in *Rookes* v. *Barnard*,[2] treating 'the matter as an exercise in abstract logic'. It is not, I believe, that an English judge is peculiarly fond of abstract logic, but he prefers it to taking sides.

In sum, in the common law there is a general warrant for judicial lawmaking; in statute law there is not. In the common law development is permitted, if not expected; in statute law there must be at least a presumption that Parliament has on the topic it is dealing with said all that it wanted to say.

I shall now consider judicial activism in the common law and the principal objections that are taken against it. The first is that, since judges are not representative, it is undemocratic. This is an objection that can rightly be taken against creativity but not against activism as I have defined it; if it is the essence of activism that it operates within the consensus, the operation cannot be undemocratic. But let us look more closely at what operating within the consensus means and at what conditions must be fulfilled. The subject-matter of the case must either be one (which I shall put in the first category) on which the public is indifferent, i.e. willing to leave to the judges, or one (in the second category) in which the view of the public is all one way; it must not be one (in the third category) on which, though it is within the province of the common law, the public holds differing views.

Mercy-killing, which I have already mentioned, is an obvious example from the third category. It is a highly controversial subject discussed by intelligent laymen more closely than by lawyers. It could not give satisfaction to the public if a solution were to be found by the use of the blunt instrument of a decision in a particular case, which depended on the composition of the court. In short, Professor Jaffe and others who argue in favour of judicial participation in the controversy are arguing in favour of judicial creativity; and what I have just written is really part of the case against that.

Now take an example from the opposite category, the second. Should a man recover damages from a friend who has given bed and breakfast to his deserting wife? This is a question on which laymen would want to be heard.

[1] Op. cit., p. 91.   [2] [1964] A.C. 1129.

They would answer it with a loud and universal No, in which the judiciary, unless inhibited by eighteenth-century precedent, would join. Activism in this category is within the true tradition of judicial lawmaking—putting the consensus into the law.

In between there is the large category, the first, in which the inclination of the layman is to leave it to the judges. Should a man receive damages from the manufacturers as well as from the seller of defective goods? The decision in *Donoghue* v. *Stevenson*,[1] revolutionary in the legal world, was hardly noticed outside it. *Rookes* v. *Barnard*[2] on punitive damages created a legal commotion surfacing in the Court of Appeal in what in less exalted circles would have been called a 'demo', but it left the public cold.

The objection which I have just been considering—that judicial lawmaking is unacceptable because undemocratic—is the only one which could have been fatal, since, Britain being a democracy, it would have gone to the root of the power. There are other objections which taken together are very formidable, but they are not total. I call them objections, but they are really factors which, to the extent to which they have to be accepted, impose such restrictions on the power as to make the judge by comparison with legislatures and rule-making bodies a crippled lawmaker. Let us see what these objections are.

There is the objection of retroactivity. The judge can change the law only by applying to the decision of a case a law different from that in force at the time the legal process in that case was initiated. I think that this objection can be exaggerated. A judge-made change in the law rarely comes out of a blue sky. Rumblings from Olympus in the form of obiter dicta will give warning of unsettled weather. Unsettled weather is itself of course bound to cause uncertainty, but inevitably it precedes the solution of every difficult question of law.

Nevertheless the objection unexaggerated is a strong one. If it does become necessary to choose between a change in the law and a real injustice caused by retroactivity in the case at bar, surely the choice must be against change in the law; that puts a limit on judicial activism. Moreover, for the method to work fairly, there should be some provision for the payment out of public funds for judicial lawmaking. This is a point which attracts little attention although the extent to which the private citizen has to pay for public lawmaking is already intolerable.[3]

[1] [1932] A.C. 562.
[2] [1964] A.C. 1129, discussed in *Broome* v. *Cassell* [1971] 2 Q.B. 354.
[3] See on this point what was said by Hailsham L.C. in *Cassell* v. *Broome* [1972] A.C. 1027 at 1053–5.

Courts in the United States have begun to circumvent retroactivity by the device of deciding the case before them according to the old law while declaring that in future the new law will prevail; or they may determine with what measure of retroactivity a new rule is to be enforced. This device has attracted the cautious attention of the House of Lords.[1] I do not like it. It crosses the Rubicon that divides the judicial and the legislative powers. It turns judges into undisguised legislators. It is facile to think that it is always better to throw off disguises. The need for disguise hampers activity and so restricts the power. Paddling across the Rubicon by individuals in disguise who will be sent back if they proclaim themselves is very different from the bridging of the river by an army in uniform and with bands playing. If judges can make law otherwise than by a decision in the case at bar, why do they wait for a case? Prevention is better than cure, so why should they not, when they see a troublesome point looming up, meet and decide how best to deal with it? Judicial lawmaking is at present, as Professor Jaffe phrases it,[2] 'a by-product of an *ad hoc* decision or process'. That this is so is of course in itself one of the objections to judicial lawmaking. Dependent as it is upon the willingness of individuals to litigate, it is casual and spasmodic. But to remove the tie with the *ad hoc* process would be to make a profound constitutional change with incalculable consequences. What is the business of a court of law? To make law or to do justice according to law? This question should be given a clean answer. If the law and justice of the case require the court to give a decision which its members think will not make good law for the future, I think that the court should give the just decision and refer the future to a lawmaking body.

However, the objection that carries most weight with me is simply that judges by themselves—sitting in banc as it were—are not as a body the complete lawmaker and it is unreasonable to expect that they should be. They can be excellent contributors and formulators, as is shown by the services they have rendered on law revision committees. But the making of law, even if it be only 'lawyers' law', requires much more than a knowledge of existing law and of its administration. Already those appellate courts which are extending the reach of their judgments beyond the facts of the case are beginning to turn themselves into law revision committees working perforce without the aids which such committees have. The aid which the judge has under the English system is limited by the assumption that all he has to do is to try the case. It consists entirely of the argument of counsel; there are no law clerks; personal research is not expected and no time is allowed for

[1] *R. v. National Insurance Commissioners, ex p. Hudson* [1972] A.C. 914 at 1015 and 1026.
[2] Op. cit., p. 35.

it. There is a limit to what counsel can do in time that is paid for by their clients; litigants are interested in the decision of their case and not in the development of the law. The persons who may be interested in that are not represented. Yet there are many people who would like to be heard on such questions as liability for careless misstatement or for punitive damages and who could speak adequately through professional bodies. New law ought not to be made until after consultation with the representatives of those who will be concerned with it. Methods of achieving this have been admirably developed by the Law Commission.

This is in my opinion the best way of lawmaking and I hope to see it greatly extended. But until it is in general use we cannot dispense with the second-best. The strongest argument for judicial activism is not that it is the best method of law reform but that, as things stand, it is in a large area of the law the only method. The judges who made the common law must not abrogate altogether their responsibility for keeping it abreast of the times. Of course they can protest, as they frequently do, that it is for Parliament to change the law. But these protestations ring hollow when Parliament has said, as loudly as total silence can say it, that it intends to do nothing at all.

Let me take one example. Ideas about sexual behaviour have recently changed with abnormal rapidity and the common law is quite out of touch. Parliament is unlikely to do anything about it and, if the more stringent rules are administered as they stand, the fabric of the law will be damaged. Take the rule which prevents a landlord recovering rent from a couple whom he knows to be living in sin. Many people would still wish to see the rule applied to prostitution and promiscuity. Some people also regard living out of wedlock as socially undesirable. But it is unreasonable now to treat every such association with abhorrence of the *ex turpi causa* type and for the law to insist that all unmarried couples should either be ejected or live rent-free. Topics of this sort are not the stuff that judicial dynamism is made of, but they offer scope for much useful modernization of the type that is now being undertaken by the State courts in America. From what I have read I doubt if the State courts, which resemble English courts more closely than the Federal, have gone much further than modernization. The example of their activity most frequently given is their destruction of immunities earlier granted by the common law, e.g. the exemption of charitable or non-profitmaking bodies, such as hospitals, from liability for negligence.[1] I can see no reason why what the judges originally granted, their mandate then being the general approval of the times, they should not withdraw when

[1] Jaffe, op. cit., pp. 4, 34, and 50.

they consider that the general approval no longer exists; if they miscalculate, Parliament can intervene just as it could have intervened initially if they were wrong in the first instance. The doctrine of common employment in England, for example, was an invention of the courts and it surely would not have been wrong for them to put an end to it when the spirit that animated it was dead. Instead they left it as a nerveless tooth which could still bite even when in decay. What stood in the way of this and other euthanasian practices was Lord Halsbury's prohibition, which prevailed from 1898 to 1966, against the House of Lords moving with the times. This rule was utterly antagonistic to the spirit of the common law. Now that the House has been set free the removal of obsolete law should be the first duty of judicial activism.

The rules of evidence and of procedure I would treat as a special subject. Here I think (though my thought, I fear, is now unlikely to fructify) that it is the duty of the judiciary to take full charge of the common law. While Parliament must have the last word, I should like to see it established as a convention that it did not as a rule intervene. At least in the first instance any change should reflect the view of the judiciary; the public is entitled to know how the judges would order their affairs—for the administration of justice is their affair—before the legislature lays down the law.[1] I agree with the views of the minority in *Myers* v. *D.P.P.*,[2] the case in which the House of Lords considered the hearsay rule. But I am touching now on a subject which needs a paper on its own—the relationship between the courts, the legislature, and the executive.

I turn now to statute law. Judges, I have accepted, have a responsibility for the common law, but in my opinion they have none for statute law; their duty is simply to interpret and apply it and not to obstruct. I remain unconvinced that there is anything basically wrong with the rule of construction that words in a statute should be given their natural and ordinary meaning. The rule does not insist on a literal interpretation or require the construction of a statute without regard to its manifest purpose. There should be, as Lord Diplock has said,[3] 'a purposive approach to the Act as a whole to ascertain the social ends it was intended to achieve and the practical means by which it was expected to achieve them'. But in the end the words must be taken to mean what they say and not what their interpreter would like them to say; the statute is the master and not the servant of the judgment.

[1] There is a statutory warranty for this; see p. 53.　　　　[2] [1965] A.C. 1001.
[3] *R.* v. *National Insurance Commissioners* [1972] A.C. 914 at 1005.

In the past judges have been obstructive. But the source of the obstruction, it is very important to note, has been the refusal of judges to act on the ordinary meaning of words. They looked for the philosophy behind the Act and what they found was a Victorian Bill of Rights, favouring (subject to the observance of the accepted standards of morality) the liberty of the individual, the freedom of contract, and the sacredness of property, and which was highly suspicious of taxation. If the Act interfered with these notions, the judges tended either to assume that it could not mean what it said or to minimize the interference by giving the intrusive words the narrowest possible construction, even to the point of pedantry.

No doubt judges, like any other body of elderly men who have lived on the whole unadventurous lives, tend to be old-fashioned in their ideas. This is a fact of nature which reformers must accept. It is silly to invite the older generation to make free with Acts of Parliament and then to abuse them if the results are unpleasing to advanced thinkers. Not that everything can always be blamed on the conservatism of judges. Statues are not philosophical treatises and the philosophy behind them, if there is one, is often half-baked. Those who want judges to search for meanings beyond words should first examine some case histories. Let me give you one which recently came to my notice and which, I can assure you, is quite typical.

The Harbours, Docks and Piers Clauses Act 1847 is not a statute infused with a high social purpose, but it is a good example of the sort of statute with which judges habitually deal. Section 74 provides that any damage done by a vessel to a harbour, dock, or pier shall be paid for by the owner of the vessel; in order to make sure that there should be no judicial quibbling about what is a vessel, the statute says 'every vessel or float of timber', but otherwise it is written in normal English. Yet when a case of damage arose at Durham Assizes in 1875, only two out of the seven judges who ultimately had to consider the case could bring themselves to believe that the statute meant what it said and actually imposed absolute liability. Note that the majority judges were taking the liberal view. The common law at that time was seeking to free itself from primitive notions of absolute liability and was at the commencement of a great development in the law of negligence; surely the Act must be made to fit in with the rational idea that liability followed upon fault.

This decision of the House of Lords in *River Wear Commissioners* v. *Adamson*[1] is one of quite a number of its sort which trouble the law of England. The point I want to take from it is that the departure from the natural and ordinary meaning of words usually leads to confusion. Five

[1] (1877) 2 App. Cas. 743.

judges are no more likely to agree than five philosophers upon the philosophy
behind an Act of Parliament and five different judges are likely to have five
different ideas about the right escape route from the prison of the text. The
House of Lords in the *River Wear* case certainly decided that section 74
should not be given its literal meaning. But beyond that, and in spite of
several judicial inquests at the highest level, the courts have not yet arrived
at any general agreement about what section 74 does mean. After a century
it is still fermenting in judicial thought. One of its legacies recently split
the High Court of Australia three to two.[1]

Today we should have no difficulty with section 74. Its language fits in
nicely with the new philosophy that negligence does not matter and that
the statutory object in such a case is simply to make clear who is to take
out the insurance policy. Perhaps Parliament in 1847 had a prophetic
glimpse of the twentieth-century philosophy, but it is far more likely that
it had no philosophical thoughts at all.

So while in theory there is room for judicial activism in the development
of a statute when the consensus is clear, I doubt whether in practice it would
be productive. The judicial expansion of statutes from the Statute of Frauds
onwards has not usually been successful. It would be surprising if it had
been. You cannot hope for effective co-operation between bodies which are
not expected to converse with each other. 'The organs of government are
partners in the enterprise of lawmaking,' Professor Jaffe writes,[2] 'courts and
legislatures are in the law business together.' He refers to the 'potentiality'
of a fruitful partnership and interaction between them. If this is meant as
more than metaphorical, ways and means as yet unmentioned will have to
be devised for effectuating the joint enterprise; one partner cannot be left
guessing about what the other is doing and why. In a country such as the
United States in which the legislature and the executive are independent
of each other, it would perhaps be possible, granted some considerable re-
laxation in the doctrine of the separation of powers, to have legislators and
judges working together in a communion which did not imperil essential
freedoms. In a country like Britain it would be impossible. For the British
Parliament, while it acts as an independent check on legislation brought forward by the executive, is not an independent legislature. Legislation in Britain is introduced by the executive and, when it has been enacted at the
behest of the executive, is frequently implemented by ministerial regulation.
Thus the executive commands both the principle and the detail of the statute. Is the judge in the case to go into partnership with the government

[1] *Geelong Harbour Trust Commissioners* v. *Gibbs Bright & Co.* (1970) 122 C.L.R. 504.
[2] Op. cit., p. 20.

of the day? On such a statute as, for example, the Industrial Relations Act 1971? Is he to ring up the appropriate Minister and get his views about the next step? Without this sort of conversation the judge, bent on developing the law, is at worst heading for a collision and at best groping in the dark; with it the judge abandons his role of arbiter between the government and the governed.

I appreciate that radical reformers may take a fundamentally different view from mine about the function of the judiciary. They may see it not as arbitrating between citizens and as holding the balance between the state and the individual but as one of the three branches of the government. They may see the need for social reform as demanding that all three arms of the government should smite in unison for its achievement. Judges should give social leadership, they say. What if they are harnessed to an Act of Parliament? They are still free to gallop with it towards the social millennium, treating the sections that rumble along behind as but the wagons that are packed with fodder for progressive judgments.

If judges were men endowed for such a task they would not truly be judges. In every society there is a division between rulers and ruled. The first mark of a free and orderly society is that the boundaries between the two should be guarded and trespasses from one side or the other independently and impartially determined. The keepers of these boundaries cannot also be among the outriders. The judges are the keepers of the law and the qualities they need for that task are not those of the creative lawmaker. The creative lawmaker is the squire of the social reformer and the quality they both need is enthusiasm. But enthusiasm is rarely consistent with impartiality and never with the appearance of it.

Why is it, I ask in conclusion, that the denunciators of judicial inactivity so rarely pause to throw even a passing curse at the legislators who ought really to be doing the job. They seem so often to swallow without noticing it the quite preposterous excuse that Parliament has no time and to take only a perfunctory interest in an institution such as the Law Commission. Progressives of course are in a hurry to get things done and judges with their plenitude of power could apparently get them done so quickly; there seems to be no limit to what they could do if only they would unshackle themselves from their precedents. It is a great temptation to cast the judiciary as an élite which will bypass the traffic-laden ways of the democratic process. But it would only apparently be a bypass. In truth it would be a road that would never rejoin the highway but would lead inevitably, however long and winding the path, to the totalitarian state.

2

The Judge as Sentencer

I

IT was sometime in the summer of 1975 that I read a report in *The Times*[1] which set me thinking. It was of an announcement by the Home Secretary—to be set, *The Times* said, 'against a background of crisis in the penal system with increased crime and severe overcrowding in prison'—of a working party to be appointed jointly by the Lord Chief Justice and himself. The terms of reference were to review the machinery for disseminating information about the penal system and to review the scope and content of training. The Home Secretary hoped that the working party might 'in the longer term lead to the setting up of more permanent machinery for judicial training and the flow of information to sentencers'.

The training of English judges in any subject other than the law itself would be an innovation. Under other systems the judiciary is a career upon which a man embarks in his youth and in which he graduates from the humbler offices to a seat maybe in the highest court. In some countries the judiciary is a branch of the civil service and a man may move from administration to adjudication and back again. In these systems it is natural that the novice should be trained in the skills which he is expected to deploy. In England the judge is traditionally one who has been a successful barrister. His training was at the Inns of Court in the substance and procedure of the law and in the practice of advocacy. Recently, and none too soon, successful solicitors have been appointed to the Bench, but they too will have been trained as practitioners and not as judges. The judge, once appointed, usually remains in the same place for the rest of his life. It is rare for a judge in a lower court to be promoted to the High Court and there are less than thirty places in the appellate courts to be filled by promotion from the High Court.

I have said that the judge is trained only in the law and its administration.

[1] 22 July 1975.

But the treatment of offenders, it may be said, is an integral part of that administration; the sentence falls immediately after the verdict of guilty and is part of the same process. So the judge, it may be said, ought to be as well equipped to pass the correct sentence as he is to preside over the trial. The trial has not greatly changed since the turn of the century, while during the same period the new science of penology has been growing. Hence, it may be argued, the need for judges to be given at least a refresher course.

The argument would have an easier passage through traditional attitudes if the English recognized such an institution as the criminal judge. But as yet they do not. There are, it is true, the justices of the peace who deal mainly in petty crime; they are laymen and their position, which is peculiar to the English system, is outside my scope. There are also the metropolitan and stipendiary magistrates, numbering now about 50 or 60, who deal in petty crime. But the judge who tries serious crime and sentences for it is still mainly part-time. When I was called to the Bar in 1929 there were only a handful of judges, all in London, more or less permanently engaged in the trial of serious crime. They were headed by the Recorder at the Old Bailey and included the Chairmen of the County of London and of the Middlesex Sessions. The Common Serjeant sat regularly at the Old Bailey but spent some time between sessions trying civil cases in the Mayor's and City of London Court; the judge of this court in return spent much time at the Old Bailey where he was known as the Commissioner. No other city in England had a full-time Recorder; the office was held by a barrister (probably one with a civil as well as a criminal practice) who sat four times a year.

The increase in criminal work during the last thirty years has altered this. The solitary commissioner at the Old Bailey has proliferated into 25 or 30 judges, and several cities besides London have permanent Recorders. But apart from this the pattern has remained the same and the division of the work has been perpetuated. The future will see the total replacement of the County Court Judge, who did civil work and no criminal, by the Circuit Judge, who does both. If the High Court and Circuit Judges now spend more time on criminal than on civil cases, it is simply because there is so much of both awaiting trial and crime must be given precedence.

So, generally speaking, the English judge is an all-purpose judge. It was not always so. Before 1873 and the creation of an all-absorbing High Court there were a variety of superior courts[1] with different jurisdictions. Even

[1] There were also innumerable local and inferior courts whose usefulness a century later is under consideration; see Law Commission, *Jurisdiction of Certain Ancient Courts*, H.M.S.O., London, 1976. The Maldon Court of Record for passing the Estates of Married Women will probably be brought to an end, but the Estray Court for the Lordship of Denbigh, which adjudicates on claims to the ownership of stray sheep, is expected to survive.

then, however, the bulk of the ordinary work was done interchangeably by the three common law courts of the Queen's Bench, the Common Pleas, and the Exchequer. What distinguished these courts from the others and linked them together was that they all worked with a jury. In them the function of the judge, whether he was sitting on a civil or on a criminal case, was much the same. It was that of presiding over the trial and directing the jury. The main difference between the two was that in the civil case the verdict of the jury determined liability and the amount of damages, if any, while in the criminal case it covered only the issue of guilt, leaving the sentence, if any, to the judge.

Before the present century this difference was not very significant. Until the middle of the nineteenth century the sentence was prescribed as death or transportation for cases of any magnitude. Then there came the comprehensive series of statutes which provided for various maximum terms of imprisonment for different sorts of offences. There was a difference in name, but not in substance, between penal servitude and imprisonment. They both meant incarceration. Imprisonment lasted up to two years and penal servitude began at three; they were for the short-term and the long-term prisoner respectively. Imprisonment could be with or without hard labour, but there was not much in that; the tough prisoner who had committed the tough crime got hard labour, the elderly rogue did not.

The result of the Victorian statutes was that the sentence was largely determined by the verdict. This was achieved by the careful gradation of offences which we still have with us. There were, for example, seven or more rungs up the ladder of assault, the lowest being the common assault, then the assault occasioning actual bodily harm, and so on up to the wounding with intent to cause grievous bodily harm, or to murder. Each of these had its appropriate slot in terms of years, up to 1, 2, 5, 7, 10, 14 years, and life. In the days when such long periods were considered realistic even for first offenders and when the gravity of the crime was the chief factor affecting the length of sentence, these categories were meaningful; they left the judge with only a limited choice. If persistence in a life of crime displaced the gravity of the crime as the operative factor, it was for a jury to decide whether the prisoner fell within the statutory description of an habitual criminal.

In the last sixty years the role of the common law judge has been revolutionized in the civil world and amplified in the criminal. The revolutionary factor in civil cases has been the decline in the use of the jury. The judge is now required not merely to preside and direct but to adjudicate, and in particular to assess damages. By far the commonest type of case he has to try is the action for physical injury caused on the highway or in a factory.

The common law judge in the course of this work picks up a good deal of information about traffic conditions; he learns rather more than he is likely to know from his own experience as a driver about the inferences to be drawn from skid-marks and the like. He learns the details, which he is likely speedily to forget, of obscure mechanical processes in the factory; he learns also, and is more likely to remember because it is of more general application, about the effect of injury on the human body and mind—the possibility, for example, of arthritis developing much later as a result of the injury, and the effect of an unsettled claim on the capacity to return to work.

Thus a twentieth-century judge has to decide many questions of fact which used to be decided by a jury. But he decides them as if he were a jury, that is, as a man with no special qualifications and as one who needs, as the juryman does, the aid of expert evidence on any subject which is outside the scope of his general knowledge. If he acquires experience in a particular kind of case he may use it to interpret expert evidence but not to manufacture it. He may never say, 'This is a subject in which I have been trained and in which I am fit to form my own opinion.'

Nor under the English system is there much inclination to see that cases in a particular field are allotted to judges with experience in that field. The Judicature Act 1873 set the tone when it created one High Court, into the three divisions of which it thrust the medley of existing courts. The judges of the High Court were to be judges of the whole court, assignable to a particular division but in theory capable of attending to the business of any of them. The theory was too extreme and the experiment of sending Chancery judges round the country on circuit was soon abandoned. But the spirit remains. The Queen's Bench Division covers a huge area: a man who has specialized in shipping disputes and has hardly seen the inside of a criminal court may spend his first judicial term mainly on criminal cases. A few concessions are made on esoteric subjects. There are judges who within the Chancery Division specialize in patent cases and within the Queen's Bench Division in commercial cases. But these specialist judges have to do as well the general work of their division.

So much for civil cases. The jury is still the indispensable instrument of the criminal trial, in which the judge still plays no more than his traditional part. The change in his role, much less emphatic than in the civil case, is due to the encroachments of penology. In England this may perhaps be dated from the first set of Prison Rules in 1899, which laid it down that the object of imprisonment should be the reform of the prisoner as well as deterrence. This imposed upon the judge the task of making the punishment fit the criminal as well as the crime. Since then there has been a variety of alternatives to mere imprisonment—probation, Borstal training for the young, corrective training, detention centres, suspended sentences, and the greater use of mental hospitals, while the growth of egalitarian prosperity has stimulated the levying of fines. Not all of these alternatives have led to the successes for which their sponsors hoped. At the same time nothing has emerged to suggest that a return to simple incarceration is what is needed. On the contrary the lack of success and the overcrowding of the prisons have spurred the search for further alternatives. A non-custodial sentence, permitting rehabilitation within the community with the imposition of forms of community service, is the current hope.

How to reduce crime by reducing the number of criminals is now the chief object of penology. Some people think that ideally crime could be eliminated by changing the conditions in which criminals are bred and by treating those who catch the disease; others think that there is an ineradicable weakness in human nature which will always produce a supply of criminals. What is certain is that the right treatment of the criminal now requires some knowledge of penology, that is, of the different types of treatment which are (and more varieties are going to be) available and of the art or science of fitting the right treatment to the right person. This takes us a long way from the role of the judge as the dispenser of the sentence that fits the crime. Hence the call for judicial training.

Hence also some alarm. The alarm is not at the idea that a person who has to take detailed decisions about the treatment of offenders should be properly trained for the job. The question is whether the judge should be that person, and the first argument against is that it would make a fundamental change in the traditional role of the English judge. In England, the judge, as I have said, is still the juryman writ large. This means more than that he is not a specialist. Embedded in it is the idea of open justice. Everything that goes into the judge's mind on fact is seen to go in by way of evidence and during its passage it is subject to the advocate's comment.

There is no point in partial training; that would produce only a half-baked expert. If the judge is to be trained, he should be fully trained. He will then be an expert who holds views of his own. His decision will cease to reflect the attitude of the ordinary man applying an intelligent mind to technical questions and will become itself the product of a technique.

I have described the judge as like a juryman, a spokesman for the ordinary citizen. The description was extensively queried when I used it in the address I gave to the Howard League for Penal Reform from which part of this chapter is elaborated. One questioner asked what suggestions I had for improving the training of the judge as an ordinary citizen! The point, though usually made with less wit, is a common one. I think that three mistaken assumptions underlie it.

The first is the assumption that to reflect the attitude of the ordinary man to the sort of question which has to be decided in the courts it is necessary to lead the life of the ordinary man, to read the same newspapers, and to watch all the same television programmes.[1] Judges of course do not lead the life of the average citizen. They are better paid and they have more than average intelligence. They are and will continue to be better educated than the average; many of the present generation obtained that by the use of their parents' money, but quite a number by their own efforts. The idea that as judges they lead specially sheltered lives is nonsense;[2] barristers are not usually rude to them, but neither are managers rude to company chairmen nor subalterns to generals.

But judges do lead the comfortable life of a successful professional man, and this is not the ordinary life. It is the sort of life led by many successful people, such as politicians, editors, writers of all sorts, and many kinds of merchants, whose job it is to know what ordinary people are thinking and how they are likely to react. The knowledge is obtained instinctively and independently of whether a man lives in a palace or a council house. To some minds it comes quite naturally. The ministers of King George V used to say that if they wanted the reaction of the average decent Briton they would get it straight from him.

Judges and barristers have unique opportunities of seeing the ordinary man in action, not in a general way but in connection with such of his affairs as the law impinges upon, and it is of course only in the area of impingement that they are professionally concerned with him. They have spent a great part of their working lives listening to him (in a great variety of types) in the witness-box; that they do so is one of the great benefits of the oral, as contrasted with the written, presentation of evidence. They do not listen to juries, but they have the opportunity in criminal cases of testing against the verdict of the jury their own notions about a case and about the character of the witnesses they have heard. They would be blockheads if they did not absorb from what is so constantly acted out before them a sense of the ordinary man's attitudes in the situations with which the law has to deal.

[1] At the other end of the spectrum Lord Goodman's requirements for a Lord Chief Justice (and if for him, why not also for his puisnes?) are that he should enjoy and absorb not only the English classics but also Marcel Proust and André Gide; *Times Literary Supplement*, 8 Apr. 1977, p. 433.

[2] Lord Hailsham in *The Door Wherein I Went*, Collins, London, 1974, pp. 257-8, reaches the same conclusion and puts it better.

This sense is what practising lawyers extol as common sense. It is this, more than learning in the law, that the good Lord Chancellor looks for in his appointments to the Bench.

The second mistaken assumption is that the judicial character is just the same as it was a generation or two ago. Since the last war (there were very few judicial appointments during the war) the quality of the judiciary has changed considerably. Its critics now are living largely on legend. Hugo Young (not a lawyer but a journalist with a keen interest in legal affairs) wrote recently of the judges as 'almost invariably good and decent men whose lives rarely qualified them for appearance in the meanest gossip column or headline. The crusty judge, the bad-tempered judge, the pompous and even the censorious judge, with one or two notable exceptions, is a figure of the past. The stereotype persists, but it is jaded and unjust.'[1]

There is no doubt that during the first forty years of the century there were on the Bench some very troublesome judges. A number of them were ex-politicians. For it was the habit of both sides to reward the faithful in this way and some lawyers went into Parliament as the surest—maybe their only—route to the Bench. This route has now been blocked and the credit for cutting it off should go chiefly to Lord Chancellor Jowitt and the Socialist Government of Mr. Attlee, himself initially a barrister.[2]

Lord Jowitt made only two appointments from his party. The better known was in 1950 of Mr. Terence Donovan, M.P., whose merits were compelling; he was one of the very good judges of his time and ended in the House of Lords.

Mr. Attlee in 1946 made a non-political Lord Chief Justice, almost the first in history. Until then the appointment had been political; the penultimate political holder, Lord Chief Justice Hewart, who reigned for the third and fourth decades of the century, was a horror.

Mr. Attlee also made the innovation of finding judicial places for members of the opposite party on their merits. In 1946 he appointed Sir Donald Somervell, a former Tory Attorney-General, to the Court of Appeal, and in 1948 Mr. Scott Reid, a former Tory Lord Advocate, as a Lord of Appeal.

---

[1] *Sunday Times*, 5 Oct. 1975.

[2] The Lord Chancellor appoints County Court and Circuit Judges and the puisne judges, i.e. all the judges of the High Court except the Presidents of the Divisions, such as the Lord Chief Justice, and the appellate judges. These are appointed by the Prime Minister, who, so far as professional qualifications go, which is a long way, usually acts on the recommendation of the Lord Chancellor. (For the present practice in the appointment of judges, see Hailsham, op. cit., p. 254; Lord Chancellor Elwyn-Jones in *Graya*, No. 79, p. 45; and Shimon Shetreet, *Judges on Trial*, North-Holland, Amsterdam, 1976, p. 71.)

Lord Somervell later went to the House of Lords and Lord Reid was one of the great judges of the century.

In 1969 Mr. Harold Wilson appointed Lord Dilhorne, a former Tory Lord Chancellor, as a Lord of Appeal in Ordinary.

The third of the mistaken assumptions is the assumption that a person who attends meetings of the Howard League and asks pertinent questions is himself an ordinary citizen. He is not. In some respects he is a more estimable type. He was probably in favour of relaxing the law on homosexuality at a time when the public as well as the judges were hostile or at best lukewarm. He was certainly in favour of abolishing corporal and capital punishment when the public and the judges wanted to retain it. In brief he is a progressive, while the public broadly and the judges more narrowly are conservative. The ordinary Englishman is against reform. He accepts it only when he is confronted with a situation in which he can perceive unfairness in the existing order, and he perceives that more easily when it affects himself than when it affects others. The success of social reform in England, and I dare say in other democracies, in the last century and a half is due to the fact that its object was to remove political and economic unfairness affecting the majority of the people. The reformers were appealing to the have-nots. The changes which they advocated were for the material benefit of those whom they asked to vote for them. It says much for the essential conservatism of the voters that the changes took so long to bring about. If and when the egalitarian society is achieved, radicals will lead a diminished band of followers along the path of social change.

The criticism of the English judiciary comes from progressive intellectuals. Progressives are often intellectual and none the worse for that. But it is important to note that there is virtually no popular criticism of the judiciary. The English distrust politicians, are slightly suspicious of academics, not very tolerant of civil servants, and often ribald about those in authority. They have a low opinion of lawyers until they become judges. In ordinary conversation they have a habit of belittling politicians and lawyers, but not judges. It is true that intemperate abuse of judges is theoretically punishable as contempt of court. But the weapon has rusted. It was not used to suppress responsible criticisms, nor could it have been used to suppress muttering. Judicial invulnerability may be due to a feeling that it is not fair play to attack the man who is responsible for seeing that play is kept fair; but the feeling, though it exists for the benefit of umpires and referees, would not be strong enough to keep down active dislike.

The English judiciary is popularly treated as a national institution, like the navy, and tends to be admired to excess. People suspect mysteries and

crafts and it is partly because the judges are free of these that they are popularly respected. Some judges are as impatient as the ordinary man of
abstruseness and pedantry in the law and often say so. Judges do not regard
themselves as arriving at their judgments by superior reasoning which the
ordinary man cannot be expected to follow. Just as in his charge to the jury
the common law judge is necessarily reminded that he is addressing laymen,
so his judgment when he sits alone is designed to appeal to laymen. He likes
to think of himself, as he often says, as 'sitting as a jury'. With some exceptions, who, as Mr. Young has written, are diminishing in numbers, he does
not think of himself as a superior person. Likewise, fewer than in the past
are puffed up with thoughts of 'the majesty of the law'. Anyway, the wig
and the robes and the pomp, which so irritate the critics, are not unpleasing
to the ordinary citizen who perhaps sees himself someday in the mayoral
robes of his home town.

Of course the English judge has to have self-confidence. He is not, as
generally in other systems, one of a more or less anonymous group of three
putting their names to an impersonal document. He declares his opinion,
usually off the cuff, and usually it is the last word on the subject. He is well
aware of that and takes the responsibility. But he may have to sustain the
public exposition of his errors in the Court of Appeal and criticism maybe
of his faulty handling of the case. No other functionary of comparable dignity
has to submit to that. The newspapers often make a feature of it.[1] In all
the other public services and indeed in most organizations, the flock gathers
round the occasional bungler with wings outspread to protect him from
impertinent observation. I once heard a distinguished statesman, after reading an appellate excoriation, say that he supposed the judge in question
would have to resign. This was probably the last thought in the judge's mind.
No judge ever has resigned because of appellate criticism; he has to be robust
enough to take it. A witty judge once said of the judicial life that the young
judge spent the first third of it in fear that he might be reversed in the Court
of Appeal, the middle third in the conviction that the Court of Appeal
was always wrong, and the last third not caring whether it was right or
wrong.

This has a palatable touch of cynicism, but it is at any rate certain that
an English judge can do his job only if he has confidence in his own powers
of judgement. This may exacerbate critics who know that in fact he is nothing out of the ordinary. But the public like to be judged by a man who knows
his own mind and speaks it. And what they may like best is the exposure
of the judicial process from beginning to end. From the first word that is

[1] Shetreet, op. cit., pp. 192 et seqq., gives numerous examples.

uttered in court to the unprimed mind of the judge until the last word of appellate criticism, nothing is hidden.

What I have written is not solely a matter of personal impression. In actions at common law and in the old Probate Divorce and Admiralty Division, which form the great bulk of civil litigation, the public have had a choice of mode of trial, and have chosen the judge rather than the jury. As I have said, trial by jury used to be the rule in all courts of common law. The first serious breach in the rule occurred in 1883. It was then ordered that, except in six special types—e.g. libel—trials should be by judge alone unless the jury was asked for. Thirty years later trials with and without a jury were about even in number. The two war periods of 1914–18 and 1939–45 considerably hastened the decline in trial by jury; jurymen were less available. The percentage of jury trials is now negligible. The main cause of the decline is not the refusal of trial by jury when it is asked for but the fact that litigants have not been asking for it.[1] It must be allowed that trial by judge alone has the attraction of being cheaper and quicker. It is true also that inertia worked in favour of trial by judge alone, since it is easier to follow a rule than to seek an exception. Even so, it is impossible to believe that if judges in the last hundred years had been out of touch with the thoughts and feelings of the ordinary man, he would not have struggled to retain trial by men of his own sort.

I am not here concerned with the quality of the English judge or comparing it with the quality of the judge bred in the tradition of the Roman law. I have been concerned to establish the character of the English judge for what he is, an epitome of the ordinary Englishman, and the character of his judgment as an elaboration of a jury's verdict. The minority criticism to which I have referred dislikes this concept of the judge. It is logical that it should, since by and large it dislikes the jury; it feels that the giving of verdicts by amateurs without reasons is a disorderly and unscientific way of administering justice.

This criticism exposes a section of the great divide that runs across the democratic process, the divide between the active progressive minority with an itch to improve society and the passive majority which prefers its habits to be left undisturbed. It is the tension created by the conflict between these two forces that keeps democracy alive and healthy. It would weaken the body politic if one succeeded in permanently subduing the other. The victory of the minority would tighten the democratic process up to the point

[1] In a sample of 285 cases during a period of seven weeks in 1956 a jury was asked for only in four; it was ordered in three of them and there was no appeal from the refusal in the fourth.

of benevolent despotism; its defeat would liquidate the process into un-
constructive demagoguery.

This is not a simple conflict with some individuals adhering to one side
and some to the other, though some of us probably have a general inclination
to one side or the other. We all of course say and think that society should
be democratic. But are we thinking of democracy behaving in the way the
ordinary man does behave if he is left to himself without elevating influences? Or are we thinking of democracy behaving in the way it can be cajoled
into behaving by a little skilful bullying from those who think, probably
quite rightly, that they know better than most? On this general issue some
of us have, as I say, a general inclination. But many let their sympathies
sway from side to side, not merely from time to time but also and more
vigorously from issue to issue. If it is an issue on which they favour action,
they deplore the immobility of the masses. If it is one on which they are
cool, they dislike the busybodies who will not leave people free to decide
for themselves. Many people are pulled both ways and yield according to
the time and the issue. Thus it is a conflict within the individual as well as
within the State.

The limit of government is determined by the law. But the limit so determined is not absolutely decisive. There are areas in which the exercise of
legal power is forbidden by convention or discouraged by public opinion;
likewise there are areas in which power is effectively exercised without
recourse to the law. Within these areas forces such as the press and the
B.B.C., trade unions and business organizations, create pressures which
swirl around the Whitehall complex, the trade unions even lapping the flanks
of Parliament with their inarticulate claims to sovereignty. But none of
them can have the direct impact of a legal decision permitting this or forbid-
ding that. So the attitude and cast of mind of the men who lay down the
law is very influential. Certainly it is their duty to hold the scales even. But
the weights are not precise and so the judges find inevitably that they have
to incline a little to one side or the other. If government is weak, if law and
order is imperilled, they will incline to government and speak with the voice
of authority. Where government is strong, they will lean against it and trans-
mit to it the *vox populi*.

When the jury sings, the melody is the *vox populi* modulated by the law
and rendered under the baton of the judge. When the judge sits alone, he
has for the last hundred years treated himself as a substitute for the jury
rather than as a servant of the Crown. But the balance fluctuates. The needle
is sensitive and even when it is as lightly breathed upon as by the suggestion
that in one aspect of their work judges should be trained, suspicion is

aroused. It is almost but not quite as if the Government were to suggest that the press should be trained in the art of political commentary; no one would believe that the training would be free of doctrine.

The character of the judge is so distinct a feature of our judicial system and its place so crucial in the balance of forces which create the tension, that any change in it is bound to cause concern. For myself I believe that in the present state of the democratic process in Britain and for so long as one can see into the future, the judge should share the popular rather than the official outlook and should judge as the ordinary man judges. Accordingly, I am against any attempt to make him an expert in anything or to qualify him or half-qualify him in any particular science. And if as an exception to this general rule I was to be compelled to select one science, it would not, perhaps surprisingly, be penology.

There is at first sight an attraction about dovetailing the penologist into the judge, but consideration shows the attraction to be superficial. A lawyer is not by nature a social worker. The two characters have not the same sort of aptitudes; they have a different set of talents and a different framework for their ideas. The lawyer's working hypothesis is that all men are reasonable; but the social worker rarely finds that the individual with whom he has to deal has just stepped off the Clapham omnibus. I am not saying that judges do not have compassion, but that the talents that led them to the vocation of the law are not the sort needed for treating the individual offender.

Penology falls between two ancient disciplines. There is the discipline of medicine, where the sin is not to cure where you can, and there is the discipline of the law, where the sin is to try to cure the man against his will. Medicine operates upon the generally valid supposition that a man wishes to be cured and that he is for that purpose willing to stay in hospital until the doctor permits his discharge; the doctor naturally is more interested in the cure than in the discharge. The law on the other hand is primarily concerned with the man's liberty. It will not without warrant allow him to be detained against his will so that he may be cured, whether it be of a disease, of an addiction, or of subversive thoughts. In the case of the criminal the warrant is for the exaction of the debt which the criminal has incurred to society. The measurement of the debt is not easy, but one thing is clear: the size cannot be affected by the creditor's promise to use it in what he considers to be the interests of the debtor.

When the period has been fixed as justice demands, the law authorizes and indeed encourages the penologist to use it for the work of reformation.

It will allow some flexibility for this purpose, being willing within limits to make the sentence longer or shorter to accommodate different forms of treatment. But only within limits. The sentence must not be longer than is justified by the gravity of the crime and must not fall below the least that retribution demands. This is the lawyer's objective. The penologist's objective is to send the prisoner back into the world changed for the better. He may not always hope for complete reformation, but at least he does not want him to leave while there is still a reasonable chance that further treatment may improve his prospects. When these objectives clash, it is the just sentence that must prevail, notwithstanding that it deprives the expert of the time he wants. To hold otherwise would be to move on to the route, though doubtless with many stages still to go, which leads as in the U.S.S.R. to mental institutions for the dissident.

An expert is by nature a man with blinkers which keep out distracting thoughts and enable him to concentrate on the job he has to do. Those who are concerned with the rehabilitation of a criminal, whether as social workers or as doctors and whether the trouble is an addiction or mental disorder or just foolishness or wickedness, find it repugnant to permit popular notions of justice to interfere with the single-minded pursuit of their objective. They find it difficult to see why a criminal has to be let out before he is cured. It is for his own good, they say, as well as society's that he is kept in. Since in their minds the cure is the thing and the detention only incidental, they will prolong the detention so as to make sure of the cure. Most judges have come across cases of unjustifiable detention of this sort. *Baxstrom* v. *Herold*, a case decided in the United States Supreme Court in 1966, is an example of it.[1] A large number of prisoners, who had been sent to institutions for the criminally insane for a certain term, were held beyond the term because after psychiatrical examination they were deemed still to be mentally ill and possibly dangerous to themselves or to others. The detention was illegal and the Supreme Court released the victims. Their subsequent history shows that the criminal detention was as unjustified medically as it was in law. Nine hundred and sixty-seven of the prisoners were, upon their release by the Supreme Court, brought into the civil process and detained in civil institutions. A check on them was made four years later, when it was found that only 2% had been sent back to criminal institutions, and that for the others the release rate was higher than it was for the average inmate of the civil institution.

Experts are not of course always on the side of severity. It is natural for

[1] The case is reported 383 U.S. 107. I have taken it from *The Future of Imprisonment* by Professor Norval Morris, Chicago University Press, Chicago, 1974, pp. 69–70.

them to dislike a sentence for a period longer than can be used beneficially for the criminal and which may even do him harm. Such a sentence has to be justified as deterrent or retributive. Whichever word is used, the task of assessing the period of detention is the same. It must be based on criteria acceptable to society as a whole and that is not a question purely for experts.

On this and other aspects of punishment the penologist and the man in the pub do not usually see eye to eye. The penologist thinks that the man in the pub has not discarded the notions about vindictive punishment that were prevalent in the last century; the man in the pub thinks that the penologist is a softy and a crank. The police as a body share the man in the pub's view rather than the penologist's and in the administration of justice the police view is something to be reckoned with. The facts are that men in pubs are often uninformed and penologists have often been doctrinaire,[1] and the function of the judge is to make the best of both.

A sentence that is passed to fit the crime and not the criminal can be determined finally and unalterably upon plea or conviction. The sentencer needs to know nothing except the facts of the crime. The same is true when the fitting of the sentence to the criminal takes account only of his character and antecedents. These can be stated briefly by a police officer. This was the sort of sentencing that was common twenty years ago. There was no social welfare report and a probation officer only if probation was to be considered.

Now that the reform of the criminal has as an objective increased in importance and that imprisonment has come to be considered as a form of treatment as well as a punishment, the inadequacy of the 'instant sentence' is becoming more apparent. So much will depend upon the response of the prisoner/patient and this at the time of the trial can only be forecast. One solution that has been found is to treat the judicial sentence as the maximum. Maximum is indeed a weak word to use since the sentence which the prisoner actually serves can be as little as one-third of the judicial sentence, and more than two-thirds of a long sentence is abnormal.[2] This shows the limited extent to which, even in relation to period, the judge determines

[1] Thirty years ago the received doctrine was that short sentences were useless because they allowed insufficient time for rehabilitation. Hence the unhappy experiment of so-called corrective training with a norm of 3 years; this, instead of the short sentence, was considered to be the right treatment for a youth who appeared to be taking to a life of crime. Today the doctrine favours the short sentence on the ground that the impact of imprisonment is made at the beginning and that the rest of it has little or no reformative effect.

[2] In an address to the Federal Bar Council on 4 May 1976 the U.S. Attorney-General said that in 1975 the average adult federal offender served less than 60% of his actual sentence.

what is really going to happen. As to the prisoner's treatment during the
sentence, e.g. whether he is treated as a star prisoner or gets special privileges
or is allowed out on licence or is trained in particular crafts, etc., the judge
has no say at all. As to the very short sentence, imprisonment is likely to
be replaced increasingly by the detention or remand centre or by some form
of community service. These must depend on what is available in the district and this is often unknown at the time of the trial.

This all goes to show how small is the influence of the judge on the exact
length of the sentence served, let alone the nature of the service. The fact is
that what happens to the criminal depends increasingly on administrative decision and this is now being recognized. In February 1977 the Home Secretary accepted a recommendation by the Advisory Council on the Penal System that the sentence passed on young offenders should no longer specify
whether it should be served in Borstal or in a detention centre or in
prison.[1]

So, even if it be assumed as a good thing that judges should in general
be trained in sciences other than the law, there are strong arguments
against making penology one of them. In summary they are that the judge
is unlikely to make a good penologist, that the rehabilitation of the criminal
depends less upon the judicial sentence than upon the manner of carrying
it out, and that what is needed when giving the sentence is an impartial
adjustment between the view of the expert on what fits the criminal and
the view of the public on what fits the crime.

If this meant that the rehabilitation of the criminal was left in the hands
of a man ignorant of all the research that has been done on the subject it
would be a distressing conclusion. But, as I have already indicated, it does
not. In the treatment of offenders there is a clear and unmistakable line of
division between the function of the judge and that of the penologist. I
should modify that: the law is clear only if it is first made clear in what
sense the word 'treatment' is being used. For in this context the word can
be used in two senses, one wide and the other narrow.

Let me take the wide meaning first. The object of a sentence is to impose
punishment. For 'punishment', a word which to many connotes nothing
but retribution, the softer word 'treatment' is now frequently substituted;
this is the wider meaning. The substitution is made, I suppose, partly as
a concession to the school which holds that crime is caused by mental sick-
ness, but more justifiably as a reminder that there are other methods of deal-

[1] *The Times*, 2 Feb. 1977. See also Lord Chancellor Elwyn-Jones in the *Magistrate*, Dec. 1976,
vol. 32, p. 188.

ing with criminal tendencies besides making the consequences of crime unpleasant.

Punishment is in four categories. The most severe is the custodial, i.e. custody in prison or some other similar institution with a gentler name. The second is a mixed bag of other forms of constraint—submission to a probation officer, some form of community service, and so on. The third is the fine. The fourth is a warning given in the form of a conditional discharge or a suspended sentence. 'Treatment' in the narrow sense is something that occurs only in the custodial category, where it embraces, first, the choice of the custodial institution and, second, the manner in which the offender is treated when he gets there. Under the second head there are differences in treatment for which prisoners can be separately grouped and even held in separate wings. Under this head also there should be put the important questions of remission, ticket-of-leave, and parole. Under the first head, the choice is very limited. It does not arise at all in the case of adult offenders; for the young there is a choice of Borstal and a detention centre, and imprisonment is discouraged.

Treatment under the first head is a judicial question and under the second an administrative one. There is no longer sufficient reason for the distinction. The regimes of Borstal training or at a detention centre are not so essentially different from the ordinary prison regimes as to justify the profound distinction between a judicial and administrative decision. In practice the choice was becoming ineffective anyway, partly because of the need to find vacancies in the detention centres and partly because the Home Secretary's overriding powers are reducing the judicial power of choice. With this distinction out of the way the situation is simple; a line can be drawn, putting justice and punishment on one side of it and administration and treatment (in the narrower sense) on the other.

If among the different sorts of prison treatment we have been considering some were designed as punishment, as in the case of imprisonment with hard labour in the old days, justice would require that the treatment should be specified in the sentence. But today the particular treatment selected does not add substantially to the punishment, which is essentially loss of liberty, and so the concern of justice is simply the length of the sentence. Is penology relevant to that? There can of course be no objection to the period of imprisonment being used for reformative purposes, but ought the judge before fixing the length of the period to be told of the treatment proposed and invited to fix a suitable sentence accordingly?

If the just sentence could be fixed to a day or a week, it would be wrong to prolong it so that the prisoner might have treatment, beneficial but unsought, just as wrong as it would be to seize an innocent man and subject him to treatment against criminal tendencies. But the just sentence cannot be fixed to a day, only within a range. It is the function of the Court of Appeal to alter a sentence that is unjust, but it will not do so simply because all its members would have given somewhat less than the judge gave. The excess must be large enough to amount to what is said in appellate terms to be an error in principle. So it is quite proper for a judge, so long as he does not go beyond the bounds of justice, when he is fixing the exact term, to have regard to the reformative treatment. Indeed, I can see no objection to his fixing a maximum and a minimum and leaving the exact term to be settled administratively. As I have pointed out, this is what is at present frequently done in substance though not in form. It is said that with an indeterminate sentence the prisoner is less co-operative than if he knows the date of his release. This seems to me to be a question for experts; justice is satisfied either way.

I do not visualize a judge passing any except the simplest sentence without hearing the experts—penologists, medical men, probation officers, social psychologists, and, last but not least, the plain social worker unadorned by degrees. He will certainly use their help on the general question of whether a sentence, particularly when the offender has never been to prison, should be custodial or not. But this is a process which has been going on from the time the oldest judge now living was born.

I I

The address which I delivered to the Howard League for Penal Reform on 30 September 1975 was the starting-point rather than a complete framework for what I have written in the first part of this chapter. I have not varied the theme of the address, which was that judges were concerned with justice and penologists with cures, and that the amount of an offender's debt to society should like any other debt be quantified as the amount owed and not as the amount which the creditor would like to spend on improving the debtor's moral character. But I have let the theme flow on to cover the broader field of the judge as a non-expert and his value to society as such. I must now return to the straight and narrow way, for in August 1976, a year after I had delivered my address, a Working Party of august but mixed parentage (it was sired jointly by the Home Secretary, the Lord Chancellor, and the Lord Chief Justice) issued under the auspices of the Home Office a Consultative Working Paper in which it took disapproving notice of some of the observations I had made.

The main feature of the Paper is a proposal for judicial training. It is recalled that in 1963 Lord Chief Justice Parker started the one-day conference on the treatment of offenders. In 1972 this blossomed into a one-week residential seminar attended by about eighty people, mainly Circuit Judges and Recorders of three years seniority and upwards. Attendance, of course, was voluntary. The new proposal is for a compulsory cramming course for the assumed novice. No one is to sit in the Crown Court, whether as low as a Deputy Circuit Judge or as high as the new Mr. Justice, unless he has attended a residential training course. In theory the course could take a year, but 'for the foreseeable future' a month, following upon the study of a 'carefully prepared package of reading material', must be taken to be 'adequate and acceptable'.[1] There will be about forty trainees. A syllabus is suggested under five heads: sentencing law and practice, penal theory, information for sentencing (which means a study of the way in which information, such as social enquiry reports, is prepared), practical implementation of sentences (which means visiting the institutions in which they are carried out, and discussing their methods), and criminology.

It is not a light thing to sentence men and women of more than middle age, by then unused to institutional life and with the atmosphere of the classroom and the syllabus long forgotten, to a month's confinement in some academic establishment. But if the authors of the Working Paper foresee any dismay on the faces of the judicial postulants, they keep their foresight out of their pages. Indeed, the only obstacle they mention as having to be overcome is the parsimony of the Treasury. They say that their proposals would cost £100,000 a year. If indeed there are judges who lack the mental equipment necessary for their sentencing duties, it would seem to be a small sum to pay for putting matters right. But we are as usual living in difficult times when public expenditure is severely constrained and, as the Working Party warns, projects 'with additional resource implications'[2] i.e. which need extra money, may be looked at askance.

When—in 1984 perhaps—the doors are thrown open to the forty trainees, there will be some questions which they will want to ask. What exactly is the relevance of all the subjects on the syllabus to the practical decisions which as judges they are shortly going to have to make? What is the experi-

[1] Paras. 18 and 19.   [2] Para. 5.

enced criminal practitioner going to be taught in a month that he does not
know already? These are immediate and practical questions. Taking the
longer look, there are more fundamental questions which the Paper does
not touch at all. If from among the many subjects which swim in and out
of a judge's ken and which hitherto he has apprehended only as an untrained
layman, penology is to be singled out for theoretical study, is the judicial
role in the treatment of the prisoner to be correspondingly enlarged? Or
is it still to be confined to a narrow choice at the outset and thereafter nothing? If so, he may fairly ask why he is being made to do penology. But if
he is to be given a larger role, where will the ultimate boundary lie between
him and the Home Secretary? Will the executive have to do what the judges
say or not? I doubt if this sort of question has been thought about. The
Working Paper concerns itself only with the mechanics of a change the
virtues of which it takes for granted.

Yet the compulsory training of judges is in England an innovation and
one whose introduction ought surely to be preceded by a thorough examination of what its effect will be upon the judiciary. Is judicial training to be
limited to penology and, if so, why? But perhaps it is not: the Paper glances
at the prospect of 'a training institution embracing a wide range of judicial
functions, civil as well as criminal'.[1] Will there be a month on each and
how many months in all will the postulant have to serve? And will a month
be long enough? The impression the Paper gives is that it is the irreducible
minimum and that a year, though not at present practicable, would be
better. A year apiece on how many subjects?

There are, however, other parts of the Paper which would leave a foreigner
with the impression that an English judge has absolutely nothing to do
except pass sentences. The flow of information which is to reach the judge,
trained or untrained, is very copious. In addition to the standard works to
be distributed, there is to be a regular bulletin which is to cover the operation
and development of the penal and probation services, local authority social
services, and the police, changing concepts of penal treatment, the nature
of different forms of penal regimes, comparative sentencing and relative
research findings on such matters as changes in sentencing practice, the large
and growing body of psychological and sociological material about offenders
and the environmental influences to which they are subject, information
on crime trends, patterns of criminal activity, regional variations, detection
rates, and so on. The judge will thus be well equipped to attend conferences,
seminars, and forums at which he will meet prison governors, probation
officers, psychiatrists, police officers perhaps, and what is described as an

[1] Para. 42.

'external element'[1] to be supplied from academic resources. Quite short meetings these would be, perhaps one or two days, 'a residential element'[2] valuable but not essential. The Working Party did not reflect on what would happen if all the other numerous bodies and disciplines which have information on other aspects of judicial work and thoughts about it to impart to judges demanded similar attention. Nor does it mention that the English judge, unlike his counterpart in most other countries, sits in court five days in the week.

The Paper says nothing specific about training the Bar. Barristers and solicitors are not mentioned as participants in the interdisciplinary conferences or included in the 'limited circulation'[3] which the bulletin is to have. The profound consequences which would follow from mixing a trained judiciary and an untrained Bar are not mentioned. Our idea of open justice requires that what goes into the judicial mind enters it in open court where it can be heard and commented upon. The self-informed judge is a product of the inquistorial and not of the adversary system.

No such thoughts as I have been canvassing disturb the smooth progress of the Working Paper. Paragraph succeeds paragraph like a file of children crossing a cornfield, their innocent faces beaming as they trample down the wheat, so confident are they that no one could have the heart to call them back as they follow their bee-line to the promised land. When it will be reached I do not know. The parsimony of the Treasury may impose a pause long enough for the omissions in the Paper to be considered. Some of them may be filled up in the final report that is promised. Meanwhile and for my purposes, it is by inspection of these omissions that something may be learnt about the character and functions of the English judge as they are at present.

I must say at the outset that the showpiece of the new scheme, the month's incarceration, strikes me, even on the assumption that judges should be penologically minded, as a dazzling manifestation of the unacceptable face of socialism,[4] that is, an excessive zeal for setting up at public expense institutions for regimenting people into doing things which any sensible person does for his own benefit, at his own expense, and in his own way.

I must also confess that had there been a cramming course when in 1948

[1] Para. 53.   [2] Para. 52.   [3] Para. 63.
[4] In the far from confident hope that someone may glance at this work when the catchwords of the 1970s are forgotten, I should explain that it was Mr. Edward Heath who as Prime Minister referred to the activities of some City gentleman, who seemed excessively anxious not to expose their incomes to a higher level of taxation than the law required, as showing 'the unpleasant and unacceptable face of capitalism'.

I was appointed to the High Court, I should certainly have been packed off to it. I had never exercised any criminal jurisdiction and not since my early days at the Bar had I appeared in a criminal court. I had never been inside a prison except once in an interviewing room. Two days after I had been sworn in, I was trying crime at Newcastle Assizes. I knew nothing at all of the subjects prescribed under four of the five heads of the syllabus and my learning under the first head was skimpy and antiquated. Most new judges in the High Court find sooner or later that they have to adjudicate in an area in which the detailed practice is unknown to them; they can always rely on a helpful Bar and in my day on an extremely well-informed Clerk of Assize.

I sat in the King's and later the Queen's Bench for just over eleven years, but owing to special assignments rather less of my time than normal was spent on crime. For seventeen years until they were abolished in 1972 I presided at Wiltshire Quarter Sessions. When I began judicial work in 1948, flogging and penal servitude had just been abolished. There was the choice of approved schools, Borstal, and corrective training for limited categories; for 90% of the cases the only custodial punishment was imprisonment. Before I finished my time corrective training was becoming obsolete, and detention centres for youths had been added. There is now the addition of community service.

I was, I believe, an orthodox sentencer. So far as I am aware, only one of my sentences, which must have totalled hundreds, was changed on appeal. This may of course have been because I was unduly lenient, which would mean fewer appeals than the average. Certainly I tended to ask myself what was the minimum sentence that would do, for I regarded imprisonment as a waste of the human spirit and felt that every day of it must be justified. But on the quite frequent occasions when I sat in the Court of Criminal Appeal I did not find that I was seriously out of tune with the others.

It is from this base that I venture out to disagree with some of the generalizations in the Working Paper. One of them is that 'sentencers are not provided with an acceptable level of training bearing in mind the complexities of the sentencing process and the extent and nature of recent developments in the penal system'.[1] I can well believe that, even without recent developments, it may be very difficult to decide upon the best prison treatment for a man and to assess his response to it, and that much knowledge, theoretical and practical, is needed for that task. But this does not affect the sentencing, which as a process is uncomplicated. In the majority of cases there is little room for choice: the judge has only to fix the appropriate term of impri-

[1] Para. 8.

sonment by applying the tariff to the circumstances of the case. The task
is highly responsible and, as in all judicial work, may sometimes lead to
anxious and difficult decisions—the imposition of the first custodial sentence
usually does; but it is not complex. Where occasionally a choice has to be
made between, say, a probation order, detention centre, and Borstal, the
judge will have the report of a probation officer. He will be one who has
interviewed the offender and should be one (though pressure on the service
sometimes prevents this; the relief of it might well be the first charge on
the 'additional resource implications') who knows both the offender and his
background. The judge always has this sort of help in every case, but it
is specially important when he has to decide on the type of sentence rather
than the length. Subject to the omission of any part of the report that might
be distressing, the evidence of the probation officer is given from the witness-
box and can be challenged by the defence. This is a vital element in the
process: not merely the public in general but often the offender's family
want to know just what is happening and why; there must be no unnecessary
secrecy. If, as is usual, the evidence was unchallenged, I personally would
accept it as far as it went. If a probation officer who knew a boy said that
he had reached the stage when a detention centre offered the best hope
of reform, I would have thought it absurd for me to form a contrary impression after looking at the boy in the dock or hearing him mumble a few sentences in the box. My concern with the proposal would be as to its justice;
I might think the punishment either excessive or inadequate. If the offender
had been on probation twice before and nevertheless the officer thought that
he still might do some good with him, I should accept the possibility but
might conclude that I could not allow it to be thought that a repeated breach
of probation carried no unpleasant consequences. As I have said, there may
well be hard questions in particular cases. The hardest one in sentencing
is, I think, when to give the offender 'the last chance', that is, when on his
record he ought to be imprisoned, but you feel or hope that he may have
reached a turning-point. No crammer can help on that; only experience or
intuition is any use.

When sentencing I did not feel handicapped by my ignorance of penal
theory and criminology; I have not from my slight subsequent acquaintance
with them discovered to what use I could have put them. I never wanted
to know how the probation officer had compiled his report, though I am
sure he would have told me if I had asked him, and I did not carry in my
head the details of the regime which are to be studied under the fourth head of
the syllabus, such as the psychiatric and medical services available in prison,
the opportunities for vocational and educational training, including the

pre-release employment scheme, home visits, security classifications, release procedures, etc. If in any particular case any of them became significant, I should expect counsel on one side or the other to explore it. If, for example, the plea in mitigation urged that a boy ought not to be cut off from a good and devoted family, I should expect prosecuting counsel to enquire about home visits. And then the family would get the answer too.

What the new judge needs to know about sentencing is the judicial approach to it. Academic writings can be interesting and useful, but the judicial approach must first be mastered. Sentencing without conformity is a social injustice; there is no room for the new judge, perhaps not for any judge, to try out theories from the higher reaches of penology. Changes in standards that follow on the best new academic thinking must of their nature come slowly and by diffusion through the judiciary. To offer a new judge a little learning is a dangerous thing; penology can be no exception to the rule that wisdom drinks deeply or tastes not.

It follows that in my opinion the only head in the syllabus that matters is the first, i.e. sentencing law and practice, and that on the assumption that the new judge is a person of independent and mature mind, not one of nature's trainees, not merely interested in his job but passionately determined to do justice, the rest is best left to him. What this first head includes is exemplified in the Working Paper as 'the range and legal basis of the various available sentencing options, the principles of the sentencing 'tariff', and the statutory restrictions, practice directions and case law which apply in different circumstances'.[1] He need not mug up the recondities of case law because counsel will enlighten him on unusual points. But he should know the general principles; above all he should know the tariff. Anyone who has had a substantial practice in crime will know all this and will be very familiar with the judicial approach; it would be an unwarrantable imposition on him to send him for a month to a novitiate.

For the man who has had no criminal practice, illustrious clerks of assize are no longer available. Almost every day, however, in any big city there must be a judge who is doing a day of sentencing. A week or a fortnight, or a month if he wants it, sitting with different judges and discussing the pleas with them, would show the newcomer the judicial approach. The opportunity would only have to be offered to be grasped. A conditional appointment to the Bench is unnecessary and undignified.

I do not agree therefore that the other heads in the syllabus are, as the Working Party says,

[1] Para. 29.

important fields of knowledge and experience, vitally and directly relevant to sentencing (including some in the purely technical legal sphere) with which the sentencer ought to be thoroughly familiar and in which a judge's resources gained from his own experience and self-tuition may be quite inadequate. To take an elementary example, a judge who is quite unfamiliar with the day-to-day conditions under which a prisoner serves his term of imprisonment can hardly be considered well qualified to determine the length of a prison sentence.[1]

The generalization is not to my mind fortified by the 'elementary example' posing the sort of question often put to a judge but usually by less sophisticated questioners. How do you know for how long to send a man to prison if you do not know what prison is like? How can you assess damages for pain and suffering if you have not suffered? How can you grant a possession order for a dwelling-house if you have never witnessed an eviction? And so on. They are all variants of the question I considered earlier: how can you represent the ordinary man if you are not one yourself? The one about prisons is not more difficult than the others to answer.

What I thought about prisons in 1948 was that they were institutions humanely run in which prisoners lived with the maximum of regimentation and the minimum of comfort. For the rest I had to rely upon my imagination—the cutting off of home and family life, of privacy, of the other sex, of new sights and sounds and the variations of the changing day, and the joy of deciding what you would do with your day; and then the vista of endless tedium. There is much else that could be added and the total would make the influence of what the Working Paper calls 'the day-to-day conditions' look small by comparison. It is not what prison imposes that is the greater part of the punishment; it is what it takes away.

When I visited a prison, as of course I did thereafter on a number of occasions, I found the regime what I expected it to be and what indeed it was commonly believed to be. A little less grim perhaps, but then on these occasions the grimmer side is not emphasized. What had previously been left to the imagination was still in the imagination. But what if I had found the regime to be harder or softer than I had thought? How should the discovery have affected the length of my sentences? By adding or deducting 10% or so from the tariff figure?

The tariff figure is a conventional one. It is no more possible to relate wicked or unsocial behaviour to a number of days in prison than it is to measure pain and suffering in pounds sterling. In neither of these spheres can a judge do his own arithmetic; the fruits of diversity would be general injustice. A judge can take into account that a prison regime will affect some

[1] Para. 12.

more painfully than others, but the application of that depends mainly on his appreciation of the individual he is sentencing. He must start from the tariff figure.

This does not mean that the tariff figure is immutable or that judges should never bother to visit prisons. The tariff figure, depending as it does on a consensus, changes slowly. Perhaps the most important element in the consensus is the state of public opinion about the gravity of different crimes; this changes over the years. At the turn of the century bigamy was, I believe, considered to be a grave crime calling for penal servitude. When I first went on circuit as a marshal in 1929 it was, unless it involved seduction, only formally treated as a punishable offence. Bigamists, with their invariable pleas of guilty, were dealt with on the first day of the assizes when the notabilities, male and female, whom the High Sheriff had invited to his luncheon attended the court. The tales of temptation unresisted and the series of bindings-over made a light and undistressing day. So already by 1929 would the series of youthful carnal knowers of the under-16s, but since in the recital of their crimes the sexual details could not, as in bigamy, be left entirely to the imagination, they were not then suited to the ladies of the county.

The nature of the prison regime is also an element in the consensus, though because of its stability over the last half-century it has not been a very significant one. I do not mean the stability of the day-to-day conditions; they have altered a great deal. But what is relevant for this purpose is the mixture of pleasure and pain in the regime as a whole as compared with the like mixture in the world from which the prisoner is excluded. If prison life is less grim than it used to be, so for the ordinary man is life in the outside world. The most potent factor affecting the tariff is not the regime but the extent to which the Home Secretary uses his powers of remission. Release on parole can be regarded either as a mitigation of the sentence or as a reward earned by co-operative behaviour. On the former view it ought to be taken into account in determining originally the length of the sentence; but on the latter it could be regarded as similar to a Borstal release. These, however, are matters which must be determined by the judiciary as a body and not individually. They are likely to be discussed informally when judges meet, as on circuit, and, most influentially, in the Court of Appeal.

But there is no getting away from the fact that it is the judges who send people to prison and it is their responsibility to keep an eye on the regime. Apart from a natural interest, this is the principal reason why they, especially the senior ones, should regularly visit prisons. It is the seniors who can best initiate change in the consensus should it become necessary. For the new judge the conventional figure must be the yardstick and it would be ridiculous for him to begin his judicial career by adding or subtracting inches to or from the yard. A man who has made one or two group excursions to prisons during his month's course is not thereby equipped to devise a new relationship between day-to-day conditions and length of sentence.

I move on to what must be taken as the most controversial statement in the Working Paper. This is its conclusion that 'a general criminal practice at the Bar' does not provide 'of itself an adequate equipment for the newly appointed judge'.[1] This is not quite what the Paper says. What the Paper does, proceeding with due caution, is to chronicle an awareness of the difficulty of maintaining the traditional assumption that a general criminal practice at the Bar provides ... etc. But sterner language later on in the Paper makes it clear that veterans must go to the crammer together with the novices so that they may be 'appropriately equipped to discharge their duties satisfactorily'.[2]

An experienced criminal practitioner must have taken part in the process of sentencing maybe a thousand or more times. He has seen and talked with the delinquents and their families, with policemen and social workers, as well as hearing them give evidence in court. He has often formed his own view of what would be the right sentence and then been able to compare it with that of the judge. He has observed the factors which the judge thought to be significant; maybe he has challenged them on appeal and heard where the judge went wrong. If he is not qualified, in so far as experience goes, to be a judge, then there can be no field of legal practice in which experience can be a qualification. Yet for centuries judicial appointments have been made on the basis that experience at the Bar is what gives a man the necessary judicial equipment. The relationship between Bench and Bar, which I shall later elaborate, is rooted in the assumption that the judge gets from the Bar the help which he needs in the selection and evaluation of the material for his decision. What the Working Party recommends is a step out of the adversary system into the inquisitorial. They recommend it without citing the errors and miscarriages which must have unseated in their minds the traditional assumption.

At first reading, however, it is the cure proposed rather than the diagnosis that attracts attention. If a working life at the criminal Bar does not provide adequate equipment, is a month's course really going to make any difference? Not, it seems to me, unless the object of the course is the limited one of relieving the practitioner of any undesirable ideas that he has picked

[1] Para. 1.   [2] Para. 22.

up in the course of his practice. Training supposes that there is a right and a wrong way of doing things and its purpose is to instruct the trainee in the right way. But then, one asks, who is to run the course? Who is to formulate the doctrine to be imparted? Someone seems to have hinted that perhaps the Home Office had it in mind to discharge this duty itself. Any such idea is denounced in the Working Paper. 'To imagine that training might easily represent a form of indoctrination is absurd,' the Paper says. Why, there *is* no doctrine, 'no right and wrong answers', 'no consensus of agreed opinion'. It is a 'highly controversial field'.[1]

Is this to be read seriously? Or are these the hasty words of men fleeing from the charge of indoctrination, pausing to discourage pursuit by scattered fire, having no time for a well-directed volley? The message of the Working Paper as a whole and the sole justification for its advocacy of compulsory attendance is that the course is simply teaching What Every Judge Needs to Know. If there is no consensus, there is nothing that a judge *needs* to know, for consensus encircles judicial authority. No judge has the right to send a man to prison because he has an individual preference for one view over another in a highly controversial field. It may be of interest to an experienced judge, and possibly of peripheral value to him, to know what discords there are on the Mount Olympus of penology. But to make this and not doctrine the essence of a course for novices is madness. And to make it part of a month's tuition!

This is the sort of thing that makes me wonder about what the Working Paper portends as well as about what it says. Were the members, consciously or not, settling for a *pis aller*? Might their thoughts, if vulgarized, have run on the following lines? 'What we should really like to see is a judge trained in penology as he is in the law. It should be a compulsory subject in the qualifying examinations for the legal professions, but this is outside our terms of reference. If we recommend anything like a year's course on the threshold of judicial appointment, the professions will jib at it and the Treasury won't stand for it. Let us therefore begin with a month.' By the optimistic eye of enthusiasm a month might be seen as better than nothing; the pessimists, who might fear that it would soon be seen to be hopelessly inadequate, might approve of it as selling the notion. Once the principle of judicial training is accepted as a sound idea, then in an age in which all advance is progress and all retreat reaction, the only solution to be found for inadequacy would be to press on with plans for bigger and better training.

Not that there is any logical reason why penology should not be made a branch of the criminal law and administered as such. It would then be

[1] Para. 10.

taught in the Inns of Court as well as at universities, practised at moots, and form part of the qualifying examinations in both professions. Such a reform would not appeal to me and I have said why not. But anyone who favours the reform must work it out far more thoroughly than the Paper does. The chief consequence, and perhaps the most unacceptable, would follow from the fact that a judge neither proposes nor recommends but lays down the law; he cannot be treated as a man putting up ideas for the Home Secretary's consideration. There is no point in making a judge a penologist unless he is to control not only the length of sentence but also the treatment during it. My preference is to separate the two, making the former a judicial question and the latter an administrative one. But if they are both to be made judicial, there cannot be a condominium; the judge must decide. That would mean treating the prisoner as a ward of court; the custodians would have for any change of treatment to obtain the approval of the judge. There are indeed those who think it would be much better if release on parole was dealt with in this way. But there is no sign that the Home Secretary is ready to relinquish any part of his domain.

The Working Party contemplates, so it says, no more than that the judge should be 'one who thoroughly understands the background';[1] he is not to aspire to be an expert. This also is a perfectly sensible objective, but here again its implications must be examined, understood, and accepted. The first thing about it to be noted is that, since there is a limit to the number of backgrounds a judge can thoroughly understand, it leads naturally to the specialist judge. The specialist judge is accompanied by the specialist Bar and very often by specialist solicitors as well. New judges, chosen from the specialist Bar, begin by thoroughly understanding the background and need no training. There are, as I have noted, specialist judges within the Queen's Bench Division, but their subjects are parochial compared with crime. Crime would require a criminal division of the High Court at least as big as the Family Division and would split the Circuit Judges between the criminal Crown Court and the civil County Courts. Is the need for expertise in sentencing a sufficient justification for such an upheaval?

I need not pursue this, for no one has suggested anything of the sort. I have glanced at it because it is the traditional way in which under the English system judges with an understanding of the background are offered to litigants. Its great advantage, which has to be weighed against the advantage of the judge with the uncluttered mind, is that it saves time. The barrister does not have to spend time in explaining to the judge the legal and factual background which is elementary to him, to the solicitors instructing

[1] Para. 12.

him, and sometimes to the litigants as well. The Commercial List[1] was instituted in the Queen's Bench Division in 1892 following upon a case which before an inexperienced judge had taken an interminable time. Thus the objective is to put the judge on an equality with those who appear before him, not make him their superior. Usually the specialist judge follows instead of preceding the specialist Bar.

What is serviceable in a specialist court would be out of place in one dealing with crime. The ordinary public does not listen to a commercial case or to a dispute about patents or the like; in such cases background knowledge shared between the judge and counsel and parties makes for speed without passing the understanding of anyone who is likely to be listening. Crime is quite different. It is of great importance that laymen should come to listen, as in fact they do, and that they should understand what is going on. This is even more important than the saving of time.

To make a judge an expert on his own in any subject is to move the doing of justice from the court to the chamber and to draw the blinds. To give him a background understanding unshared with the Bar is to admit experts as well as the parties to the chamber, but to leave the parties without effective counsel. To give him a like understanding shared with counsel is to open justice to all those who are likewise familiar with the background, but to leave the public bewildered.

The Working Party's proposals on background for the judge are innovatory in three respects. First, the background is to be acquired not by lifelong experience but by eleventh-hour academic training. Secondly, it is to be acquired not in a matter of interest only to a small section of the public but in one of universal concern. Thirdly, it need not be shared by the Bar. The judge is to become learned in matters beyond the range of the barrister with the substantial criminal practice. The Working Party notes that training might be appropriate either as part of basic legal education or as part of experience gained in legal practice, but considers that such matters are outside their terms of reference.[2] Yet they say that a well-informed judge is dependent upon a well-informed Bar and they say it without apparently appreciating the extent to which their proposals divorce the two.

There is an ecology for the legal organism as for others. In the English system judges feed off the Bar. The Bar supplies the material which enables the judge to decide a question of law and argues about how the question should be decided. No judge attempts to read all the current law reports and the spate of legal articles. A specialist judge may read the more important in his own line, but he would do it for his own interest and, if any case came

---

[1] The Commercial Court was not created until 1971.   [2] Paras. 13 and 14.

before him in which new developments were relevant, he would expect counsel to present them to him. There is no time in his schedule allotted to legal research and, if in connection with any case the judge had to do a lot of it, counsel would not have done his job properly.

This dependence of the judiciary on the Bar, much greater than in most other countries, has not been created for its own sake. It has flowed naturally and inevitably from the fact that the whole of the legal process is public and conducted almost entirely by word of mouth. Everything that might affect the judgment must be known to counsel so that they can comment on it and challenge it if they wish. This does not mean that the evidence and argument in court may not be viewed in light from the background, but that there must be a common source of light. If the judge perceives some point that counsel has not taken, he must be able to put it to counsel for comment. If in this 'highly controversial field' he is tempted to apply the Puffberg theory of recidivism (if there be such a thing), but doubtful to what extent it has been demolished by Dr. Pinkerton-Smith, it is useless to discuss the matter with a barrister who has heard of neither. But if it might affect the sentence he is about to pass, that is what he should do. In short, if the judge is to become a penologist, under the existing system counsel must become penologists too.

Of course the ecology can be altered. There is nothing absurd in a system which leaves it to a judge to fix the appropriate sentence after making his own inquiries and collecting for himself the material which he thinks he needs to have. To a greater or smaller extent this is the system followed in many countries. But in all of them the judge is allowed time and given facilities for the pursuit of his inquiries and research. This is the inquisitorial as opposed to the adversary system. Its adoption in England would mean a fundamental reform.

The first thing to ask about a fundamental reform is whether the reformers know where they are going. There is nothing in the Paper to show that the Working Party do, or even that they are conscious that they are stepping off the beaten track. When that question is answered satisfactorily, it will be time to ask whether there is a need for the reform and, if so, whether the size of the proposed change is proportionate to that need. This means that in the matter of sentencing the options open to the judge, as they are now, must be identified; there must be a clear statement of policy as to whether they are likely to be diminished or increased; in relation to each of them it must be demonstrated in what respects principles of penology, unrevealed by practical experience, are going to help the judge to make the right choice. It is not enough to generalize about sentencing being a vital responsibility and it is not in this connection encouraging to come across in the Working Paper a sentence such as the following:

> It seems to us that in the light of present-day thinking we should give less prominence to the idea of the effect of penal treatment upon individuals, and be less optimistic about the likelihood that research findings will in the foreseeable future come to assist judges in their case-by-case task in the sense of offering prescriptive guidance as to the appropriate form of sentence.[1]

Then what is the point of it all? Case-by-case tasks are what constitute judicial work and judges have no business outside it.

I turn now to the proposals in the Working Paper for increasing the flow of information to judges and for arranging what the Paper calls 'interdisciplinary contacts'.[2] I have already pointed out the difficulties that would arise if other disciplines were to claim the same privileges. I shall not pursue this further but shall look at the proposals as if they were framed to affect only the judge who spends his full time, or at least the great bulk of it, on crime. He will be a judge who works 'office hours'. that is to say he will be in court or in his chambers from 10.0 a.m. to 5.0 p.m., and after that may spend an hour or so looking through the notes of the evidence he has taken, framing in his mind the lines of his summing-up and marking the passages in the notes or in the documents exhibited which he may want to refer to. If he is not doing that, he will be looking at the headnotes at least of cases in the Criminal Appeal Division and reading through the *Criminal Law Review* or some such journal. He will certainly have some contacts of his own. He will meet chief constables and prison governors, on circuit if he is a High Court Judge, or within his own district if he is a Circuit Judge. He will occasionally visit prisons, Borstals, and detention centres, and the like, where he will meet the staff. He will accept invitations to address societies, not only of magistrates and lawyers but also of social workers and other bodies concerned with criminal law and administration. All this he will do as a matter of private enterprise. It is certainly to be encouraged, but its organization into what the Working Paper calls rather grimly 'continuation training'[3] is

---

[1] Para. 56. In its application to crimes of violence Lord Chancellor Elwyn-Jones, speaking on 22 Apr. 1977, put the point more bluntly. 'For a long time criminologists emphasized that the treatment of offenders must fit the criminal and not the crime. Experience has shown, however, that this approach has not produced significant results; and the fact remains that the paramount object of sentencing must be the protection of society. The severity of a sentence and the length of a custodial sentence should be primarily related to the offender's criminal act and to the protection of the public.' *Magistrate*, vol. 33, p. 111.

[2] Para. 51.

[3] Para. 52.

a different matter. This is the aspect of it on which I want to make my first comment.

A judge's time for extra-judicial activities, that is, outside office hours, is limited. Such activities have to compete with the need for a reasonable amount of leisure in a mentally exacting job. Indeed the wise use of leisure is a part of the job. A research scientist, for example, could work every evening and all weekends without, if he preserved his health, making his research any less acute. A judge who did likewise would truly be living in the ivory tower which his critics always suppose to be his chosen habitation. A knowledge of what is going on in politics and what is interesting people generally is the stuff of social talk; a judge needs it, as also he needs to read outside the law.

Then, penology is not the only claimant for inclusion in a list of extra-judicial activities, even if the list is entirely limited to the criminal field. A judge is quite likely to have a special interest in other features of criminal law and administration; there are several judges on the Criminal Law Revision Committee and there is often a judge presiding over a committee on some particular subject. There are bodies concerned with the running of the profession and with legal education on which some judges will be serving.

Many judges devote quite a lot of time to their Inn of Court or to their old university. At both they will meet students, often when addressing a university or college law society. At the latter they will meet academics and at the former their fellow benchers and others of the Bar. The latter contacts are to my mind the most important. Contacts within the discipline are just as worth while as contacts outside it, and a judge, since he is usually working alone, does not get them to the same extent as in many other disciplines. The Inn of Court is the place at which there is fostered the unique relationship between Bench and Bar in England which contributes so much to the swift passage of judicial work.

In short, many judges may reasonably regard the proposals in the Working Paper as demanding a greater share of their free time than their value can justify. Criminology and penology are young sciences without as yet an imposing record. They have not, as many of the other disciplines have, demonstrated how theory and research can be used to produce concrete results. Everyone can see the enormous benefits brought in the last half-century by advances in medicine, for example; by contrast, penology does not point to a reduction in the crime rate or to a record of success in the reform of criminals, or even to consistency in theoretical development: consider the recent changes from the long to the short sentence and from the sentence that fits the criminal to the sentence that fits the crime. It should not be given up in despair, but as a recruit to judicial thinking it is not in a position to make its own terms of entry.

My second comment concerns the method of conveying information to the judge. For this purpose I think that the information should be considered in two categories. The first is the general and factual, what the Working Paper calls 'routine information', of which, as the Paper rightly says, there is at present no shortage.[1] It consists of crime statistics and official reports, e.g. of the after-care department of the Home Office. It is proposed that the bulletin should include a digest of these. This will be useful, but why should it be in a bulletin produced specifically for judges? The information will be just as useful and interesting to practitioners and social workers. It will be like that excellent pamphlet, *The Sentence of the Court*,[2] to which the Paper refers. This pamphlet keeps the profession more or less up to date with the different ways of dealing with offenders, particularly those under age. It is really a supplement to the textbooks and has the same sort of value; its publication might not be attractive to private enterprise, and if the Government will subsidize it, so much the better.

The other category consists of the rest of the bulletin, which I have already summarized. This is information of a less factual sort, such as on changing concepts of penal treatment, psychological material, environmental influences, and so on. The material in it will be of little practical use to a judge unless it is related to a particular choice which he has to make. The proper person to make the appropriate selections and to relate them to the case is the counsel for the prosecution acting under the advice and with the assistance of the penological experts in the prison service or in other departments. I am coming back to the point I have already made. Why is all this aimed directly at the judge? Why does the Working Party ignore the function of counsel? Surely under our system it is the business of prosecuting counsel to bring to the attention of the judge all such matters as ought to affect his mind in passing sentence. At present counsel is still briefed in the way he was when the sentence was decided solely on the circumstances of the case and the offender's record; when he puts the police officer in the box his duty is virtually done. Since the Working Party feels quite rightly that a judge needs more than this, I cannot understand why they did not (unless they want to move from the adversary to the inquisitorial system as unobtrusively as possible and to phase out the profession) call attention to the need for change. The prosecution can study all the material at leisure, consult the penological works and back numbers of the bulletin, and present

[1] Para. 62.
[2] *A Handbook for Courts on the Treatment of Offenders*, H.M.S.O., 3rd edn. (1978).

the judge with the material relevant to the choice he has to make. Surely this is better than relying upon the judge to spend an evening or so a month wading through current material without any idea of what use he may be able to make of it. It is unreasonable to expect him as he reads it to pigeon-hole items in his mind ready to be picked out when required. The process of passing sentence occupies perhaps half an hour from the time the judge is told the facts of the case until the job is done. He is working in open court in the public eye, not in a library with books and files which he can consult at leisure, with time to verify things half-remembered.

My third comment is on conferences, seminars, and 'continuing contacts with members of the services involved'.[1] To take conferences first. Most judges attend from time to time conferences on topics in which they are interested. I take as an example the activities of the British Maritime Law Association in which all the 'maritime disciplines' participate. Judges are there mixing with all those who as litigants will be opposed to each other—insurers and insured, shipowners and cargo-owners, and so on. But this sort of mixture, which comes about naturally in the commercial world, cannot be so easily secured in the criminal. There is an important element missing, consisting of the criminals themselves. There are of course some very articulate ex-prisoners, and it would be an excellent, if so far uncontemplated, thing if they were invited to attend. But offenders are never likely to be represented in force. They are likely to regard all the people attending the conference as belonging to the 'other side'.

The same thing applies to the continuing contacts. It is difficult to have contacts with able and dedicated professionals without being brought to share, at least to some extent, their outlook, assumptions, and sympathies. What is the harm in that, it may be asked; all these people are simply concerned, as is the judge, with the good of the offenders they are looking after, and the judge is meeting them only to get background information. This, however, is not how the offenders will see it: the articulate ones will ask why the judge is not getting background information also from the people who dislike being looked after. The art of acquiring background information from one side only without allowing it to crystallize into prejudgement is not easy to acquire. Moreover, judges are not always very good at keeping background information in the background. They are not immune from the temptation to air superior knowledge. As long as fifty years ago there were judges who thought that they knew all that there was to know about prisons. I recollect a case in which a judge rejected out of hand the evidence of an expert witness for the defence that the facilities for psychiatric treatment

[1] Para. 64.

in a certain prison could not provide what was needed for his patient. The judge said that he knew that they were perfectly adequate. Perhaps he was right and, if so, justice was done. But whether he was right or wrong, it was not British justice that was done.

Lastly the Home Office has played and is playing a large and unconcealed part in the movement to train judges in penology and inform them about prison regimes. The Home Office is the department concerned with the enforcement of the law and has the superintendence of the police as well as of prisons. It is not interesting itself in the judicial attitude to sentencing purely out of concern for the competence of the judiciary; if that comes within the sphere of any department it would be the Lord Chancellor's. The Home Office is naturally anxious that its policy on prisons should be understood, and it cannot be indifferent about whether or not judicial sentences fit in with it. But in another of its capacities it might be equally anxious about law enforcement; the police might reasonably want the judges to know something about their problems and policies. Indeed all government departments whose activities may be criticized and who sometimes come before the courts would probably like the judges to know about their problems and policies. Pushing the thing to extremes, is there any reason why the imparting of information should be the privilege of government departments? One can imagine how delighted a trade association would be to arrange conferences, exhibitions, and bulletins, not to mention contacts, so that judges could have the background information which would be so useful to them in understanding disputes about the merchantability of their products.

One does not want to be pedantic about this. But where the independence of the judges may be touched or appear to be touched, it is a good thing to have a protocol. Protocol should, I think, decree that in the acquisition of background information a judge should be left to his own devices. If he is left to himself to find his own sources of background information where he thinks he needs it and if in the acquisition of it he behaves in a discreet way, he will not be criticized. But when his sources are organized for him, questions will be asked. As the Working Party says, its programme must 'avoid encroaching in any way, either in reality or in appearance, on the independence of the judiciary'.[1] It says later that 'there would be an advantage in entrusting the task of dissemination of information to a body which was not regarded as speaking with the voice of the Home Office or of any other government department'.[2] This is drawing it far too mild. It is out of the question that bulletins should be prepared or contacts organized for

[1] Para. 10.   [2] Para. 62.

the judges by any government department. If such tasks really need to be undertaken, it must be on the initiative of the judiciary itself and by means of arrangements which it alone creates.

There is certainly a case for the creation of an institution such as the judicial conference which flourishes in the United States. Leaving on one side the question of whether it should organize contacts for judges, there is to my mind a strong case for settling judicial policy more openly than at present. I have indicated, for example, the 'customary processes'[1] by which changes in the tariff can be brought about. The time may have come for the judiciary, as it came for the Conservative Party, to put things on a more satisfactory basis, not only in relation to sentencing practice but also in relation to legal procedure generally.

The Judicature Act, which created the new Supreme Court in 1873, provided in s. 75 for a Council of Judges of the Supreme Court[2] to assemble once at least in every year. Among its powers was the 'enquiring and examining into any defects which may appear to exist in the system'. It was to report annually to the Secretary of State about any provisions which it would be expedient to make for the better administration of justice and which required the authority of Parliament. This section was re-enacted in s. 210 of the consolidating statute of 1925.

It is for the Lord Chancellor to summon the meeting. All Lord Chancellors respect the law but some are more respectful than others. Although the statute requires that there should be an assembly at least once a year, it has met only intermittently. If it has inquired into any defects in our system of justice, it has not, I think, exposed its conclusions in an annual report. The judiciary is now too large to achieve much simply by assembling. But there is a basis here for an organization on American lines.

[1] This is a catchword of the 1960s, being the phrase used in 1963 by the retiring Prime Minister, Mr. Harold Macmillan, to describe the methods by which his successor was selected.

[2] I am grateful to the Lord Chancellor's Department for giving me information about this little-known body.

3

The Judge in the Adversary System

ENGLISH judges have spent much less time than you might imagine in actually adjudicating. True, that equity judges have always adjudicated, but, looked at over the ages, their total of 'judge hours' is comparatively small; it was not until 1813 that the first Vice-Chancellor came to help the Lord Chancellor and the Master of the Rolls. What the common law judge did for nearly seven out of eight centuries was to preside at a trial by jury and order that judgment be entered in accordance with the verdict. He began himself to adjudicate in the ordinary civil case in 1883. The first trickle of non-jury cases has now become a flood. But in criminal causes, in which now he spends on the average two-thirds of his time, he is still only the president.

This is the background to any discussion of the adversary system in England. For trial by jury no other system is possible. It was not selected for its superior qualities; the only alternative was not practicable.

The alternative is the inquisitorial system. The essential difference between the two systems—there are many incidental ones—is apparent from their names: the one is a trial of strength and the other is an inquiry. The question in the first is: are the shoulders of the party upon whom is laid the burden of proof, the plaintiff or the prosecution as the case may be, strong enough to carry and discharge it? In the second the question is: what is the truth of the matter? In the first the judge or jury are arbiters; they do not pose questions and seek answers; they weigh such material as is put before them, but they have no responsibility for seeing that it is complete. In the second the judge is in charge of the inquiry from the start; he will of course permit the parties to make out their cases and may rely on them to do so, but it is for him to say what it is that he wants to know.

The centrepiece of the adversary system is the oral trial and everything that goes before it is a preparation for the battlefield. An inquiry could be held orally within a single day, but in a case of any complexity it is a long process whose centrepiece is the dossier. I propose now to make a brief comparison of the two systems, mainly as they affect the civil process, and taking as typical of the adversary system the non-jury trial in England.

In the adversary system, and in so far as it involves the judge, the case begins and ends with the trial. Before the judge goes into court he will have only the pleadings which contain a bare statement of the issues in the case. He has them, I suppose, because they are the only documents which the parties have filed with the court. If he is curious to know what the case is about he will look at them, but he is not expected to have studied them; indeed, unless some question arises about whether or not a point is within the pleadings, they are not likely to be referred to. The judge will obtain his first knowledge of the case from the opening statement of counsel for the plaintiff. This will be followed by the oral evidence of the plaintiff and his witnesses, of which the judge will take a note; the evidence of minor witnesses whom the defence does not wish to question may be in writing. The questioning is conducted by counsel, the judge intervening mainly to clarify or to develop a point and very occasionally to run a line of his own. Documentary evidence, e.g. correspondence between the parties, will be put in as an exhibit as it becomes material.

At the end of the plaintiff's case counsel for the defence will present his case in the same way. At the end of that there will be closing speeches by counsel. Points of law will be dealt with by counsel in one or other of his speeches. Immediately upon the conclusion of these, unless the case is one of exceptional difficulty or complexity when judgment may be put into writing, the judge delivers a judgment in which he states his findings of fact in narrative form and gives his conclusions and his reasons for them. The victorious party will ask for an order for costs which he will normally get, any variation from the usual order being settled by the judge then and there. In nine cases out of ten this is the end of the litigation.

The successive stages of this process are not subject to any time-limit, though the judge may intervene to stop waste of time. It is the general experience that trials take longer than they used to; it is now, I believe, rare for a trial to last less than a day, but there is much variation. A 'heavy' case may last for a fortnight or more. Then the opening speech may last a day or more, and if there is a lot of law in it counsel may spend hours reading out the authoritative judgments in earlier cases on which he relies. Likewise the plaintiff or defendant or their principal witnesses may be cross-examined for a day or more. The documents put in may rise to a pile of a foot or two on the judge's desk, all except a few strays being properly arranged in

bundles and paged for reference.[1] Everything goes at the speed of slow talk
with pauses to find the right page in the document or law report: 'Did you
say page 53, Mr. Jones? No, my lord, page 63.' Argument is never presented
in the form of written briefs.[2]

Depending upon the size of the case, there has been before the trial a
great deal of preliminary preparation, but the trial judge has not been concerned with it. Each party prepares his own case separately and, so far as
he is permitted to do so, conceals his preparations from the other side. If
the trial were nothing but the battle which in some respects it resembles,
each party would want to leave his opponent guessing about the shape of
his array. To some extent this is permitted, but not to the point where the
opponent would be taken by surprise. It is at this point that the analogy
with the military finishes. In the art of war surprise is everything, but then
in war victory is as likely to go to the unjust as to the just and there does
not hover over the battlefield an umpire with power to adjourn. If there
has been insufficient disclosure, an adjournment (for which he must pay
the costs) is the best result for which a defaulting party can hope, as well
as the most usual one; the worst is to have the evidence on the unpleaded
point excluded.

The rules[3] require each party in his pleadings to set out 'in summary
form ... the material facts on which he relies for his claim or defence as
the case may be, but not the evidence by which these facts are to be proved'
and to 'be as brief as the nature of the case admits'. Contentions of law do
not have to be pleaded. The rules[4] also require each party to prepare lists
of documents in his possession or power, not only of those on which he
is himself relying but of all documents relating to the matters in the action.
The opposite party is entitled to have inspection of these documents unless
objection, e.g. on the ground of privilege, is taken. These processes frequently give rise to disputes. Are the pleadings sufficiently detailed? Further
facts have come to light: may there be leave to amend? Have all relevant
documents been disclosed, e.g. the contents of a document that has been
disclosed may suggest another that has not? Ought the objection to inspection to be upheld? Such disputes are settled in the first instance by a subordinate judge known as a master or registrar. But they may be taken from him
to a judge (not usually the judge who will try the case) and thence sometimes

---

[1] There would be trouble if they were not. In my limited experience of dossiers their most
unattractive feature is that the documents are arranged anyhow and there is no continuous pag-
ing.

[2] A classic account of the judge's function in the adversary system is given by Lord Justice
Denning in *Jones* v. *National Coal Board* [1957] 2 K.B. at 63.

[3] R.S.C. O.18 r.7.   [4] R.S.C. O.24 r.1.

to the Court of Appeal. These interlocutory proceedings may take up a lot of time and cost a lot of money.

I now contrast with this the inquisitorial system. While the system is in general use on the Continent, there are different procedures in different countries and I shall confine myself to the essential features. There is at or near the beginning of the proceedings a full statement in writing of his case by the plaintiff followed by a similar statement in reply by the defendant. These statements set out evidence rather than issues. They must cover all the facts upon which each party relies and indicate the means by which he proposes to establish them. They resemble the opening statement of the English advocate, not the English statement of claim; they are written to convince and not to conceal. Relevant documents are annexed. These statements, maybe followed by a rejoinder and a rebutter, form the backbone of the dossier. The rest of it is made up under the supervision of the judge. If the court consists, as is usual on the Continent, of three judges, one of them will act for this purpose as the *juge des mises en état* or *juge rapporteur* (to give the French terms), i.e. the judge in charge. He will call on one party or the other to produce such further material as he thinks the court may want, or he may instruct the *greffier*, or registrar of the court, to obtain it. He may obtain reports from experts, which will go into the dossier. He may decide that certain witnesses ought to be orally interrogated and, if he does so decide, he will undertake the task himself in the presence of the parties. The questioning will be done by him; sometimes the parties or their advocates are allowed at the end of his examination to put further questions; sometimes they are allowed only to suggest further questions to be put by the judge. Either way there is nothing to match the hostile cross-examination that is such a distinctive feature of the English trial. The judge's note of the evidence will be put in the dossier.

The dossier is completed by a note or summary or perhaps a draft judgment by the judge in charge. The other judges study the dossier and the three will discuss the case. They decide whether a hearing, the *audience publique*, is necessary or desirable. If there is one, the advocates will be allowed a limited time; even in a heavy case it is unlikely to last for more than half a day. The judgment will be expressed briefly and in writing.

Let me now consider what are the qualities to look for in the administration of justice and see how far they are present in each system. I do not place them in order of merit and I do not at this stage consider the important question of expense. Let us look at them at first as if money was no object.

One attribute, about whose value different opinions are held, is openness. The British consider it to be essential; they say that justice should not only be done but should be seen to be done, and the English system observes this precept in the spirit and in the letter. This is in their opinion the distinguishing mark between justice in the forum and administrative or faceless justice. The British civil servant is just and incorruptible, and when the administrative decision arrives with the post, first-class mail, no expense spared (except for an instruction to re-use the envelope for your reply), clearly and politely expressed in the civil service passive ('credence is not attached to your statement that ...', etc.), and is found to be favourable, there is no complaint. But when unfavourable the recipient wonders who it was who really took the decision, some understrapper perhaps, and whether he really understood this, that, and the next thing. The contrary view to all this is of course that the process does not matter unless it can be shown to be irregular; what matters is that there should be a clear and well-reasoned decision at the end.

The importance of the *audience publique* is that it removes to some extent the facelessness. It cannot compare in this respect with a process which allows the public and the press as well as the litigants to see the judge at work from start to finish, but at least it lets them see what sort of men the judges are, and, if there is some debate, as there may be, to assure themselves that they have studied the case; some litigants suspect that some judges only pretend to read papers.

Akin to this question of openness there is the element of verbal pugilism which is so characteristic of the British trial and which, except for a possible encounter in the *audience publique*, is entirely absent from the dossier systems. Moreover in the *audience publique* the pugilism is expressed only by an exchange of forensic eloquence; there is no cross-examination of the parties and it is in cross-examination that the British trial comes closest to fisticuffs. Fisticuffs are hardly needed for the pitiless exposure of deceit where that is present, and, where it is, there is no other forensic art which approaches cross-examination in effectiveness. Where his opponent is a villian the ruthless exposure of the villainy must be much more satisfactory to the innocent and injured party—and incidentally a much greater deterrent to villainy—than the simple non-attachment of credence. But the fact is that in most cases there are no villains. Nevertheless, in many of them, the plaintiff or the defendant, naturally not unprejudiced, has a tendency to suspect at least minor forms of villainy on the other side. Hence the temptation to fisticuffs. It is display fighting, very stylized, descending in bellicosity from the 'I suggest to you that your evidence is nothing but a tissue of lies from start to finish' down to the 'I put it to you that you are entirely mistaken'. Doubtless it was suited to a nineteenth-century jury and has now become a traditional part of the process. Probably too it allows a losing litigant (a winning one needs no soothing) to get off by proxy what is on his chest: 'Pretty well told him he was a damned liar, my man did.'

In so far as the object of a trial is to give satisfaction to all, this is important; it has no part in the process of adjudication. Solicitors, nevertheless, like to please their clients and for that purpose to pick a good fighter. At least they did, but times may be changing and litigants getting less pugnacious. There is, however, a little more to it than a display of pugnacity. Opportunities are offered in the open trial, by way of judicial comment made during it or in the judgment, more discursive than the Continental type, to acknowledge the good points made by both sides. Sometimes a loser may feel that he has won a moral victory on what mattered most to him; sometimes he may feel that he has scored a point or two, enough to amount to a consolation prize.

But for all this there is a price to pay in terms of convenience. The convenience of the litigants is the next quality in the administration of justice which I shall consider. There can be no doubt that the dossier system scores heavily here. The taking of statements from parties and witnesses is common to both systems. But while in the dossier system they may not be further troubled—and, if they are, it will be only for some of them and for a short appointment—under the English system this will be only the beginning of their sorrows. They will almost certainly lose a day in attendance at court and may have to travel some distance to it. This is not so bad for the parties, since it is their fight, but it can be very burdensome for the independent witness. It is not only his time that is taken up. To have to appear in public and as part of a performance with strange rites may be an unusual ordeal for him, very different from the informal interview at which a statement is taken. He may be told to speak up; to answer yes or no if he can; not to make speeches; to deliver his answer to the judge and not to the questioner whom he has been facing; to speak more slowly; to pause in mid-answer while what he has said is being written down—'follow my Lord's pen', he will be adjured. Although he has come, as he sees it, only to help in the doing of justice, he may be subjected to a hostile cross-examination and not allowed to answer back. He may conceivably find his credit attacked on matters outside the ambit of the case, having been given no notice of the questions and being offered no chance, except by his denials, to rebut the accusations. The rule is that the cross-examiner cannot go behind the witness's denial, but this does not displace the slur.

Moreover, it is far from certain that the day upon which he is summoned to attend will be the day of the trial. The clerks and administrators who make up the lists must try to fill the judicial day. For the time that the court-room is empty, the whole cost of it—the hypothetical rental, the upkeep, the salaries of the judge and court officials—will be wasted. In a mixed system the judge at least could occupy himself with written work, but in the English system, except for the occasional reserved judgment which normally he would write out of court hours, the judge has no written work. It is not easy to estimate the length of a case. If the second case in the list is not reached, the parties and witnesses will be told to come back on the next day; or, worse still, if that day is occupied, to await a summons for another day unspecified. It would not be out of the way for a witness to attend on three days so as to give half an hour of evidence.

The administrators are up against an even graver hazard than the erroneous estimate, namely, the collapse of the case. In crime this happens rarely enough, when there is an unexpected change of plea to guilty, but it is a regular feature of the civil list. A high percentage of cases are settled when opposing counsel meet at the door of the court. This makes it necessary to put into the list many more cases than are likely to be reached. In the settled case the witness may find his journey is wasted but at least he does not have to come again; in the unsettled case, unless it is first in the list, the witness may find not only that his journey is wasted but that he has also to come again. In general, the difficulties of arranging a list are so great that a witness may be told no more than that he may be wanted during the next week and not notified of the actual day until the evening before. This makes life very difficult for the man or woman with appointments to keep. The administration of justice is deemed to take precedence of all else, and a witness who without an acceptable excuse fails to attend can be severely fined.

It is time now to come to the fundamental question, though I doubt if I shall be able to answer it without hedging. Is an equally good result, that is the just result, obtainable from both methods: if not, which is to be preferred? I have already made the point that the objects of each method are formally different, the one being to decide whether the prosecution or plaintiff has discharged the burden of proof, the other being to ascertain the truth. In practice there is not, at any rate in the civil case, all that much difference. The English say that the best way of getting at the truth is to have each party dig for the facts that help it; between them they will bring all to light. The inquisitor works on his own but has in the end to say who wins and who loses. Lord Denning[1] denies that the English judge is 'a mere umpire' and says that 'his object, above all, is to find out the truth'. The real difference is, I think, that in the adversary system the judge in his quest for the truth is restricted to the material presented by the parties, in whose production he has played no part and which he cannot augment, while in the inquisitorial system the judge can find out what he wants to know. Put in a nutshell, the arbiter is confined and the inquisitor is not.

Are the facts more thoroughly prepared under one system than under the other? It can be argued that to have an experienced judge in charge of the inquiry is a clear advantage; it can also be argued that two prejudiced searchers starting from opposite ends of the field will between them be less likely to miss anything than the impartial searcher starting in the middle. So there may not be much difference in the preparation of the facts. But when it comes to their presentation, there is.

Under the dossier system there is no difficulty about presenting the whole of the witness's story in a smooth sequence. If it has emerged under questions the questioning has been done impartially by the judge; a witness who has been put forward by one party or the other is treated no differently from one who has been selected by the judge. This is in complete contrast to the English system, under which the advocate for each party calls his own client and his own witnesses. Whereas under most Continental systems the advocate is discouraged, if not prohibited, from interviewing a witness before his examination in court, the English advocate has in front of him a 'proof', or written statement of evidence which the witness has already given; he examines him from that. This is known as 'examination-in-chief' (in the United States as 'direct examination') and is quite different from cross-examination. The theory is that the witness is partisan; an advocate refers to him in court as 'my witness' or 'your witness'. So questioning in examination-in-chief is very restricted. The witness may not (except by consent on parts of the evidence not in dispute) be asked leading questions, i.e. questions whose form is suggestive of the answer which the advocate wants; the witness's answer, if unfavourable or even astounding, may not be challenged. Thus as a rule it is thought to be too dangerous to call a witness who has not previously given a proof.

Cross-examination on the other hand is uninhibited. Its object is to challenge and discredit, taking care not to let in incidentally material helpful to the other side. Thus if the witness has in chief proved impervious to all jogging of the memory which falls short of the forbidden lead, and consequently an act or event, maybe vital to the plaintiff's case, remains un-

[1] See footnote on p. 56.

proved, the defendant's counsel will keep well away from the point. Likewise he will not seek to improve upon the surprisingly favourable answer lest on reconsideration the witness modify it. Many are the tales told of the un-skilful cross-examiner who by asking one question too many has made his opponent's case for him. It is always open to the judge to probe, but the tradition is strong that he is an arbiter and not an inquisitor and that the coming to the aid of a party in distress might impair his impartiality.

The scope for this sort of tactical manœuvre is one of the chief distinctions between a trial and an inquiry. While it is true to say that the double search by both parties is likely to discover all that is relevant for and against, this is not the same as saying that it will all be presented at the trial. Indeed it can happen in a civil case that a key witness will be left on the sidelines. Both parties may fight shy of calling the man who has something to say for both sides, each party doubting whether he will do his side more good than harm and each hoping that the other side will call him so that he can have the inestimable benefit of cross-examining him, leading him to all that is favourable and challenging him on all that is not. If the exis-tence of such a witness is revealed in the course of the trial, the judge can call him, if neither side objects, but this is a course that is very rarely taken.

The rules of evidence constitute another impediment to a full presentation of the facts. Ideally it must always be best to let the parties prove what facts they like and for the court to sift them and to give each its due weight. But for the sifting there must be a trained mind. A jury would find it difficult to differentiate in value between firsthand and secondhand evidence; our ancestors' solution of the problem was to exclude altogether the second-hand: hence the need for rules on this and similar points. These rules were continued, though with some modern relaxations, into the non-jury trial. Although it is a pity to exclude altogether secondhand evidence, which can often be useful and which a judge is competent to evaluate, there must be some limit to its admissibility in oral proceedings if they are to be kept within bounds.

It is indeed one of the advantages which written proceedings have over oral that in them irrelevance and prolixity do not much matter; the worthless can be skimmed and discarded in comparatively little time. In oral proceed-ings surplus matter is less easily disposed of. It is the business of the skilful judge to keep it to a minimum. Likewise he seeks to minimize the time taken by unimpressive points without letting the advocate feel that he is being denied a fair hearing. But in perceiving and excluding what is irrelevant, in curbing prolixity without abruptness, and in handling bad points, there is inevitably some waste of court time, and court time is much more expensive than paper.

So much for the presentation of the facts. The disadvantages which I have just been pointing out have to be set against the big advantage which to my mind is given to a judge who has the whole story, as it were, played out in front of him. He can resolve on the spot the small point that worries him whereas the dossier cannot be questioned. He can form an opinion of the sort of man the witness is and so get an impression, more lively than any dossier could give, of how he is likely to have behaved in the events he is narrating. It is often and rightly said that the playing out is in slow motion and that much of it is rendered three or four times over in speeches, in examination, cross-examination, and re-examination. But, disregarding for the moment the question of expense, the slow motion is itself an inducement to minute inspection.

The great virtue of the English trial is usually said to be the opportunity it gives to the judge to tell from the demeanour of the witness whether or not he is telling the truth. I think that this is overrated. It is the tableau that constitutes the big advantage, the text with illustrations, rather than the demeanour of a particular witness. On that I would adopt in their entirety (this being the highest form of judicial concurrence) the words of Mr. Justice MacKenna:

I question whether the respect given to our findings of fact based on the demeanour of the witnesses is always deserved. I doubt my own ability, and sometimes that of other judges, to discern from a witness's demeanour, or the tone of his voice, whether he is telling the truth. He speaks hesitantly. Is that the mark of a cautious man, whose statements are for that reason to be respected, or is he taking time to fabricate? Is the emphatic witness putting on an act to deceive me, or is he speaking from the fullness of his heart, knowing that he is right? Is he likely to be more truthful if he looks me straight in the face than if he casts his eyes on the ground perhaps from shyness or a natural timidity? For my part I rely on these considerations as little as I can help.

This is how I go about the business of finding facts. I start from the undisputed facts which both sides accept. I add to them such other facts as seem very likely to be true, as, for example, those recorded in contemporary documents or spoken to by independent witnesses like the policeman giving evidence in a running down case about the marks on the road. I judge a witness to be unreliable if his evidence is, in any serious respect, inconsistent with these undisputed or indisputable facts, or of course if he contradicts himself on important points. I rely as little as possible on such deceptive matters as his demeanour. When I have done my best to separate the true from the false by these more or less objective tests, I say which story seems to me the more probable, the Plaintiff's or the Defendant's.[1]

---

[1] From 'Discretion', a paper read at University College, Dublin, 21 Feb. 1973, printed in the *Irish Jurist*, vol. IX, new series, p. 1.

In the presentation of the law, if it is complicated, I believe that the ideal,
money being no object, is the written brief followed by an oral discussion
of the points that trouble the judges. If I had to choose between making
the whole presentation either oral or written, I should have to gamble on
the quality of the advocacy. If it is good and clear, there is nothing to equal
the oral; if it is bad, it is best to study it in writing.

I can now no longer delay my arrival at the complex question of costs. I do not
know of any work comparing in a detailed manner the costs of obtaining
justice under the two systems, the adversary and the inquisitorial. I am not
sure that they can be compared with any precision, but I should like to see
the attempt made.

One could begin perhaps by taking a common sort of claim, e.g. for personal injuries in a road accident, and comparing the cost to the parties of
proceeding to judgment in England and in, say, France. I do not think that
one would get very far this way because the method would leave out of
account, as I shall seek to show, so much of the full cost of litigation. Nor
can it be assumed that in France or any other country the operating cost
of the dossier system is as low as it should be or that there are no French
critics of French procedure as there are English critics of English. At the
end you would arrive at a total sum in francs to be compared with a total
in sterling. But there would be other factors to be taken into account besides
a possibly erratic rate of exchange, as for example the rates of professional
remuneration in the different countries. In England it is still probably true
to say that the barrister's brief fee in a case that is fought is large enough
to compensate him for underpaid work in cases that are settled before
trial.

Another way would be to take the same sort of case, construct for it a
new English dossier procedure, and then calculate what would be par for
taking it round the course under the existing procedure and under the new
and compare the two. This method would permit the ascertainment, though
some of it would be speculative, of what I have called the full cost of litigation. This would be under four heads: court time, judicial time, lawyers'
time, parties' and witnesses' time.

Under the first head, there is in England a large amount of fixed capital
invested in the construction of courtrooms. The investment is continually
increasing and always behindhand. During the whole of my time at the Bar
and on the Bench there were in the East Quadrangle of the Royal Courts
of Justice in the Strand two temporary courts, shacks they might impolitely
be called, to stem the overflow. It should be possible, I suppose, to calculate

the annual cost of a courtroom and appurtenances allowing for interest on capital and amortization, to add to it the cost of maintenance and the wages of staff, such as ushers, and to express the total as a notional hourly rental. Under the adversary system this would be quite an appreciable sum and under the dossier system very little.

Under the second head, the cost of judicial time, the balance should on the face of it incline the other way, but appearances may be deceptive. Undoubtedly, European countries have a much larger judiciary than England has. Of course the European figures are swollen by the general practice of sitting at first instance in a bench of three; this is not a necessary feature of the dossier system. Even so the Continental judges, particularly the one in charge of the dossier, must spend more time on it than the English judge does on the trial. Against this there must be put the cost of judicial time expended under the adversary system on interlocutory work.

By the cost of lawyers' time under the third head, I mean the time spent on the preparation and presentation of the case by the advocates on both sides. Here there is a feature of the English system which, if it adds to the cost as in the smaller case it may do, would have to be disregarded as irrelevant since it is not essential to the adversary system: this is the division of the legal profession into barristers and solicitors.

Subject to this, let me take separately the cost of preparation and the cost of presentation. The former should be less under the dossier system, since if the work is done under judicial direction the issues to be prepared should be reduced and duplication of work avoided. The question whether a written presentation of the case is less costly than an oral presentation is one on which opinions differ. It is suggested that counsel's fee for preparing a written submission would be just as high, if not higher, than for delivering an oral one. Here I think it would be necessary to distinguish between what I might call study time and performance time. Study time, i.e. reading or writing time, can be given when it suits the convenience of the advocate, while performance time requires him to be in a particular place at a particular hour and often to be kept waiting. This should be reflected in a difference in the rate of remuneration.

But, assuming the rate to be the same, let me examine the proposition that the written statement would cost more. I do not doubt that written composition is more laborious than the delivery of an opening speech. But in the written procedure it is not on the composition that money is saved; it is on the studying or reading time as compared with listening time. A written script can be read in half (sometimes much less) the time that it takes to listen to it being delivered with the customary pauses and fumblings, unrecorded colloquies between counsel, and the like. In a substantial case with two counsel and a solicitor for each side present in court as well as the judge, there are six listeners to one orator. If the six listeners are turned into readers, the saving of six half-days would enable the composer to be paid, say, 50% more than the orator and still leave a considerable surplus.

Under the fourth head I have already said enough to indicate the economies that would be made if parties and witnesses were not required to attend court. These economies are not fully reflected in the saving of witnesses' fees and expenses; regard must be had also to the saving of disruption.

These rather amateurish calculations hardly do more than indicate the sort of factors to be assessed. Even a professional calculator would, I think, be left with a lot of room for guesswork. At this stage my guess is that the dossier system should prove a lot cheaper.

Another approach is to consider the cost of obtaining justice in relation to the amount at stake. One of the most elementary duties of a civilized State is to provide for its citizens a system for settling disputes. This obligation would be meaningless if the price to the citizen was out of proportion to the value in dispute. The Welfare State could of course provide the citizen with free legal aid in all disputes, but this would not eliminate the need for keeping the cost proportionate to the object. A Welfare State cannot survive if it pays more than a reasonable price for the benefits it confers upon its citizens. The only way of determining whether the cost of a lawsuit is reasonable or not is to ask if a reasonable man would think the expenditure worth while if it had to be paid out of his own pocket. The answer to that question depends largely on the amount at stake; expenditure which would be reasonable in an attempt to recover £100,000 would be unreasonable if the dispute were about £10.

There have always in England been local courts to cater for the small litigant. The principle was, so to speak, codified in the County Courts Act 1846 which created courts with a jurisdiction of up to £50 (now £2,000) in the ordinary case. If it be right to suppose that judicial and forensic qualities are to some extent commensurate with salaries and fees, then the quality of justice in the County Courts is lower than in the High Court. But the procedure, excising some trimmings and perhaps cutting some corners, is the same. Contrast this with the Small Claims Courts which were created in 1972 with a jurisdiction up to £100 (increased now to £150) and provided with an entirely new system of justice. The system does not permit any legal representation, dispenses with the law of evidence, permits the court to make inquiries on its own, and allows written submissions from either party. This is virtually the inquisitorial system. Indeed, where there is no legal representation, and save in the exceptional case of the skilled litigant, the adversary system, whether or not it remains in theory, in practice breaks down. Where both parties are unrepresented, the judge is left with no alternative except himself to ferret out the relevant facts; when one side only is represented, the judge finds it difficult to do justice without constituting himself to some extent the advocate for the other.

So at the impoverished end of the scale, i.e. below £150, we do have the inquisitorial system. There is no inherent virtue in the sum of £150; it is simply a cut-off point. Would it not be better to make the point of division flexible: should it not be the point at which the cost under the adversary system ceases to bear a reasonable proportion to the amount at stake? If we were to accept this as a general principle, it would still leave a lot to be discussed. What is a reasonable proportion? How do you ascertain the amount at stake, which is not necessarily the same as the amount claimed? What provision will be made for exceptional cases, since money is not always the only thing that matters in a lawsuit?

I shall not in a lecture designed as a comparison between two systems let these inquiries lead me on to the construction of detailed procedural steps. I shall not do more than advocate two broad measures. The first is that inquisitorial methods should be officially admitted into the procedure of the High Court as constituting one mode of trial. The second is that there should be a more elaborate selection of the appropriate mode than there is at present. This will require some modification of the adversary system. There is not at present enough material disclosed sufficiently early in the litigation to enable such a selection to be made.

But the heart of the system has already been broken so as to ensure that at the trial neither party is taken by surprise. This results in a partial and measured disclosure, the measuring often necessitating expensive interlocutory procedure. This seems to me an unsatisfactory compromise. Why should there not be a full disclosure at the outset, all cards face up on the table? This or something like it is what already happens under our Admiralty procedure in the case of collisions at sea.[1] The judge will then have at the outset the material that will enable him to decide upon what is really at stake, whether it be money or a reputation, and so to decide, in relation to the value of the subject-matter as well as its nature, upon the appropriate and economical mode of trial. If the amount in dispute is large and the parties, unconcerned with the scale of costs, want the trial to proceed in the old way, there is no reason why it should not. Or in cases where the parties

[1] R.S.C. O.75 r.18.

are concerned with costs, it may be that the adversary system, with economies effected by some substitution of written for oral procedure, will seem likely to reduce the bill to a reasonable level. But there will be cases in which it will only be by the use of the inquisitorial system that a reasonable level can be reached and then neither party should have the right to insist on greater expense.

What is a reasonable relationship of costs to amount at stake? I can only express my opinion and I say it should be about 20%. £5,000 is an average sort of figure for the two bills of costs in the High Court; and I personally think that if a plaintiff has to put down £500 to get the thing started with the prospect of finding another £500 if he loses, that would be as much as he should be expected to face. I am talking of the minimum, i.e. 'taxed costs', and leaving out of account the costs, often substantial, incurred on both sides which, though not unreasonable, are disallowed in the bill presented to a loser. Checking this guess would require a great deal of research in an area not much explored. The figures of course exist in solicitors' files, but cases differ so much that the investigation of a large number would be necessary in order to produce a fair average percentage.

Of course no solicitor could give an assurance that his bill would not exceed a fair average percentage unless he was prepared either to gamble or to take enough cases to make the simple pay for the complicated. But if the mode of trial was such as to keep the costs within the given percentage in the average case, it would mean that the litigant who hit the norm on the head would not be paying more than he could be expected to afford, and this would set a standard from which the abnormal would benefit. If ever the Welfare State breaks through the 'poverty barrier' in Legal Aid to help all litigants, it would have the resources to guarantee the excess of any bill over the given percentage and the power to collect from those whose bills were smaller. But I am sure that, within the framework of our present modes of trial, we could not arrive at a percentage which the State would find acceptable.

It is true that only a small number of people have to dig into their purses to finance their own litigation. Government Departments pay their litigious way, but they can hardly be thought of as digging into their purses. Big business corporations pay half and put the other half against Corporation Tax. But ordinary folk insure against having to finance their own litigation, if it arises, by paying premiums or subscriptions to insurance companies and to trade and professional associations. These are the bodies who conduct the bulk of England's litigation out of funds provided mainly by non-litigants (since it is only a tiny percentage of the subscribers who get involved) in the same way as the healthy pay for the cure of the unhealthy and the short-lived for the annuities which sustain long lives.

This sort of litigation is concentrated on one type of case, i.e. accidental injury on the highway, in the factory, or in the hospital. Probably all the bodies which conduct it keep records which would show over the period the relationship of costs to amount at stake. The National Coal Board,[1] for example, meets every year a large number of claims for accidents in their mines. Their records show the sums paid out and the costs incurred. The National Union of Mineworkers must have similar figures from the trade union side. I estimate the costs of both sides added together would be about 15% of the damages paid. But then of course the vast majority of these cases would have been settled before the full costs of a lawsuit had been incurred. For cases fought to a finish a figure of 30% would not be unusual. And this is what might be described as economical litigation. Many economies can be made when the lawsuit is within a well-charted field and the solicitors on the one side are familiar with the ways used by those on the other.

Lawsuits between ordinary citizens of limited means are so uncommon that it is difficult to find out anything about them. The main reason why they are uncommon is, I think, because the cost would be prohibitive. Yet the obligation on a State to provide justice is not discharged by devising a single and inflexible mode of trial whose cost is beyond the reach of the ordinary citizen. Its obligation is to provide as many modes of trial as are necessary to cover the variety of disputes that may commonly arise so that for each type there may be selected a mode that will offer a reasonable standard of justice at a reasonable cost. To neglect this obligation in pursuit of a single mode which is considered to be the best is bound to end in a denial of justice to many. This is not merely a matter of proportions and estimates. Everyone knows, every lawyer particularly knows, that for the ordinary citizen unqualified for Legal Aid (and for many who qualify, only subject to their making a large contribution) a lawsuit is financially quite out of the question. The citizen who is up against an insurance company or a trade union, or any other powerful litigant, must take what is offered to him and be glad that he has got something. If he is up against one of his own kind, the result depends on bluff and brinkmanship rather than upon justice.

---

[1] I am much indebted to the Board for information which produces estimates realistic enough for my purpose.

The question whether the inquisitorial system should have any place in our criminal process gives rise to entirely different considerations. For trial by jury is an essential part of our criminal procedure, and the presentation of the case to a jury is incompatible with the inquisitorial system. It might no doubt be argued that the benefits of the inquisitorial system are greater than those conferred by trial by jury. But this would raise too large an issue to be settled here; for my part I am not willing to abandon trial by jury in cases of serious crime. Moreover, the open trial is one of the great advantages of the adversary system; its importance in civil procedure may be questionable, but in crime it is supreme.

What I want to consider here is the use of the inquisitorial system in the preparation of the criminal case. In Europe generally the preparation is, like the preparation of the dossier in the civil case, done under judicial direction. In France, for example, the figure, so familiar to addicts of crime fiction, of the *juge d'instruction* plays a dominating part in the investigation of crime; so does the less dramatic procurator-fiscal in Scotland. In England there is no judicial equivalent.

This has not been ordained as part of a deliberate policy. Until the early part of the nineteenth century the justice of the peace, in his role as examining magistrate, investigated crime, made arrests, questioned suspects, granted bail, prepared the depositions of witnesses for the prosecution, and, if he thought that they showed a case to answer, submitted a bill of indictment to the grand jury. His duties were laid down by statutes in 1554 and 1555. He sat in private, often in his own house. By 1848, when the Indictable Offences Act was passed, this investigating procedure had developed into a preliminary hearing. It was the formation of police forces that made this development possible; the first of them was in London, the Metropolitan Police Act being passed in 1829. The police took over the responsibility for the investigation; the magistrates retained the judicial side. They controlled the grant of warrants for arrest on information laid by the police (though in many cases the police could arrest without warrant) and likewise the grant of bail; they heard in the presence of the accused the witnesses for the prosecution whose statements had been taken by the police and decided whether or not to commit for trial; since the police rarely presented a case which was too weak to be committed, the committal was usually unopposed.

Soon everything fell into the hands of the police. On paper the extrusion of the judicial inquisitor would seem to mark the triumph of the adversary system. With the aid of the police the prosecution would assemble for the trial all the facts that told for the accused's guilt, the defence lawyers would produce all those which told for his innocence, battle would be joined, the stronger would win, and the weaker be defeated. So it should have been in theory. But, as it has recently been put,[1]

The theory of the adversary system has proved too strong for modern ideas of criminal justice and so in practice it has been diluted. The theory is based on the presumption that the resources of the parties are sufficiently near to equality to ensure a fair fight. The presumption may be sound enough in criminal proceedings when they come to trial, now that legal aid is available. But in the preparation of the criminal case it is manifestly unsound. For in criminal cases the State has in the police an agency for the discovery of evidence superior to anything which even the wealthiest defendant could employ.

The police have a duty to make enquiries in a quasi-judicial spirit. By quasi-judicial in this context we mean that the enquiry is to be conducted as much with the object of ascertaining facts which will exonerate as of ascertaining those which will convict; and that the facts when ascertained are to be assessed impartially. It is because this quasi-judicial duty exists that it is not unreasonable to expect a suspect to make a voluntary statement to the police; no such expectation could reasonably be entertained if he were simply giving advance information to the enemy.

All things considered the police have discharged this peculiar obligation, though not impeccably, remarkably well, at least well enough to enable the system to work. The general conclusion of a Royal Commission reached half a century ago is about as true today as it was then. This was that the police did not press for the conviction of people whom they believed to be innocent, but did occasionally strain the evidence against someone genuinely believed to be guilty.[2]

The great advantage of this amalgamation of roles is that it has enabled an accused to be brought to trial with a speed unmatched in any other country. For most of this century trial followed arrest within a matter of weeks rather than months. In the last decade delays have been much longer, but they have been caused not by the police but by the insufficiency of judges and courts to keep abreast of the increase in crime.

Undoubtedly a practical, resourceful, and adaptable man can fly quite a long way contrary to theory, but theory, if it is sound, must in the end get him down. The role we have assigned to the police is theoretically unsound. There is a great difference between playing fair with an opponent, which the police are rightly required to do, and holding the balance even between

---

[1] *Report to the Secretary of State for the Home Department of the Departmental Committee on Evidence of Identification in Criminal Cases*, H.M.S.O., ordered by the House of Commons to be printed 26 Apr. 1976 (hereafter referred to as *Identification Report*), paras. 1.17 and 5.98. A number of points considered in this report and hereafter referred to in this lecture have been considered also in Sir Henry Fisher's *Report on the Confait Case*, H.M.S.O., ordered by the House of Commons to be printed 13 Dec. 1977 (hereafter referred to as the Fisher Report); see especially paras. 2.29 and 2.53.

[2] *Royal Commission on Police Powers and Procedure*, H.M.S.O., 1929, Cmd. 3297, pp. 100–103.

him and yourself. The latter activity is discountenanced by the legal maxim that no man can be a judge in his own cause. The police would not be as useful to society as they are if they were not ardent against its enemies and did not make their apprehension and conviction the cause for which they fight. It is unnatural to fight quasi-judicially. The face of the police officer is not 'sicklied o'er with the pale cast of thought', and, once he finds a reasonable quantity of pros, he will act decisively without too much anxiety about the cons. When a police officer charges a man it is because he believes him to be guilty, not just because he thinks there is a case for trial. For the policeman the arrest and charge ends the matter; what follows is for him the solemnization which society as a matter of decency requires. The process may be likened to the progress from the betrothal to the altar; occasionally something goes wrong in between, but this should be abnormal. This is why it makes sense to police chiefs to talk of juries acquitting the guilty; they are referring to the acquittal of those whom they rightly arrested.

It is at this stage of the process, i.e. when the police have made up their minds, rather than at the earlier stage when they are still hunting, that the interposition of a judicial mind would be useful. Nine times out of ten it will find nothing new, but every now and again it will find in the material dredged up by the police something of importance to the defence which the police have ignored.

Is there not, you may ask at this juncture, some obligation on the police to pass on to the defence discoveries which might be helpful to them? Twentieth-century judges do not appear to have been very forward on this point, especially when their efforts are compared with those of their nineteenth-century predecessors, who gradually forced the prosecution to disclose before the trial every scrap of evidence that it was going to use against the accused. On the disclosure of material favourable to the defence virtually all that the courts have done is to ordain that when the police have taken a statement from a person who can give material evidence but whom they decide not to call as a witness, they must supply the defence with his name and address; save in exceptional cases, they are not required to supply the defence with copies of statements they have taken or documents they have discovered. This meagre offering is in practice supplemented by arrangements between counsel for more generous disclosure. Since April 1973[1] the matter has been under the consideration of the Home Office. On 24 June 1977 the Prime Minister announced a Royal Commission to investigate the pre-trial process.

[1] *Identification Report*, para. 5.1; Fisher Report, paras. 29.17 to 29.37. But see now *R*. v. *Leyland Justices* (1978), referred to at p. 83 below.

At the heart of the difficulty is the tendency of the police, once their mind is made up, to treat as mistaken any evidence that contradicts their proof of guilt. This tendency played a part in two of the most notorious miscarriages of justice in this century.

In the case of Timothy Evans in 1950 the accused confessed in quite convincing detail to the murder of his wife. Later the police took statements from two witnesses which made Evans's account of how he had disposed of the body extremely unlikely. These statements should have been made available to the defence in case they wished, as at the trial in fact they did, to challenge the confession. But the police, being satisfied with the confession, simply assumed that the witnesses must be mistaken and indeed persuaded the witnesses that they were mistaken and got them to alter their statements. The original statements were not supplied to the defence who challenged the confession unsuccessfully. Evans was convicted, and so some years later was the true murderer.[1]

In the Virag case in 1969 the criminal was surprised while stealing coinboxes from parking meters. He was chased and in the pursuit shot and wounded a policeman. Six witnesses picked out Mr. Virag as the criminal, first, from an album of photographs, and then, after his arrest, on identity parades. Then on four of the stolen coin-boxes the police found fingerprints which were not Virag's. Much later they were found to be those of the true criminal. But at the time the police were unable to envisage the possibility that the six identifying witnesses could all be mistaken. They concluded that Mr. Virag must have had an associate and that the fingerprints were his. There was no other evidence that he had an associate and the facts of the case would have made the theory difficult to sustain. The theory never had to be tested because the police never disclosed the existence of the fingerprints. Mr Virag was wrongly convicted.[2]

These are celebrated examples of a situation that probably arises quite often. I do not mean that quite often injustice results, but that quite often there is concealed in police files material which the defence might be able to make some use of. Indeed, this is what accounts for the reluctance to disclose. Why should the defence, the policeman asks himself once he is convinced of guilt, be supplied with material which they will use to divert attention from the real issue? Diversions of this sort are a familiar form of defence; often the advocate has nothing better to offer. The police have to accept these forays as part of the game, but need they provide the ammunition for them?

[1] Ludovic Kennedy, *Ten Rillington Place*, Gollancz, London, 1961.
[2] *Identification Report*, Chapter 3, especially paras. 3.104 to 3.112.

This is what makes me doubt whether the problem can be solved by rules. The police cannot simply be made accountable to defence lawyers, some of whom rightly or wrongly they may distrust, as if they were inquiry agents for both sides. Much of what they get is confidential, e.g. from informers; the police guard their sources even more jealously than journalists. Any attempt to make them hand over this sort of information, even if it were thought in theory desirable that they should do so, would be frustrated in practice; information which they did not wish to disclose would not be recorded in writing.

For these reasons there cannot be a simple rule requiring disclosure. Nor can there be a rule with exceptions; a framework of this sort would be too rigid. Things can be left as they are, i.e. in the discretion of the police, but with clearer and more detailed administrative guidelines. I do not think that this would provide a satisfactory solution because I do not, for the reasons I have indicated, think that the police can be expected to exercise a judicial discretion. I do not indeed see any solution other than by the creation of a judicial intermediary.

This is the point where the inquisitorial system scores heavily over the adversary. In searching for a pattern of judicial mediation under the adversary system, we should naturally begin by looking at our civil procedure which has elaborate arrangements for the disclosure of documents by both parties. I have already[1] stated what they are and indicated how long the process could take; it is indeed one of the few processes in the adversary system which I feel might benefit from less writing and more talk. By contrast, the *juge d'instruction* could practically conduct the whole business on the telephone. More remote than the police, he can direct the investigation for the benefit of both sides. He is a man qualified by training and inclination to take a more detached view than the police could take and should perceive more readily than the police can what would be of real significance to the other side. The disclosure to him of a confidential document does not mean that it is automatically seen by the defence and that its contents may be passed on to all the criminal underworld. As a result of it he can order further inquiries to be made or devise a way of disclosing to the defence as much as they ought to know without revealing the whole. This does of course mean that everything is not open and above-board; it is not in the spirit of the adversary system, but it is very practical.

Another consequence of the slide of our adversary system into the police inquisition has been the diminishment of defence activity. In civil procedure the solicitors for plaintiff and for defendant are equally busy in preparation.

[1] See p. 56.

In the criminal trial there is much less for the defence solicitor to do and to some extent he expects the police to do it. Most criminal defences are entirely paid for by the State; if they were prepared as thoroughly as a civil defence the bill would be very large: since the police are there to investigate, why double the cost? So the costs of a defence will always be far below the cost of the prosecution, and the legal aid fees payable to defending solicitors, while adequate, are not stimulating. In Dougherty's case in 1973 the accused's alibi was so imperfectly presented that he was wrongly convicted;[1] the resulting criticism, when the truth became known, was directed against the police rather than against the defence solicitor. This case and the Virag case, which I have already mentioned, were the subject of a joint investigation by the committee which produced the *Identification Report*. At the outset of its Report the Committee observed:

A foreign jurist, studying the two cases on which we have to report, might be tempted to attribute the whole trouble in both of them to the lack in the English system of any officer of justice such as the *juge d'instruction*, whose function it is to apprise himself of all the relevant facts, whether they tell for or against the prosecution, to decide upon what charges, if any, the accused is to be arraigned and to place all this material before the court trial. If there had been such an officer in Dougherty's case, he would have discovered well before the trial was due to begin that the accused had a cast-iron alibi. In Virag's case he would have unearthed material which could have caused the prosecution's case to have been presented quite differently and might, notwithstanding the apparent strength of the identification evidence, have produced an acquittal.[2]

Here there were two cases in which there ought not to have been a conviction. In the one (Dougherty) there would not have been and in the other (Virag) there might not have been a conviction, if there had been a proper preliminary investigation. There are also cases, probably many more, in which there has not been a proper preliminary investigation and which therefore collapse at the trial. The consequence then is not injustice but a great waste of time and money. Such cases die unrecorded deaths and it is impossible to say how many of them there are. In theory they should be killed off at the committal stage and, if the examining magistrate had an inquisitorial function, they probably would be. But since the adversary system prevails at that stage as elsewhere, the magistrate waits for the defence to take the initiative. In practice the defence rarely does so. The principle, which we have noted in civil procedure, that neither side must take the other by surprise, applies in criminal procedure only against the

[1] This case is further discussed at p. 190.
[2] *Identification Report*, para. 1.6.

prosecution: the prosecution must disclose everything, the defence (except for an alibi defence) nothing. So if the defence were to expose its case before the magistrate and to fail in its attempt to defeat a committal, it would have given up for nothing the advantage of surprise. To defeat a committal the defence must show 'a strong or probable presumption that the jury would acquit the accused',[1] while to obtain an acquittal at the trial itself there need not be more than a reasonable doubt of guilt. The odds are against the defence at the preliminary proceedings and for him at the trial. So it is very rare for the defence to put up a fight before the magistrate. This may be one reason why under the French inquisitorial system there are fewer acquittals at the trial than under the English; in France the weeding-out is more thorough.

I cannot hazard a guess as to how many prosecution cases collapse at the Crown Court because of inherent defects which a more thorough examination would have disclosed, but I can give an example of the sort of thing I have in mind. At Doncaster Crown Court in November 1976 two members of a firm of scrap merchants were charged with attempting to obtain money by deception from the British Steel Corporation. The Corporation's method of buying scrap was to issue permits to merchants on an approved list. Each permit specified a grade of steel and entitled the merchant to send a wagon-load of steel of that grade to one of the Corporation's plants. The price, of course, varied according to the grade. On arrival each load was examined by one of the Corporation's scrap examiners. If he accepted it at the stated grade it was paid for accordingly by the Purchasing Department. If he was not prepared to accept it he could either reject it or suggest that it be accepted at another grade. The prosecution's case was that, at least on the twelve occasions which they selected for indictment, the merchant, having obtained a permit for grade 1, loaded the wagon with inferior grades, top-dressed with grade 1, in the belief or hope that the examiner would look only at the top. So he was said to have made a false representation that the contents of the wagon were all of grade 1 when he knew that they were not.

The Corporation's way of doing business was no doubt neat and efficient on paper, but it presupposed a respect for forms which is far from universal. It presupposed also that the purchase and sale of scrap would always be in a buyer's market, i.e. that the Corporation could offer according to the grade a fixed price as a 'take it or leave it' price. When, as frequently happened in times of short supply, the merchants were unwilling to sell at the Corporation's prices, the system broke down. What then the merchant ought to have done was to tell the Corporation that he had, for example, some

[1] Halsbury, *Laws of England*, 3rd edn., vol. 10, p. 365.

grade 4 scrap for sale but that he would sell it only at a grade 1 price. There was no provision in the permit form for this, so what the merchant did was to decide the price he wanted for his load and then label it with the grade that corresponded with the price. If this variation was well known to the officers of the Corporation who handled the scrap, there was no deception. The permit then became, not a representation of the quality of the scrap, but a statement of the price at which it was being offered for sale.

The preliminary hearing occupied three or four days, during which the defence laid the foundation for their case, ascertained what sort of documents they would need to support it, and gave notice to the prosecution to produce them. The trial lasted for twelve working days, by which time the prosecution was about halfway through its evidence. By then so many instances had been given of the purchase of loads after a full examination had shown that only the top dressing, if that, fitted the grade on the form, that the prosecution threw in their hand. The daily cost of the trial alone, apart from anything else, was about £2,000.

It may be said that this is only an example of insufficient care being taken over the decision to prosecute. But what are the factors to be taken into account in making this decision? There must of course be a prima facie case based on credible evidence. This requirement was satisfied: on the face of it, and assuming that the system was being operated as it was intended to be, there was a reasonably clear case of deception. Is it then part of the duty of the police to look beneath the surface for possible defences and to consider whether, notwithstanding the prima facie case, there is 'a strong and probable presumption' of innocence. If this is part of the duty of the police, it would help them a lot, I think, if they were told so plainly. Plain speaking on this point would have to be accompanied by the admission that what the police were being told to do was in effect to take over the function which the adversary system has designed for the examining magistrate, if, but only if, the defence invokes his aid.

If we intend to put this duty on the police, we should first arrive at a realization of what we would be doing. We should be telling the police to hold informally a preliminary trial in secret. For if the police look at both sides of a case and decide that probably the accused is innocent, they are exercising a judicial function in what is the first stage of the legal process. It is true that in theory all that they are doing is to decide not to prosecute and that this does not prevent anybody else from prosecuting. But this is pure theory. In fact he whom the police do not prosecute is acquitted with less pain than if he is tried and found not guilty, and also spared some perhaps not undeserved odium which publicity would have brought him.

The examining magistrate would then become even more insignificant than he is. The function which he was intended to discharge in court would be discharged by the police in camera. We should be breaking with our tradition that justice should be openly administered. Open administration is an attribute of justice, not merely a safeguard for the defence. It requires that where there is reasonable suspicion, innocence as well as guilt should be publicly demonstrated, otherwise there will be room for doubt and dissatisfaction. Thus, in Dougherty's case, would it have been entirely satisfactory to the witnesses who were convinced that they had seen him shoplifting and to those who had heard their version, if they learned no more than that the police had accepted an alibi?

This is not necessarily a plea for tradition. There are strong arguments for secret investigation as it is practised generally in Europe and in Scotland. It is less expensive and can spare innocent people hurtful publicity. The only point I am ready to make at present is that if we decide to break with our tradition of open justice, it would be better to make a clean break. The tendency at present is to drift towards the inquisitorial system without an official inquisitor. We leave the inquisition to the prosecution, administering to them one of our favourite nostrums by exhorting them to act fairly. Would it not be better to impose an undisguised judicial figure between the prosecution and the defence? It would be his clear and publicly proclaimed duty to investigate both sides using the police as his agents. He should be an impartial figure to whom the accused might be expected to talk far more freely than he does to the police. He should be also a single person of standing and accountability, such as a *juge d'instruction* or a procurator-fiscal, so as to ensure that his decision to drop a prosecution is accepted as authoritative and impartial.

We should have to face the fact that under a system of this sort the trial becomes less important. It is not then a prima facie case that is committed for trial but a case in which a judge is already satisfied that there is a high probability of guilt. To that extent the case has been tried in secret before it 'goes public'. The public trial would be more than the showpiece which it is under a totalitarian regime, but it would be a review rather than an original proceeding. It would follow the lines drawn by the inquisitor. It might expose points which he had overlooked or give effect to doubts which he overrode or revive considerations which he thought irrelevant, but it would be a review out of which ratification would be the expected, though not the inevitable, result.

I have already made it plain that there is nothing in our criminal process to correspond with our procedure in the civil process for settling interlocutory disputes. This does not mean that there are not in the criminal process any such disputes. But until the case comes to trial it is the police who are in control of the process. It is they who decide, at any rate in the first instance, how the dispute is to be solved. I should like to examine in this connection two pre-trial processes.

The first is the interrogation of the accused. In theory there is no interrogation of an accused, only of a suspect. But there is a point at which the suspect becomes de facto the accused; this is the point in the course of questioning when the suspicions of the interrogator are confirmed and it is not a point that is easily fixed. Nor is it always easy to distinguish between questioning on the one hand and the offering of an opportunity for explanation on the other. The second process is the identification of the accused when identity is not admitted. This is done by means of the identification parade, the arrangements for which are, as for the interrogation, in the hands of the police.

Police questioning of suspects has been a subject of concern to lawyers at least since the turn of the century; the first set of Judges' Rules offering guidance to the police on how the questioning should be conducted was formulated in 1912. It has always been a cardinal principle that no suspect or accused is obliged to answer any question at all, that he must be told of his right to keep silent and warned that, if he speaks, his words may be put in evidence, that no adverse comment may be made upon his silence, that he must not be pressed or enticed to answer against his will, and that only a voluntary confession, free of inducement by promise or threat, is admissible in evidence. From this one might suppose that police questioning is so unproductive as to play little or no part in the criminal process. On the contrary, admissions in a written statement signed by the accused form a significant part of most cases for the prosecution and in many an essential part. The admissibility of such statements is often resisted by the defence; sometimes the confession is so complete that resistance is the only alternative to a plea of guilty. The usual grounds for resistance are that the police misunderstood what the accused said or that they put words into his mouth or pressed him too hard or threatened him with loss of bail or the like. Allegations of physical threats are rare and of their being actually carried out rarer still; if as happens very occasionally, such an allegation is proved, it is sensational. On the other hand, the police stoutly resist proposals that interviews should be tape-recorded or conducted by a magistrate on the ground that their investigations would be hampered.[1]

---

[1] In 1972 the Criminal Law Revision Committee accepted this view; Cmnd. 4991, paras. 47–52.

There is a distinction, clear enough in principle though difficult to apply, between asking for information needed for an investigation and obtaining admissions needed for proof. Questioning in the first category is administrative in character, and in the second judicial. There is certainly a case, the merits of which have often been canvassed, for entrusting the latter to a judicial officer. I do not mean, however, to pursue this point, but to look at the existing practice in the conduct of investigations and identification procedures. Both are regulated in the same way. They are in the control of the police, but the police are required or expected to follow rules of conduct laid down either by the judges themselves or with judicial approval. For interrogation there are the well-known Judges' Rules to which I have already referred. For identification, there is a set of rules prepared by the Home Secretary in consultation with the Lord Chief Justice dealing with the conduct of parades and the use of photographs in identification procedure. The sanction attached to these rules is that of adverse comment by the judge at the trial and possibly the disallowance of evidence obtained in breach of the rules.

The sanction is appropriate to cases of deliberate disobedience, but inappropriate when there is a genuine dispute about what the rules require. Thus there may be a genuine dispute over the police arrangements for an identification parade. Examples are given by the Home Office Committee which reported on identification procedures. Should the parade be held up till the defence has found a solicitor able to attend? Is a foreigner entitled to demand that all the others on parade should be foreigners too? And so on. It is the duty of the police to treat such objections fairly, but, if they reject them, there is no appeal. The defence can obtain no redress until the trial. The procedure then is described by the Committee as follows:

Objection is taken by the defence to the admissibility of the evidence on the ground that the parade was unfairly conducted; the judge breaks off to hear evidence on this issue, usually in the absence of the jury; on the basis of his findings he sustains or overrules the objection, and the trial then proceeds. The disadvantage, especially from the point of view of the defence, is that the judge is being presented with an accomplished fact. Objections which might have been compromised or dissolved before the parade took place must now be decided starkly; once a parade has been held under faulty conditions, it becomes impossible to hold another one under improved conditions. The judge does not like to apply the drastic remedy of excluding altogether vital evidence upon which the prosecution may depend and so he tends to override objections which, considered in advance, he might have thought quite reasonable. This is said to be the present experience of defence advocates. It is under the existing procedure open to the defence to invite the judge to exclude evidence emerging in an unfair parade under his general discretion to exclude evidence prejudicial to the defence. But it is said that, while the judge may be led to make an adverse comment, he will only very rarely exclude the evidence.[1]

The same sort of situation can emerge in an interrogation. Police questioning often takes place late at night or in the early hours of the morning; they claim that catching criminals cannot be kept within normal hours; critics say that the police like to interview a man when he is not at his best. Objections to the time and mode of questioning, to the topics introduced, or to the degree of pressure applied can be quite genuine. Here again the accused's only remedy is to protest at the trial. It is a hit-or-miss procedure. It allows the police perhaps rather more latitude than they should have, but, if they overstep the mark, the accused can hit the jackpot: a case against him which is 90% sound can by the exclusion of a small but vital admission be utterly destroyed.

The police are generally fair and reasonable; the accused, who, whether innocent or guilty, may fear that obstructive behaviour will prejudice his chances at the trial, is generally co-operative. So the system works well enough. The Home Office Committee saw no practicable way of inserting into it an interlocutory judgment. But if there were a judicial figure giving a neutral direction to the inquiry, he would be the natural person to decide points of this sort. Indeed it may be argued as a matter of theory that, if an adversary system cannot provide for interlocutory adjudication of interlocutory disputes, it ought to give way, at least in its interlocutory processes, to one that can.

The frugality over interlocutory procedure practised in criminal matters is astounding when it is compared with the cornucopia in the White Book on civil procedure. This frugality is highly prized and rightly so. Speed and simplicity are the great virtues of English criminal practice. We have to remember, however, that these virtues were bred in a system that was a good deal rougher than we would tolerate today. It is an ancient and historic system: there can be marked among the milestones nearest to us the grant to the accused 142 years ago of the right to be defended by counsel, 80 years ago of the right to give evidence, 71 years ago of the right of appeal, and most recently and more gradually of legal aid. The fact that for so many years the accused was denied procedural rights which we now take to be elementary explains to some extent the tenderness towards the defence in such other respects as the burden of proof and the concealment of bad character. It is still to my mind a blot upon our procedure that it rests upon a unilateral inquiry into crime with no clear method of ensuring that facts favouring the accused are fully presented; where there is a wrong conviction,

[1] *Identification Report*, para. 5.43.

this defect is more likely than any other to have played a part in it. It is perhaps inevitable that suggestions for reform are so often countered by reminders of undue tenderness displayed to the accused at the trial; the police already have a difficult task, it is said, do not let us make it any more difficult. But it is not satisfactory to trade advantages against disadvantages in a general way; it is better that each item should be rightly balanced within itself.

Pre-trial procedures are likely to increase. Our forefathers did not, for example, bother about identification parades. It seems to have been an 'Assistant Judge of the Middlesex Session' who first called the attention of the Metropolitan Police to the need for something better than a confrontation; at any rate he made in 1860 'some remarks' which were fruitful.[1] By 1960 the psychologists were just beginning to suggest that they might have something to contribute to the doing of justice which could not easily be accommodated within the shape of the trial. They believe that they can tell judges and juries something about witnesses, their powers of observation and recognition, their reliability and their truthfulness, which may not emerge under the traditional processes of examination and cross-examination. We may have to invent a procedure for that.

We shall certainly cling to speed and simplicity for as long as we can. Thoroughness in preparation is excellent but has to be paid for in time. The delay in bringing a case to trial is the most formidable criticism of the French system. Maybe some of it is unnecessary: all legal procedure attracts barnacles and should be regularly scraped. Still, there may come a time when we are forced to choose between a longer delay than we have and a rougher justice than we should like to admit.

My conclusion is that on balance there is a vacancy in our system for the post of judicial intermediary. Anyone who fills it is, I think, more likely to be given an administrative than a judicial title. The Englishman would not be soothed by the sound of a *juge d'instruction* rustling in with his dossiers; he would take more kindly perhaps to an officer like the procurator-fiscal whose value has been proved in Scotland. Could not, it may be asked, the function of an intermediary in England be discharged by the prosecuting solicitor who should be able to take a more detached view than the police of what is due to the defence? But how detached is the modern prosecuting solicitor? Most police authorities now have their own legal department; only a few still employ outside firms. The Chief Constable makes the decisions. He takes advice from the solicitor but not instructions. Indeed, it is the other

[1] *Identification Report*, para. 5.29.

way round; it is for the solicitor, subject to the standards of his profession which the police would always respect, to prepare the case in accordance with the instructions he is given. So the prosecuting solicitor has neither the appearance of independence nor enough of its substance to act as an intermediary.

The Director of Public Prosecutions has enough of the substance. The Director conducts prosecutions for serious crimes, such as murder, and takes over any other prosecution which is sufficiently complicated or difficult to deserve his attention.[1] But these form only a small proportion of the cases brought before the Crown Court. His department is in London (there are no regional offices) and is tiny compared with the 500 *juges d'instruction* in France. The Director has weight and authority as well as independence. Until recently he has come to his office from outside as a barrister or solicitor of distinction with great experience both of prosecution and defence. To a lesser degree many of his officers have that experience also; it is important that they should have been against the police as well as on their side. At present their function is to take the select material given to them by the police and shape it into a case for the court. Within this field they are the dominant partner, but they have neither the time nor the mandate to dig out points for the defence. Nor is it the practice to bring them into interrogations or to consult them about identification parades.

There is room here for a judicial growth. The Director's men are already more than half way to umpirage. There is here the nucleus of a semi-judicial group. Meanwhile the existing quasi-judicial function of the police is being increasingly absorbed into the judicial process proper. A striking example of this has recently been given. Compliance with the rules of natural justice is demanded from any tribunal or person who exercises judicial functions. But no one until the case against the Leyland Justices[2] had ever contended that the prosecution had an obligation to observe natural justice in its relations with the defence. In this case a conviction was quashed because the police, who were prosecuting, had failed to notify the defence of the existence of witnesses who might be helpful to the defence and whom the prosecution did not intend to call. The Divisional Court held that this was a denial of natural justice and that it was immaterial that the blame for it fell on the prosecutor and not on the tribunal.

[1] He acts under the superintendence of the Attorney-General; Prosecution of Offences Act 1879 s. 2.
[2] *R.* v. *Leyland Justices, ex p. Hawthorn, The Times,* 25 July 1978.

4

The Judge and the Aequum et Bonum

THE first—ought one to say the whole?—duty of the English judge is to administer justice according to law. In this commandment has the phrase 'according to law' a qualifying effect or is it just added to give *embonpoint* to the word 'justice' which might look, if made to stand by itself, too thin to be impressive? To be sure, the language of the law does sometimes mistake rotundity for dignity, but in this case the phrase has a significant meaning. If it is going too far to say that it clarifies the word 'justice', at least it explains the sense in which the word is being used.

Judgment according to law is *not* invariably the same thing as judgment according to the merits of the particular case from which the judgment flows. The hallmark of judgment according to law is conformity with a set of rules. The rules should be designed so as to ensure justice in the normal case and also in any foreseeable exceptions, at least to the extent that provision for the exceptions does not make the rule intolerably cumbersome. But to frame a set of rules that would do complete justice in every case which could be brought within them would be, if not theoretically impossible, at any rate practically unattainable. So lawyers perforce accept the distinction between justice according to law and justice on the merits, or *ex aequo et bono* as they call it, and the public washes it down with the proverb that hard cases make bad law.

Yet there remains something distasteful about the idea that the justice of the case clashes, albeit only occasionally, with the law and has to defer to it. It is especially distasteful to the British mind, which is fond of good plain justice without legal flavours. Is a clash absolutely inevitable? The good citizen deals justly with his family, his neighbours, and even with his adversaries without being trammelled by the law. Why cannot the just judge in society dispense justice in the same way?

To begin with, there is the difference between the good citizen as an individual and in the society to which he belongs. The good man practises justice as a virtue for its own sake. The State, which is the administrative organ of society, has not hitherto been in the least interested in justice as a virtue. It may be that the time is coming when the State will concern itself with the virtuous behaviour of its citizens to the same extent as it does today with their health and welfare, but, when our legal system was brought into being, the State did not concern itself with any of the three. What motivated the State was the maintenance of order. It is because a sense of injustice is the most potent breeder of disorder yet invented that the State has to concern itself with justice.

Mark that I say a *sense* of injustice. This from the State's point of view is what is significant. If three good citizens in three different parts of the country reach in a matter of domestic justice three different decisions because they apply three different principles for the determination of the responsibility or the assessment of compensation, the probability is that none of the three individuals involved will know anything about the other two cases. Because there will be no comparison, there will be no sense of injustice; each individual will, if he accepts that he has been treated fairly and reasonably as an individual, be satisfied with the result.

Even if there is a comparison, it does not follow that it will give rise to a sense of injustice. That must depend on whether the individuals think of themselves as belonging to the same group, i.e. as being members of the same society. If they do not, the unsuccessful would shrug it off. Thus if an English, a French, and a German judge deliver three different judgments on the same set of facts because each judge is applying a different principle, no one is upset; each judge is right according to his lights.

So we allow that each community may have its own ideas of what is just. As we reach out towards a world community, we begin to formulate general principles which we say all communities should adopt. Subject to that and in the application of the general principles we accept that results may differ. But within the community they must be the same and this can be ensured only by the existence of law. A sense of injustice is more easily aroused by the apprehension of unequal treatment than by anything else. The administration of justice is rarely criticized in Britain, but when it is, the complaint is not usually of specific injustice but of the rendering of different judgments in similar cases; a common complaint is that magistrates in different counties impose different penalties for the same sort of motoring offence. Thus for communal justice law is indispensable. Fidelity to the law, notwithstanding that it may mean the harsh judgment—even the unjust judgment if all that is being considered is the aequum et bonum in the particular case—is the price that men have to pay for life in society.

This follows ineluctably from the nature of human society and its need for law and order. We have to accept that every now and again, but fortunately quite rarely, a judge is confronted with having to deliver a judgment that seems to him, as he knows it will seem to the public, to contain too much law and not enough justice. When this happens there is a temptation to alter the mixture a little. The rest of this lecture consists chiefly of an examination of the various ways in which under our legal system, looking first mainly at the civil and then mainly at the criminal, the law is diluted to meet the justice of the particular case. But before that there are two things that I ought to do. First, I ought to state more precisely what I mean by the aequum et bonum. Second, I must strike a fairer balance between the attractions of the law and those of the aequum et bonum than I have done so far.

I do not mean by the aequum et bonum something totally distinct from the law. I am contrasting it with the text of the law, whether that is written in a code or a statute or a binding precedent. I am not contrasting it with the idea of law. I am not supposing that a judge who is thinking about the aequum et bonum would not also be thinking about a framework of general principles. For it is only within a framework that a dispute can be shaped into issues to be resolved. The boundaries can then be drawn to include what is relevant and exclude the irrelevant and thus reduce the material to a size that can be handled judicially. If the parties when preparing their material had no notion of what the judge might think to be relevant and if the judge himself did not think about it until all the material had been placed before him, only exhaustion could bring the process to an end. The dictum that a judge should first ascertain the facts and then apply the law to them is a warning rather than an instruction and is to be observed in the spirit rather than in the letter. He should not until he has all the facts reach his final conclusions. But it would be impractical for him not to think about the law at all until the evidence was complete. The process of selecting the facts that are going to matter legally is a continuing one, set in motion at the start; it is a channelling that begins broadly and ends narrowly.

So when the parties to a contract agree that disputes between them shall be decided *ex aequo et bono*, they are not imagining a judge with a vacant mind. They expect his mind to be well stocked, if it is a trade dispute with a knowledge of trade customs and practices, or if the dispute is on a higher plane, with some principles which in general they would both respect. They do not want him to decide without the law, but they want him to take in the application of the law as much freedom as he thinks to be needed to satisfy justice.

An English judge would not be attracted by the idea of applying his own law. If he were, he would repel the attraction because he is acting not by virtue of an *ad hoc* authority given to him by the parties but by virtue of a mandate from the Crown to apply the law of the land. He would always accept the spirit of the law. He would, at any rate when he is applying a statute, accept the clear policy of the law; he might, for example, think it to be socially unjust that employers should have to answer for their employees' misdeeds, but he would know that constitutionally this was no business of his. The attraction of the aequum et bonum for him can arise only when he feels the law to be too constrictive in a particular case. It would be too facile to describe this as a conflict between the spirit and the letter of the law, for a judge is not bound to construe a statute literally and he should interpret the text purposefully, as Lord Diplock has said.[1] But written law, whether it is derived from statute or from precedent, is naturally much less flexible than a statement of policy, and it is the gap between the text of the law and the policy inspiring it which leaves room for the aequum et bonum.

So when lawyers talk of the aequum et bonum—those of them, that is, who will admit to having some truck with it—they do not see it as an escape from fundamental principles. The sort of aequum et bonum which they are trying to handle is something which has unfortunately been squeezed out in the processing of a principle into a rule. The squeezing may happen in several ways. There may be an omission in the wording of the rule unnoticed at the time when the rule was framed, and then many English lawyers would like to use the aequum et bonum, as in other systems lawyers are allowed to do, to repair the omission. Or the particular case which the judge is considering may belong to a category for which the rule makes no provision at all; and the lack of provision may be due either to inadvertence or to a deliberate refusal to make an exception because of the convenience of having a general rule. To what extent in these circumstances the system permits judges to be influenced by the aequum et bonum, or to what extent judges, if not permitted, may be deflected by the aequum et bonum, are the questions I am posing.

Statute sometimes overrides, as inexpedient, solutions based on the aequum et bonum and favoured by equity or the common law. Limitation of actions provides an example of this. In this field there has been for some centuries a running battle between the aequum et bonum and statute. Statute has conquered ultimately, of course, as it is bound always to do, but has left the aequum et bonum restive under its heel.

[1] See p. 14.

Equity judges were ready to accept that there must be a *finis rerum*, an end to all things, even to justice, since under the wear and tear of time justice can decompose. Moreover, speed is an attribute of justice, and delay can be oppressive. So the court should consider in the circumstances of each case whether or not there has been unjustifiable delay. This is the equitable doctrine of laches; the principle of limitation is accepted but applied according to the aequum et bonum.

But Parliament has thought it more convenient to fix arbitrary periods within which specified categories of claims must be made. The Statute of Limitations 1623 was the progenitor. When the equity judges were at the height of their power, they took part of the Statute into their own hands. They observed that under it the period of limitation began to run from the date when the cause of action arose, not the date when it became known to the plaintiff. Clearly this could be a source of injustice, particularly if the defendant was keeping quiet about his trespasses in the hope that they might not be noticed until it was too late to sue. So equity judges invented the doctrine of concealed fraud and said that in such cases time would not begin to run until the plaintiff knew of the interference with his rights. Today judges would not be so bold. But at least until 1963 when the law was made more flexible, some of them were apt to express such displeasure when the Statute was pleaded as to discourage its use.

This concludes what I have to say about the sort of aequum et bonum I am talking about. The other part of my preliminary task is to redress the balance between the attractions of the aequum et bonum on the one side and those of the law on the other. I have pointed out that we have to have law, whether we like it or not. What I now want to stress is that a good many people like it and I want also to mention some of the considerations which might dispose even the most ardent lover of the aequum et bonum, if not to welcome the law, at least to make the best of it.

In the first place, judgment according to law by imposing a norm also secures it. Against the number of cases in which the law hinders the good judge from expressing the aequum et bonum, there must be put the number in which it prevents the bad judge from giving effect to idiosyncratic notions. For most of the law's history the public has looked upon it as a protection against corrupt or stupid judges. When the public thinks of the law as obstructive, it is a high mark of confidence in the judiciary.

Akin to this consideration is the thought that the law is a protection for the judges themselves. For the law does and ought to embody the collective wisdom. No judge who applies it can be accused of partiality. A judge who has to reach his conclusion without its guidance or who feels sufficiently confident to reject the guidance puts his personal reputation at stake.

In the second place, the law instructs the citizen how to behave justly. This, you may say, is a simplistic statement. The ordinary citizen does not need the law to know how to behave. He behaves well because he is brought up to accept the same standards of conduct as those which form the basis of the law; the object of the citizen who regulates his activities by the law is more likely to be to keep just on the right side of it and take advantage of any loopholes.

The truth is, I think, that the good citizen does not bother about the law until a dispute occurs or some other sort of situation arises in which, wishing to act with justice, he has to decide what to do. If there were no law, there would be no lawyers to consult. He could seek the advice of three wise men, but they might all differ, as wise men frequently do, each giving cogent reasons for his own opinion. The perplexed citizen would then be like a man today who is told that the answer to his legal problem depends upon whether it is governed by French, English, or German law, and that the answer to that depends upon whether it comes before a French, English, or German court.

The last remark shows that lawyers are not always able to provide the good citizen with the comfort he seeks. But the existence of law does enormously reduce the number of cases going to court because it diminishes the areas of uncertainty and enhances the possibility of a settlement, which, when freely negotiated, is always the best solvent of a dispute. Moreover, a great deal of the administration of justice is simply adjustment. The good citizen may know that he ought to pay something; but how much?

Finally, it must be said, that the divergence between justice according to law and the aequum et bonum could often be narrowed by the improvement of the law. The law could never be made to fit every case perfectly, but it could be made to fit better than it does, or to fit more frequently than it does, if it was kept under continuous inspection with immediate correction when its application was seen to result in injustice. Unfortunately this is not the sort of service which the State provides, notwithstanding that it is continually creating new and not always well-constructed law. A government often behaves as if it expected an Act of Parliament to run smoothly for ever, or at least until it collided with some upsetting new thought. Of course, if from a government point of view the Act has ceased to earn its keep, if, for example, it is not bringing in all the taxes expected of it, the renovators will be set to work at once. But an Act which is not the protégé of a powerful government department may have to go on running without an overhaul and with its dents unrepaired until it is fit only for the scrapheap.

As lawyers you may think that I have taken too long in defending the concept of justice according to law. But it is a concept which the public dislikes and with which lawyers themselves are not always happy. It is a common enough feeling to desire the end and to dislike the means. The public desires order and dislikes law, though without law there would be no order. The judicial qualities which the public singles out for praise are common sense and humanity; devotion to the law is less admired than a willingness to strain it. It is not surprising, therefore, that from the earliest times the English legal system has accommodated various devices designed to enmesh the legal result with the justice of the case.

I want now to look at four of these devices at work in civil procedure:

1. Stretching the law
2. The jury
3. Judicial discretion
4. Arbitration.

Stretching the law or moulding the facts to fit the law is the time-honoured method by which the judge consciously or unconsciously—probably half-consciously, and not permitting himself too acute an analysis—makes room for the aequum et bonum. But it is a condition of the use of this and of all other methods and devices having the same object that the object should not be admitted. The supremacy of the law must not be defied.

Why not be frank about it, one may ask. Why this unacknowledged stretching; why not face up to what everybody knows to be the case, namely, that the strict application of the law sometimes works injustice, and give the judge—or perhaps a superior judge with a special jurisdiction—power to override the law in a particular case and without creating a precedent? This indeed (except that it quickly ran to precedent) is just what was done in England in the fourteenth century by the creation of equity. On the ground that they were denied justice at common law litigants went to the Lord Chancellors for equitable relief, and the Chancellors gave it in a measure which, the common lawyers scornfully said, varied with the length of their feet.

But this was in the early days when English law was in the making and was being made piecemeal. There is no Mount Sinai in England, nor has there been an Emperor Justinian. At common law if a suppliant alleged a wrong which the King was prepared to right, a writ was issued summoning the defendant to one of his courts, King's Bench, Exchequer, or Common Pleas. So there grew up a patchwork of causes of action. It was the incompleteness in the system rather than the injustice in the exceptional case that led to equity. It was an incompleteness which, if it existed today, would be cured by law reform, but which in medieval conditions was more conveniently remedied by the imposition of a superior jurisdiction. It is, however, at least two centuries since equity turned itself into a system of law and more than one since it ceased as a system to be separately administered. In a mature system a judge who openly refused to apply the law would have to claim a dispensing power. Ever since its use by the Stuart monarchs the dispensing power has been thought of as an instrument of tyranny. The consequence of casual injustice would have to be grievous indeed before the English would reconsider the Bill of Rights.[1]

So the judge cannot openly dispense. But he can stealthily stretch or mould. When I speak of him as moulding the facts, I do not mean that he deliberately turns them to the shape he wants. I am thinking of the way in which the story as he listens to it takes shape in his mind. The inflow mixes with what is there already and it is out of the mixture that the shape grows. What is there already is an accumulation of experience including tendencies, prejudices, and maybe bias. I do not mean a conscious bias; let the litigant who thinks that the judge has a conscious bias in his favour bemoan his fate, for if it moves the judge at all, it will move him the other way. I mean the unconscious biases which any man may have and which he cannot eradicate because he does not realize that they are there. Among them is one which, if not laudable, is at any rate the least harmful of the lot, and that is a bias in favour of the justice of the case and against any law that seems to deny it. Once a judge has formed a view of the justice of the case, those facts which agree with it will seem to him to be more significant than those which do not. A judge's longhand note, necessarily incomplete, will consist mainly of what he thinks to be significant; the insignificant, being omitted, will disappear from memory.

In smaller cases, those tried below the level of the High Court, judgments are final on questions of fact. But it is not just the power to find the facts that is crucial, it is that power coupled with the lack of record. Without the record, without maybe a full summary of the judgment, it is difficult to review the reasoning, and if the reasoning cannot be reviewed, the judgment is equivalent to a verdict. Even the judgment in the High Court, which is not conclusive on fact, used without the record to be difficult to

[1] 'That the pretended power of dispensing with laws or the execution of laws by regall authoritie as it hath been assumed and exercised of late is illegall.'

review. The transcript of the evidence has made a world of difference to
appellate proceedings. I believe that it would make almost as much difference in an appeal from a judge whose finding of fact was conclusive as
from one whose finding could be directly challenged. For if an appeal court
thinks that a judge has gone seriously wrong on the facts, they will set the
hounds of the law on him. Is his finding of fact sufficiently supported by
the evidence? Was his approach to the facts erroneous in law? These are
questions of law, and unsatisfactory answers to them will undermine the
finding of fact.

Three appellate judges, who have not seen and heard the parties and are
studying the case on paper, are less likely than the trial judge to be lured
from the law. But they are not impervious to the justice of the case. Cases
that are thin on the merits will be scrutinized more carefully, burdens of
proof will be less easily lifted and doubts on the law will be resolved so as
to favour the aequum et bonum. 'Your Lordships will be glad to hear that
I shall present a pure point of law uncorrupted by any merits' was how Theo
Mathew[1] once opened his case in the Court of Appeal. As a skilful advocate
he made the best of it; but only the crabbed practitioner, and this is true
from the solicitor's clerk to the law lord, relishes the unmeritorious point.
The climate is against it. The litigant who wants to rely on it will, unless
it seems certain to bring him victory, be mildly discouraged by his advisers.
Phrases such as 'the court may be against you' will be used and he will be
warned that the court may comment. Publicity and the judicial comment
are powerful allies of the aequum et bonum. They go very far to secure the
small man against the oppressive use of legal technicalities. Probably the
whole way if the opponent is a government department or a body with a
public reputation to maintain.

So much for the influence of the aequum et bonum on the facts. What is
its influence on the application of the law? Does the wind of the law blow
equally upon the meritorious and the unmeritorious litigant? No, it does
not. At all judicial levels and in all systems the law is sometimes stretched,
a little shamefacedly perhaps. When that happens the case is described from
the Bench as 'very exceptional', the qualification 'in the particular circumstances' is sprinkled over the judgment, and the distinction without the difference unexpectedly honoured. Thereafter an advocate will be discouraged
from using the case as a precedent. 'It was a case which turned entirely on

[1] The doyen of the junior Bar in the 1920s and 1930s and the author of such delightful books
as *Forensic Fables* (by 'O'), complete edn., Butterworths, London, 1961.

its own facts,' he will be told irritably, and it will be said to be a pity that it was ever reported. So far as possible it will be hushed up.

As I have said, stretching the law is not peculiar to the English system. So I shall take an example from the proceedings of the Administrative Tribunal of the International Labour Organisation, a court which decides claims made by an international civil servant against the Organisation that employs him. The Tribunal follows in the main the principles of French administrative law; so the decision has no binding force as a precedent and need not be hushed up.

The case of *re Ballo and Unesco* (Judgment No. 191) was decided in 1972. Herr Ballo was employed by Unesco under a contract for a fixed term of two years, later extended to three. In 1971 a question of a further extension came up and the Director-General decided against it. Under English common law that would have been an end of the matter. But under administrative law an employee has in such circumstances an expectation that his contract will be renewed. What that amounts to is that some reason must be given for non-renewal and it must be a reason which cannot be successfully attacked as an abuse of power. This doctrine, like our own, requires whoever takes the decision, the Director-General or in our case the Minister, to apply his mind correctly to the issue; his appraisal can be faulted only if he has taken into account irrelevant facts or failed to take into account relevant ones.

Everyone in Unesco except the Director-General himself thought very highly of Herr Ballo and wanted to keep him, that is to say, all his immediate superiors who were high-ranking officials; and the Advisory Board was unanimous for his re-appointment. The Director-General said, however, that he could not endorse these laudatory assessments; he had himself seen Herr Ballo at work on a number of occasions and he was not impressed. The Advisory Board means no more to a Director-General than his Cabinet does to an American President, and everyone knows of the celebrated occasion, whether it be fact or fiction, when President Lincoln, having taken the opinion of each member of his Cabinet in turn and each of them having said No, rose from the table saying that he thought the Ayes had it. An added complication arose from the fact that Herr Ballo was a Czech and the Czech Government, with whom he apparently had become *persona non grata*, wrote to say that they would not agree to his re-appointment. No one suggested that this influenced the Director-General in the slightest degree—indeed it was his imperviousness to influences of all sorts which was the feature of the case—but equally no one wanted to see the Czech Government accommodated or Herr Ballo having to look for work in Czechoslovakia.

The Tribunal quashed the Director-General's decision, saying that, by resting his judgment entirely on the limited part of Herr Ballo's work which he himself saw and treating as of no account the unanimous opinion of those who were familiar with the whole of it, he had failed to take into consideration essential facts. Another view of the case could have been that the Director-General was dealing with opinions and not with facts and that his only fault was a refusal to substitute the opinion of others for his own. Only a nice distinction divides the two views. And where two results are almost equally defensible he would be an inhuman judge who, in deciding between them, succeeded in pushing the merits out of his mind.

To return to the law of England. The more flexible the law the more easily it can be stretched. Is not the common law, it may be asked, more flexible than the Continental codes and, since so much of English law still consists of the common law, is not English law more amenable than most to the aequum et bonum? I doubt it.

The formation of the common law in its infancy was no doubt influenced by the aequum et bonum. It is possible to imagine the first judgments as a set of principles, each of which produced the aequum et bonum in its own case. But what begins as a number of principles soon turns into a body of precedents. As new types of cases came to be decided the search for the appropriate precedent seemed, because of the social need for a coherent body of law, to be more rewarding than the elevation of the aequum et bonum. I dare say that medieval judges gave as much thought to squeezing old cases into new precedents, broadening the precedents but never bursting out of them, as medieval clerks did in trying to squeeze new causes of action into old writs.

No doubt the common law was continually being expanded as, much more sluggishly, it still is. But the shape of the expansion has little or nothing to do with the aequum et bonum of the case in which it is enunciated. Consider some of the notable expansions in recent years. *Donoghue* v. *Stevenson*,[1] which brought the manufacturer of an article into an area of liability up till then monopolized by the seller, was decided as a bare point of law on demurrer. Whether there really was a snail in the ginger-beer bottle is unrecorded in legal history. The object of the expansion in this and similar cases was to fill out or clarify the unwritten code in a satisfactory manner. It was, for example, unsatisfactory in principle that liability for negligence should be confined to physical injury and not extend to financial damage;[2] likewise, that the tort of intimidation should be confined to the use of physi-

[1] [1932] A.C. 562.
[2] See *Candler* v. *Crane* [1951] 2 K.B. 164, and *Hedley Byrne* v. *Heller* [1964] A.C. 465.

cal threats and not extend to economic; and when the House of Lords in
Rookes v. *Barnard*[1] sought to tidy up the law of punitive damages, it was
because they considered the law to be in a mess and not because they wanted
Mr. Rookes to have more or less money.

I have no doubt that the common law is of its nature more flexible than
statute. I say 'of its nature' because a judge who takes the precedents too
literally can seriously damage their flexibility. But here I am comparing the
common law not with statute but with the Continental code, and I think
that the Continental judge treats the code more liberally than the English
judge treats statute. I have suggested that the English judge in his use of
flexibility is concerned more with the shape of the law than with the aequum
et bonum. I do not know that this is equally true of the Continental judge.
I think it may be that the power of the English judge over the common
law, theoretically so much greater than the Continental judge's power over
the code, makes him feel more responsible for the shape of the law and so
more resistant to the aequum et bonum.

In the end my feeling is that the aequum et bonum stretches a code just
as often and as far as it does the common law.

For six-sevenths of our legal history trial by jury was the chief conductor
of the aequum et bonum into the legal process. In the civil process it is
no longer that. Nevertheless, because of its importance (and because it continues to play a great part in the criminal trial), it must be put high on the
list of the modes which favour the aequum et bonum.

Not that the jury was created in order to favour the aequum et bonum
nor that its dominion over the facts was enough of itself to let it in. What
makes the jury different from the ordinary fact-finding tribunal is the independence from the judges that its history has given it. When an inferior
tribunal finds the facts, it may be made to put them into the form of a 'case
stated' so that the court may decide for itself any emerging question of law
which arises from the facts. Included among such questions there may be
the question whether there is any evidence sufficient in law to support the
tribunal's decision. If the High Court thinks that the facts are insufficiently
stated, it may send the case back to the tribunal with a demand for specific
findings. All this places great difficulties in the way of a tribunal which is
pursuing justice on the merits rather than according to law.

In the procedure of the case stated the dominating feature is that it is
the judge who is applying the law to the stated facts; this is what gives
the superiority to him. In the case of a jury which is returning a general

[1] [1964] A.C. 1129.

verdict, the process is the other way round. It is the jury which is applying
to the facts the law stated to it; this is what gives to the jury the superiority.
It is assumed that it will apply the law as stated by the judge, but no one
can be sure that it does since it gives no reasons and does not say what facts
it finds; its verdict is Yes or No.

This is the perfect accommodation for the aequum et bonum. Here are
twelve men and women who come to court without any legal knowledge.
They must all have had occasion to apply general notions of fairness in matters of domestic justice and the need to reach unanimity will rub out the
quirks that sometimes misdirect the single mind. The English are not too
fond of legal ways of doing things, but they have a great respect for
the idea of law, associated as it is with order. They will therefore listen
attentively to the judge and they will follow the law if they can. They will
reject it only if in the particular case they feel that it does injustice. The
door is not wide open to the aequum et bonum, but it is not bolted
and barred against it. It will be admitted when the jury seriously feels
the law to be inadequate. Admitted in this way it can go into the composition of the verdict while leaving the law untouched. The law of the case,
if it is cited in the textbooks, will be the law which the jury was told
to apply and not that, never to be formulated, which in truth they did
apply.

This is, I dare say, a somewhat idealistic picture. The door that is opened
to let in the aequum et bonum can let in also ignorance and prejudice. Nevertheless, on balance the civil jury as an institution has earned great respect.
It would not have survived for six centuries if it had not. It was respected
by those who administered the law as much as by laymen. Its decline in
its seventh century in civil cases was not because it came to be distrusted;
lawyers shook their heads at its aberrations but envied it its capacity for
meeting the justice and the common sense of the case. But cheapness, convenience, and predictability have a great appeal, especially to practitioners
anxious to sell their wares. The customers themselves may perhaps have
been impressed by an improvement in the independence and understanding
of judges and in their manners, an improvement which muffled the solemn
warnings of Blackstone's bell.[1] The decline was gradual. Sixty years after
it was admitted, the non-jury trial was still serving only the minority, but
a substantial minority, of 45%. Two wars created a shortage of jurors and
accelerated the decline. For the last twenty years the proportion of jury trials
has dropped slowly from about 3% to about 1%.

A study of the jury points to two matters on which lawyers and jurymen

[1] See p. 172.

habitually differ; the first is about what is relevant and the second is on the virtues of compromise.

As to the first, a lawyer thinks in terms of logical relevance and is pleased with a structure which separates issues and assigns to them distinct modes of trial. Thus guilt or liability is one issue, and punishment or compensation another; in the criminal trial guilt is for the jury, and punishment for the judge. But if you are interested not in the law generally but only in the particular case, there is really only one question: 'What punishment, if any, does he deserve? What compensation, if any, ought he to be paid?' In criminal cases jurymen are always told to disregard as irrelevant the consequences of their verdict. But their natural inclination makes them ask themselves whether as a result of it the person they convict will be sent to prison or, in the days of capital punishment, executed. It is contrary to human nature to expect a jury, unconcerned about the logic of the law, its attention attracted and held only by the circumstances of the case that has brought it into a court which normally it would never visit, not to bother about the consequence of the verdict. In civil cases juries are told not to consider damages until after they have found liability, but their verdicts have often shown that they prefer compromise to disagreement and that they consider a plaintiff, as I dare say he himself would agree, to be better off with half a loaf than with no bread.

The common law insists on a black or white solution that often goes against the grain of the English love of compromise. This came out strongly in the ordinary highway or factory accident case, in which quite often there was some carelessness on both sides. The sensible thing would be to divide the responsibility according to the degree of blame. This was introduced into our maritime law in 1911.[1] But the common law continued until 1945[2] to insist that only one person could be held responsible and that it must be he who had the last opportunity of avoiding the accident. This was unpopular with American juries as well as with English.

There is no doubt also that in accident cases juries were inclined to find against a defendant whom they believed to be insured.[3] To the lawyer insurance is absolutely irrelevant. But outside the courtroom we should all think it rather hard that a plaintiff, at any rate if he was not himself seriously to blame, should not get the benefit of the insurance. If juries took the view that the defendant should be treated as having insured the plaintiff as well as himself, they were on the way to a solution that many people now think

[1] Maritime Conventions Act 1911.
[2] Law Reform (Contributory Negligence) Act 1945.
[3] Insurance was not made compulsory until the Road Traffic Act 1934.

should be accepted by the law. In this respect as well as in their dislike of the 'last opportunity' rule, they help to bring the law into line with popular justice.

But the benefit conferred by the jury system in this respect is outside the scope of my present subject. I am considering to what extent the civil jury admits the influence of the aequum et bonum and whether, when it does, the result is satisfactory. The answer must be that it admits it to a limited extent—quite strictly limited if it is compared with the criminal jury—and that the result is mixed. Frequently it is, at the best, rough justice. For example, the effect of the common law before 1928 was to present to a jury which thought apportionment to be the just solution a Hobson's choice between the plaintiff and the defendant. If they had thought to avoid the choice by returning a verdict of an apportionment, such as the law now demands, it would then have been rejected as contrary to law. The civil jury cannot flout a law it dislikes; the best it can do is to ignore it secretly. This produces some mysterious verdicts.

Let me illustrate with one of the last civil jury trials at which I presided. The plaintiff was a workman whose job took him down a shaft. On his way up again he knocked his head quite lightly against a protuberance on the wall of the shaft. The knock was recorded in the factory accident book and the bruise treated, and nothing more was heard of the matter for a number of years. Then the plaintiff began to behave in an odd way and with unaccountable violence. When he toppled a grandfather clock on the head of his landlord and injured himself as well, he was taken to hospital. The medical men diagnosed a tumour on the brain which had caused a personality change. They searched his previous medical history for anything which might have caused the tumour and alighted on the knock on the head.

The plaintiff sued his former employers. At the trial the great issue was the cause of the tumour and there was much medical evidence on both sides. Everyone agreed that there was a pre-existing abnormality in the brain which might have remained dormant but which might have been triggered off by a severe enough blow. The defence contended with the help of their experts that the knock recorded could not have been severe enough and that, if it was, there must have been countless other knocks in the course of the plaintiff's life which could just as probably have pulled the trigger.

In these circumstances there were two principles of law to be applied, both commonplace to lawyers but perhaps not immediately persuasive to laymen. The first is quite a modern one. The law has by a change of policy which occurred about fifty years ago imposed a strict duty on employers to make working conditions safe. In this respect standards have changed; this type of injury used to be more or less an occupational risk.

The plaintiff's cause of action was in negligence, negligence being the word which the law uses to describe the breach of the duty to take care, whether the duty be strict or lax. Negligence in the popular sense means something more than an error of judgment or slight inadvertence, something rather reprehensible. When the duty imposed by the law was light, there was no difference between the popular and legal meanings of the word. When the judges altered the effect of the law by tightening the screw, they continued, as is their practice, to use the same terminology. This practice leads to a divergence between legal and popular meanings, and lawyers begin to talk of legal negligence, legal fraud, legal misconduct, etc. In the case I am considering the lawyers, having regard to the strictness of the duty, had little doubt that there was legal negligence; the protuberance was unlikely to cause any serious damage, but it was capable of causing some and it should not have been there. The defence did not concede the point, but they hardly fought it. But the removal of minor protuberances in a shaft might be seen by a layman as a counsel of perfection.

The second relevant principle of law in the case is that a wrongdoer, whose act is an effective cause, albeit only a minor cause, of injury—only a 'triggering off', as it is called—is responsible for the whole of the consequences. If there is another cause of the injury and it too was a legal wrong, each wrongdoer has been able since 1935[1] to sue the other and make him contribute his proper share. But if there is another cause and it is *not* a legal wrong, the single wrongdoer must pay for the whole damage including that attributable to the other cause for which he was not responsible. The defence in the case I am considering had to accept the triggering off as an effective cause, but it was a very minor one, hardly more than a piece of bad luck; if it had not been that bump it would have been another one. It may not seem so convincing to a layman as it does to a lawyer that the employers should have to pay for the lot.

In the result and to the astonishment of all, the jury found for the defendants, thus negativing any negligence on the part of the employers. It is not the decision which the judge would have made. The stone which the lawyers had all but cast out was made the foundation of the verdict. The hours devoted to the physiology of the brain counted for nothing beside the minutes given to the protuberance and the shaft.

I suspect that the jury found the legal approach altogether too sophisticated. They were offered the choice between nominal damages if the bump

[1] Law Reform (Married Women and Tortfeasors) Act 1935 s. 6.

played no part in causing the plaintiff's disorder and a very large sum indeed if it did. They thought that the latter would be ridiculous—fancy having to pay in five figures for a bump—and why should they have to condemn the defendant as negligent if all the plaintiff was going to get out of it was a few pounds? What they probably wanted to do was to give the plaintiff a small golden handshake as a solace for his misfortunes and as a sort of insurance against the possibility that they might just be mistaken in thinking that the defendant had nothing to do with them. No doubt this is what they would have done if they had been settling the thing round a table *ex aequo et bono* instead of in court, and it would have made very good sense to a lot of people.

In some cases the attraction of the aequum et bonum to a jury that cannot entirely free itself from the law produces a verdict that is neither one thing nor the other and far from a good mixture. This may be due to the dislike of a law from which there is no escape and the dislike may be due to an insufficient understanding of its purpose. Many judges do not go beyond the incantation that 'the facts are for you and the law is for me'. It is for them, they feel, to lay down the law, not to justify it. On the facts, they might allow that the jury does the job better than they would do it themselves, but only if it is kept harnessed and within the shafts; if not blinkered, it might shy.

Myself I feel that the judge should briefly explain the law as well as propound it. It is quite possible to do that without inciting the jury to question it. If there are apparent imperfections in the law, it is possible to point out that for the sake of uniformity there has to be a law which is the same for everyone, that this is the one which has been approved by experience, and that the jury will not mend matters by trying to revise it in the jury-box. This should help to ensure that the jury do not lightly reject the law and do not hanker after the aequum et bonum unless they see in it a clear and compelling alternative. That they will nevertheless reject the law in some case, especially in criminal cases, is certain. If, for example, a man of good character whose wife had disappeared preferred bigamy with an acquiescent partner to the divorce court (this in the days when divorce was difficult and costly) no amount of explanation would be likely to convince a jury that the accused in order to be acquitted ought to produce something more than a convenient supposition that his wife must be dead.

I have been speaking about the jury when it is returning a general verdict. The jury when it is returning a special verdict is, at least so far as the aequum et bonum is concerned, an entirely different institution. For a general verdict the only question put to a civil jury is: 'Do you find for the plaintiff or for the defendant and if for the plaintiff, for how much?' The successful party then asks for judgment in accordance with the verdict. For a special verdict the jury is asked a separate question about each of the issues of fact in dispute and it gives an answer on each, which is not necessarily monosyllabic. That is the end of its duties; it finds no general verdict either for or against the plaintiff; after hearing such legal argument as may be necessary, the judge gives judgment on the facts found according to law. Thus the special verdict reduces the status of the jury to that of an ordinary fact finding body, allowing only limited scope for the aequum et bonum.

A jury is not obliged to return a special verdict. It is symptomatic of the relationship between judges and juries that the jury is not usually told that it could refuse. Indeed its rights are never explained to it. Jurymen are not assured that they are answerable only to their own consciences nor told in a criminal case that a verdict of acquittal returned contrary to the direction of the judge must nevertheless be accepted. If he were sitting in judgment upon others a judge might say that he thought it rather unscrupulous to bring a bunch of laymen into a process dominated by professionals and not to explain to them their rights. But, as I have suggested, most judges would answer by saying that the working of the system requires the jury to be bridled. If the horse takes the bit between its teeth there is nothing to be done about it; it cannot be punished for it, but it should not be taught how to do it.

It has become the practice to take a special verdict in cases such as libel and malicious prosecution in which there is more than one issue on the pleadings. Sometimes the complexity of the case and the refinement of the law (in malicious prosecution, for example, the question whether the prosecutor honestly believed in the guilt of the plaintiff is an issue for the jury while the question whether he had reasonable grounds for his belief is an issue for the judge) result in an examination paper being laid before the jury. Sometimes they misunderstand and give inconsistent answers. Their failures in this respect may have contributed something to their decline. But a jury struggling with a special verdict is not doing what it is within its genius to do.

I come now to the third of my heads—the discretion of the judge. This does not mean, as might be thought from the sound of it, a discretion given to the judge to modify the law so that justice may prevail in a particular case. What it means is that the judge is put on a looser rein and in certain parts of the country left to find his own way. For the law leaves certain areas more or less uncharted. They are the wild spaces which the motorist sees on his map, framed in by the motorways and trunk roads, avoided even by the first and second class roads, crossed only by thin white lines, sometimes dotted, quite far apart. In these fields that are at best only roughly mapped, the judge must act—more or less, according to the state of the map—in his own discretion. This is another way of saying that he must decide each case largely according to its particular merits. It is thus that the discretion of the judge admits the aequum et bonum.

There is no official admission. The aequum et bonum is not recognized by name. The way it is let in is by prescribing that from decisions given within the field there shall be no appeal. If formally you do that and if, formally or informally, you ensure that no reasons are given for the decision, you prevent the creation of law; by eliminating the law, you leave the aequum et bonum in control. Observe that success really depends on stifling the reasons. For very many years there was practically no appeal from the decisions of Lord Chancellors in equity, but by giving their reasons they constructed a system at least as rigid as the common law.

The extent of the discretion depends, as I have said, on the state of the map. If it is quite unrouted, there is an absolute discretion; if there are some guide-lines, there is a limited discretion. It is closely connected with the right of appeal. To say that a judge has an absolute discretion is the same as to say that there is no appeal at all from his decision. To say that he has a limited, i.e. qualified or conditional, discretion is to say that there is a limited right of appeal from his decision. A limited right of appeal and a verdict without a reason stated were what made for so long the jury trial the doorway for the aequum et bonum into the legal process.

I can think at the moment of only one class of case in our civil procedure in which a judge has something like an absolute discretion. This is in his decision to allow or refuse the costs of an action or to apportion them between the parties.[1] He is not required or even expected to give his reasons and consequently there is no law on the subject. In following the aequum et bonum he is not displacing the law since there is none to displace.

Cases of qualified or conditional discretion are far more common. In them there is some law to be followed and some principles not to be ignored—some routes and some signposts. They leave the judge with plenty of latitude, but his immunity from interference on appeal is conditional upon his following them so far as they go. 'Principle' may mean one of two things. If the principle which has not been observed can be stated by the appellate court, an error in principle is virtually an error in unformulated law since the principle has only to be stated by an appellate court to become a binding

[1] See, for example, *Donald Campbell* v. *Pollack* [1927] A.C. 732.

precedent and so law. Alternatively, error in principle is a convenient way of saying that the judge has gone very wrong and has strayed outside the reasonable but undefined bounds of his discretion.

There are two broad categories of case in which a judge has a limited discretion. The first comprises decisions in which the need for finality, if the administration of justice is not to be intolerably delayed, outweighs the need for correctitude. By far the largest proportion in this category is comprised of decisions on points raised in the course of the proceedings, i.e. interlocutory judgments. An unlimited right of appeal on such points could be used to delay the proceedings inordinately. So there is an appeal from an interlocutory judgment only when it can be shown that a point of law or of principle is involved. This piece of legal machinery is like a sieve: small disputes drop through it and are taken out of the process; the serious dispute, in which some point of principle can plausibly be advanced, continues on its way. The machinery helps also to shorten the argument in the Court of Appeal. If the court is not initially impressed, it will not be long before the appellant's counsel is reminded from the Bench that the court has no power to interfere with the judge's discretion; but, if the appellate judges are impressed and the respondent's counsel is reduced to tendering to them a similar reminder, he is likely to be told that there is clearly a point of principle involved. No doubt a point of principle is an elastic conception and can be stretched more easily than the law itself to favour the aequum et bonum. But this brings us back again to stretching the law.

The other large category of protected judgments consists of those composed of what I might call, taking the words from the Latin proverb,[1] the *non disputanda*. These are matters in which one well-qualified opinion is as good as another. Justice in such matters does not stand upon the point of a pin but within a range. Whether a sentence of imprisonment should be nine or ten years or compensation (when damages are at large) £900 or £1,000 is not an appealable question. If, however, the judge goes outside the range he is said to err in principle. If the nature of the case permits, the Court of Appeal will be more specific about his error. If he has given reasons, they will say that he has—or if he has given no reasons, they will say that he must have—taken into account factors that he should not have regarded, or failed to take into account those which he should. But this is not necessary if he has gone right outside the range. What is the range? One hears it said that an appellate judge asks himself, whether the sum or the term fixed is within 50% more or less of what he would have fixed himself. But if this is a guide it is a very rough one. When three, or at least

---

[1] *De gustibus non est disputandum*, meaning that there is no accounting for tastes.

two, appellate judges feel that the result is beyond the bounds of the *non disputanda* then in the eyes of the law it is injustice.

Of course the fixing of a sentence and the assessment of general damages are subjects which are less governable by the law than most. They depend more than most on the justice of the particular case. The less law there is, the more room for the aequum et bonum. But there is some law in the form of precedents about what considerations are relevant and in the form of judicial experience about the extent of the range. A judge does not begin an assessment of compensation by looking at the facts and asking himself what sum, subject to the law, would be appropriate: that would get him nowhere. He begins by applying the law, by excluding in accordance with it the irrelevant, and then by asking himself what sum within the permitted range would be appropriate. This can be expressed by saying that in deciding what is appropriate the judge has a limited discretion. It could be phrased as accurately by saying that within the range the law does not operate, only the aequum et bonum.

I come now to arbitration as a gateway to the aequum et bonum. It may be said that arbitration is outside the legal system. But its efficacy depends on the willingness of the system to enforce the award. Anyway, it has by statute[1] been brought within the legal system, though at the cost of narrowing the gateway.

Two people may agree that, if any dispute arises between them, they will not go to law but will submit it for settlement by the parson according to the aequum et bonum. If both of them keep their promise, well and good. But what if, after a dispute arises, one party is told that a law whose application the parson might in the circumstances regard as harsh has only to be mentioned to ensure his victory before a judge? If he is tempted and issues a writ, the other party cannot compel him to go to the parson. For the agreement not to go to law is invalid, being an attempt to oust the jurisdiction of the court and so contrary to public policy. The parties are in the same position as if they had made a gaming and wagering agreement or contracted to pursue some other activity upon which the law frowns. Of course many people do resolve their disputes in accordance with what a third party, ignorant of the law, thinks to be fair, just as many people make bets and pay their losses, but the law will not help them. This does not mean that parties may not validly agree to arbitrate, but that they may do so only within the framework of the law and the law will not recognize the aequum et bonum.

When a dispute actually arises, the court may have to be satisfied at the

[1] Now the Arbitration Act 1950.

outset that it is suitable for arbitration, and thereafter that the proceedings are conducted as a lawyer thinks they should be. I do not mean that the court will act inquisitorially but that it will intervene at the request of either party so as to secure these objectives. It assumes that the parties will wish the proceedings to be conducted in the same manner as in a court of law, though it permits some laxity if the parties so agree. The penalty for any departure from the procedure, assumed or agreed, or for any behaviour which might in the opinion of the court lead to a miscarriage of justice, is the removal of the arbitrator for legal misconduct. As a quid pro quo the court will make available to the parties such aids to prolonged litigation as orders for interrogatories, disclosure of documents, and security for costs; and is ready to confer upon them such benefits as the use of affidavits, the appointment of receivers, and interim injunctions. But in relation to the aequum et bonum the most important statutory provision of all is the one by which the court reserves to itself the right to decide all questions of law, even when the parties have agreed that the arbitrator's award should be final in all respects. This is done by the procedure of case stated. Here again it is not unknown for parties to agree in advance that they will not invoke this procedure, but the court would not enforce such an agreement. 'There must be no Alsatia in England,' Lord Justice Scrutton said grandly, 'where the King's writ does not run.'[1] Outside England there are many Alsatias. The usual principle is that an award is as final on law as it is on fact. The case stated procedure has been adopted in some only of the common law countries, e.g. Australia and India. It does not apply in e.g. the United States or Scotland.

So English law would not enforce a submission to arbitrators permitting them to decide as they thought best. 'Arbitrators must in general apply a fixed and recognizable system of law which presumably and normally will be the law of England, and they cannot be allowed to apply some different criterion, such as the view of the individual arbitrator or umpire on abstract justice or equitable principles.'[2] The courts began imposing legal solutions in 1802, when they interfered to correct errors of law on the face of the award. Since then the policy of a series of Arbitration Acts has been to turn arbitrators into subordinate judges with limited jurisdiction. Small disputes over the quality of goods escape the statutory juggernaut simply because

---

[1] *Czarnikow* v. *Roth* [1922] 2 K.B. at 488. 'Alsatia' was the popular name for Whitefriars, between the Thames and Fleet Street, which was a sanctuary for debtors until its privileges were abolished in 1697.

[2] *Orion* v. *Belfort* [1962] 2 Lloyds R. per Megaw J. at 264. But see now *Eagle Star* v. *Yval* [1978] 1 Lloyds R. 357; and see Dr. Mann's note in 94 L.Q.R. p. 486.

there is no scope in them for any principle of law, and the tendency of arbitrators to make a compromise award has not been eradicated.[1] Otherwise the
aequum et bonum is given no more rope in arbitration than in litigation. A
point of law turns the arbitration room into a costly antechamber to the court.

As a general rule nineteenth-century lawyers were keen—too keen, it is
now thought—on freedom of contract. But there is one freedom which they
never permitted, freedom to contract out of the law. There were many misfortunes against which they saw no need to protect the unwary citizen—
they said robustly that he should be taught to look after himself—but the
misfortune of being judged by someone unlearned in the law, 'the cadi under
the palm-tree',[2] was not one of them. Within their own domain even nineteenth-century judges liked to be paternalistic.

The reason advanced by lawyers, one with a professional rather than a
universal appeal, for the insistence on the case stated is that the development
of the law would suffer if decisions on debatable points were not published
in the law reports. So there must be an annual tribute of disputants to feed
the minotaur. The next step would, I suppose, be a prohibition placed on
the settlement of cases containing interesting points of law.[3]

Then it is argued that the State must not be put into the position of having
to use its executive power to enforce a manifestly unjust award. This object
could be achieved by treating it as an implication in every arbitration agreement (which surely it is) that the process and the result should be in conformity with the principles of natural justice. The object does not require
that the process should be a facsimile of legal process or that the final result
should be determined by lawyers. Why is it contrary to public policy to
prefer justice from the cadi under the palm-tree to justice according to law
and precedent? There are good reasons for preferring the latter as I have
pointed out: there is the reason that justice should be the same for all and
the danger that the cadi may be a bad cadi. But in an arbitration the cadi
is the choice of the parties, not thrust upon them, and since they have chosen
arbitration in preference to litigation, they have sought individual treatment;
they have preferred bespoke tailoring to ready-made and are willing to pay
for it.

[1] In *Howards* v. *Aylwin* [1958] 2 Lloyds R., Diplock J. was asked at 560 to take judicial notice
of the fact that most awards by commercial arbitrators were compromises, but refused to do
so.
[2] The cadi under the palm-tree is—or at any rate as a character in English law is to be deemed
to be—one 'who has to do the best he can in the circumstances, having no rules of law to guide
him': *Metropolitan Properties* v. *Purdy* [1940] 1 A.E.R. per Goddard L.J. at 191.
[3] I am forced to admit that I am saying these uncharitable things about some very distinguished
lawyers who would vigorously present a different point of view.

Legal reasoning on this point has boxed itself in with the false assumption that nothing lies between justice according to law and injustice. Thus when the Tasmanian legislature provided that the Supreme Court should not in deciding a certain type of case 'be bound by the strict rules of law or equity', the Privy Council held that the decision which emerged was not judicial. The matter was, they said, placed 'in the hands of the judges as the persons from whom the best opinions might be obtained and not as a court administering justice between the litigants'.[1] The decision of the best persons would not be corrupt, but it might be unjust in the sense of being influenced by considerations of what was politic or expedient. Thus the decision in a dispute between an employer and a workman might be shaped so as to avoid a strike instead of being given strictly according to the merits.[2] I think that it is to be implied that when parties refer a matter to arbitration, whether they speak of arbitrators or of persons from whom the best opinions may be obtained, they want a just decision in their case and not a political decision designed to promote some worthy objective outside it. But it does not follow that they want a decision according to the strict rules of law. There is room in between.

It is time we thought again about this. Arbitration is an ideal way of giving to those who want it a judgment on the merits of their case without injuring the fabric of the law. If we are unwilling to think again as a matter of principle, we may find ourselves having to do it as a matter of expediency; otherwise England may be put out of bounds as a place for international arbitration. Let me take this point further.

Businessmen of different nationalities are now becoming increasingly reluctant to plump for the law of one nation rather than the other. It is not simply that an argument about whose law is to prevail gets in the way of the rapid and successful negotiation of the contract. It is, my experience tells me, exceedingly dangerous for a party to permit a contract of any complexity to be governed by a law with which he and his advisers have only a superficial acquaintance. The contract may not run smoothly, and then without a foreign lawyer at his elbow he risks walking blindfold into many pits. English law in particular digs pits for the unwary because of its hospitality to implied terms which often make the point upon which the foreigner is relying of no avail.

Consequently arbitration clauses are no longer invariably based on the 'fixed and recognizable system of law' which the English court demands. Sometimes the parties decide to leave it to the arbitrator to apply to any

---

[1] *Moses* v. *Parker* [1896] A.C. 245.
[2] *United Engineering* v. *Devanayagam* [1967] 3 W.L.R. 461.

point in dispute whichever of the two systems of law he considers to be the better in relation to that point; this is halfway to the aequum et bonum. Sometimes a party is willing to accept in general the law of the opposite country, but not the whole of it. If, for example, a multi-national company is entering into a long-term contract with the government of a developing country, it may be happy with the law of the country as it is but suspicious of future changes. It is now not uncommon to provide that the governing law shall be the law of the country at the date of the contract. The exclusion of a few years of recent legislation may create no practical difficulty; but is it theoretically admissible? I doubt if an English court would allow the parties to contract out of any part of the law of England; suppose that they provided that the contract should be governed by English law as at the death of Queen Anne! Again, a party may in general accept English law but wish to introduce the principles of public international law as well; an English court does not recognize international law as part of the law of England. Sometimes the parties do not want to be governed by any national system at all, but want to make their own ground rules. Where there is an elaborate contract, filling several hundred pages of print, the parties have taken to saying that the contract provides its own law and all that the arbitrator has to do is to interpret it, presumably in the light of the aequum et bonum. The I.C.S.I.D.[1] clause, for example, seems to be wide enough to allow the parties to make their own rules:

The Tribunal shall decide a dispute in accordance with such rules of law as may be agreed by the parties. In the absence of such agreement the Tribunal shall apply the law of the Contracting State party to the dispute (including its rules on the conflict of laws) and such rules of international law as may be applicable.... [This] shall not prejudice the power of the Tribunal to decide a dispute ex aequo et bono if the parties so agree.

There is another aspect of international arbitration to be noticed. English law assumes that businessmen will be able to make contracts which will last for years, meeting all contingencies with an exceptions or *force majeure* clause and with the aid, if there is a complete upheaval, of the doctrine of frustration. The assumption worked well enough in settled times. Today circumstances change so rapidly that often an elaborate contract can be kept alive and meaningful only by adaptation. Frustration kills it stone dead and a *force majeure* clause offers only partial relief. What is needed, and what is often now inserted in the contract, is a clause requiring the parties when circumstances alter to consult together and, if they cannot agree on the adaptation, to submit the matter to an arbitrator for settlement. In English law such

[1] International Centre for Settlement of Investment Disputes.

a clause is unenforceable. It is ancient doctrine that the court will not make a contract for the parties, and I do not see an English judge undertaking the task. Arbitrators, who could be chosen for their knowledge of the conditions in which the contract has to operate, are in a different position, but in deciding what alterations would be fair, they would have nothing to guide them except the aequum et bonum. There have been several international awards in which effect has been given to this type of clause.

All these new ideas use the aequum et bonum in one form or another. If they emerge in an agreement which provides for arbitration in London, it is not yet clear what the attitude of an English court would be. But if arrangements of this sort are not to be respected, and if international arbitrators are to be required to state a case, they will take their business to Alsatia and not to London. Yet if English law lets the aequum et bonum into international arbitrations,[1] can it continue to deny the facility to its own nationals? If it does, our much respected Institute of Arbitrators may be driven into changing its name to the Institute of Persons From Whom The Best Opinions May Be Obtained.[2]

I have now examined the main features of our civil procedure for signs of the aequum et bonum. I have not found as much of it as might have been hoped from the discretion of the judge and the apparent flexibility of the common law. I have not examined to what extent the aequum et bonum may come alive in the workings of the numerous statutory tribunals which now play so great a part in our legal system; I do not believe that there are yet sufficient data for an assessment.

I have reached three conclusions: first, that in the past the happiest home of the aequum et bonum has been in the jury; second, that it still flourishes in the English judge's unwelcoming attitude to technicalities and in his willingness, whether or not he knows it himself, to stretch law or fact on occasion; third, that in arbitration procedure it has been far too sternly repressed.

I turn now to consider the aequum et bonum in criminal procedure. At once I find it necessary to draw a very sharp distinction between two parts of the criminal law. The first is the old and traditional part which consists of indictable crimes punishable chiefly by loss of liberty. The second is the modern and statutory part (meaning by 'statutory' that the origin of the offence is in the statute and not in the common law compound of custom

---

[1] As is proposed in the Queen's Speech for the 1978–9 Session. 'Bill should prevent loss of legal cases to other countries' is how it is headlined in *The Times*, 2 Nov. 1978.

[2] See *Moses* v. *Parker*, cited p. 107 above.

and morality which a statute has codified) consisting of summary offences punishable chiefly by the fine. In the first category the aequum et bonum is extremely influential; in the second it is barely recognized.

I start by considering crimes in the first category. Manifestly the proverb that hard cases make bad law is quite unacceptable. You cannot tell a man who has not behaved badly that he must stay in prison because he is a 'hard case'. The aequum et bonum in its relation to crime requires that every man should have his just deserts, no more and no less, in accordance with the good citizen's idea of justice and notwithstanding the letter of the law. To what extent is this requirement (which, when the law and merits are in conflict, our civil procedure meets only surreptitiously) met by our procedure for indictable offences?

There is no way of meeting it completely. What we do in serious, i.e. indictable, crime is to jettison one half so as to save the other half. We do not allow the prosecution any share at all of the aequum et bonum, with the result that many a man who, if he got his just deserts, would be in prison, remains at large. The gift to the accused of the whole of the aequum et bonum makes it theoretically possible to ensure that he will not be punished unless he is guilty both in the eyes of the law and on the merits. How far in practice do we ensure it?

Do we ensure that a man is heavily punished only for wickednesss? That is what it comes to. We seek to do it, first, by defining the act to be punished as one that is, if done intentionally, judged to be wicked by the moral standards of our society and is not just made wicked by law; and, second, by making it a universal principle that to be punishable the act should be done intentionally, i.e. the requirement of *mens rea*. The law covering indictable offences does, I think, give effect broadly to the good citizen's idea of what is wicked.

Basically our criminal process is designed to secure that a convict who is guilty in law will be guilty also on the merits. On this basis there are other factors working to the same end. The first of them to be noticed is the elasticity of the sentence. In the civil process compensation is not adjustable to degrees of moral blameworthiness, but the sentence is. Where there are absurdities (such as the extraordinary decision in 1921 that while a reasonable but erroneous belief in the death of a spouse is a good defence to a charge of bigamy, a like belief in a divorce is not[1]), they can be corrected in the sentence, which can be light or even nominal.

To this there must be added three out of the four factors which I have

---

[1] *R*. v. *Wheat* [1921] 2 K.B. 119. But it will be all right if the accused believed not in the dissolution but in the invalidity of the marriage: *R*. v. *King* [1964] 1 Q.B. 285.

examined in relation to the civil process. Arbitration is obviously inapplicable, but the other three work potently for the defence.

First, the law works for the defence without having to be stretched. When the indictable offence is defined by statute, as most now are, the rule is that the statute must be strictly construed, i.e. strictly against the prosecution and in favour of the defence. The act has to be caught by the spirit of the words and to be within their scope as well as within their reasonable meaning.

Second, the jury is 100% active instead of 2% or 3%: no case is triable on indictment without a jury. A special verdict is asked of it only very rarely and for an exceptional reason; otherwise, it has all the latitude given by the general verdict.

Third, judicial discretion is transformed. While the prosecution is always bound by the law, the judge has throughout the criminal process a wide discretion to override procedural law in favour of the defence. He is given what is virtually a dispensing power. The rule of law must give way whenever he considers that it would bear too heavily upon the accused. A common example is the exclusion of relevant evidence tendered by the prosecution, e.g. evidence which would reveal incidentally the accused's bad character.

This discretion is in its origin absolute: the prosecution has no right of appeal. So at the start it was pure aequum et bonum; the judge displaced the law by what he thought to be fair in the particular case. But while the prosecution could not appeal from the positive, the defence could appeal from the negative. If a judge, for example, refused to exclude relevant evidence as unduly prejudicial, the court of appeal might hold that he ought to have done so. They could do this only by holding that he was wrong in principle in refraining from exercising his discretion; and this would be the making of a rule, the turning of the aequum et bonum into law.

The result of all this is that to obtain a conviction the prosecution must succeed both on the law and on the merits. For the defence the gap between justice according to law and justice on the merits is closed. But if through human error the prosecution was to succeed unmeritoriously, there are two further tests for it to pass. One is the Court of Appeal, which in the last decade has begun to concern itself seriously with the merits as well as the law. The other is the Home Secretary, who has never concerned himself with anything but the merits.

When criminal appeals were first permitted in 1907, the new court concerned itself hardly at all with the merits of the case; merits were for the jury. To be sure, the statute creating the court gave it wide powers of intervention. However, many judges in 1907 disliked the idea of a criminal appeal. They felt that the verdict of a jury properly directed in law—they would always of course correct the law—should be unassailable and that to allow an appeal from it cast an unnecessary doubt on its reliability. This feeling, coupled with the normal judicial distrust of innovation, resulted in a very narrow exercise of the new powers. The court looked primarily to the verdict and to the summing-up which had led to it and only secondarily to the evidence, which it would not re-assess. It was not taken to be a sufficient ground of appeal that the verdict was against the weight of evidence or that the prosecution's case was very weak. It became true that in such circumstances the court would scrutinize the summing-up with extra care and that then minor misdirections of fact might be considered as sufficient to vitiate the verdict. But the principle applied was that when the accused had got the verdict of a properly directed jury, he had got what the law gave him and it was not for an appellate court to look behind the verdict into the merits of the case.

There is no doubt that the court had the power to look into the merits, and it could on rare occasions be persuaded to exercise it. In a case in 1931 the appellant was convicted of the murder of his wife on a theory of the facts which was possible, but hardly probable. The trial judge, who subsequently became Lord Wright, though a great lawyer, was no orator; indeed, he was a master of the monotone sinking sometimes to the mumble. It was thought at the time that the jury must have misheard or misunderstood or, at the very least, failed to be gripped by a summing-up which the Court of Criminal Appeal described as completely fair and accurate and as one which might have been expected to have resulted in an acquittal. The court quashed the conviction on the ground that the verdict could not be supported having regard to the evidence.[1]

Parliament can, as we know, do anything it likes. But it has not yet found a way of suggesting to the judges in statutory language that they should be less sticky about the use of their powers and that a few more cases like R. v. Wallace would do no harm. In 1966 it sought to convey this idea by means of a delicate re-phrasing. Whereas in 1907 it had told the judges to allow the appeal if they thought the verdict unreasonable or such as could not be supported having regard to the evidence, in 1966 it told them to allow the appeal if they thought the verdict under all the circumstances of the case to be unsafe or unsatisfactory. The judges did not pause to ask themselves whether a verdict that was unreasonable or unsupported by the evidence could ever have been safe or satisfactory, or otherwise to analyse the

[1] R. v. Wallace 23 Cr. App. R. 32.

textual differences. Under the leadership of Lord Justice Widgery, soon to be Chief Justice, they took the hint. In a striking judgment the Lord Justice laid it down that the judges must ask themselves 'the subjective question' whether 'lurking doubts' caused them to wonder whether injustice had been done; the reaction need not be based strictly on the evidence but 'could be produced by the general feel of the case as experienced by the Court'.[1] This entails a fresh and wide re-examination of the merits.

There is another respect in which, also in 1966, the appellate powers were extended to favour the defence. When considering statutes of limitation earlier in this lecture, I dealt with the difficulty of reconciling the aequum et bonum with the time bar. A similar difficulty arises when fresh evidence, relevant and credible and capable of altering the result, is discovered after judgment has been given. Here again there is a quarrel between the aequum et bonum and the legal principle of finality. The compromise that is reached in a civil suit is to admit the new evidence only if it can be shown that it could not with the exercise of reasonable diligence (which includes of course, indeed usually means, the diligence of the solicitors) have been produced at the trial. The Criminal Appeal Act 1907 gave the court an unlimited discretion to admit fresh evidence. One might have supposed that this would lead to the admission of any fresh evidence which was credible and influential, except perhaps in cases in which it appeared that the accused had deliberately withheld it from the trial court in the belief that he could make better use of it on appeal. In civil cases of course the principle of finality is much more stringently enforced. But while the loss of a civil case is usually the loss of money or money's worth, and compensation is obtainable from a negligent solicitor, it is impossible for a civilized community to tell a man who may be unjustly imprisoned that he must serve out his term and look to his solicitor for compensation at the end of it. Even if it is his own fault and not his solicitor's, the appropriate punishment for negligence is not the same as the punishment for a crime which *ex hypothesi* the criminal did not commit.

Considerations of this sort did not, however, commend themselves to the judges of 1907 or their immediate successors. It was another unfortunate provision, they doubtless felt, in this innovatory Act. What had they to do with fresh evidence? They had no power to order a new trial and surely they were not expected to re-try the case themselves when it had been established for centuries that only by the verdict of a jury could a man be condemned. The situation had always been satisfactorily dealt with in the past by requiring a person who had fresh evidence, which he believed could prove

[1] *R.* v. *Cooper* [1969] 1 Q.B. 267.

his innocence, to beg for a pardon for a crime which he was maintaining he had not committed. So they declared at first that it was only in exceptional circumstances and under exceptional conditions that they would admit fresh evidence, though eventually they came to formulate rules that were substantially the same as those in civil procedure.

In 1964 the court was given power when it admitted fresh evidence to order a new trial and in 1966 its power to admit was re-worded. The discretion was repeated in the old wide terms and a duty to admit if there was a reasonable explanation of failure to adduce the evidence at the trial was imposed. But what if there was no reasonable explanation? Was the prisoner to continue to serve a life sentence, maybe, because of his failure to adduce one? Was the reiterated grant of full discretion to serve no wider purpose than its 1907 progenitor? At first it seemed so, but during the ensuing decade the door has been slightly opened, though still held in position by the time-honoured doorstop of 'wholly exceptional circumstances'.

The judiciary's insistence on finality and its reluctance to yield to the aequum et bonum on this point cannot be understood unless it is realized that there is beyond the Court of Appeal, as its judges well know, a tribunal where the aequum et bonum is all that matters. This ultimate tribunal is the Home Secretary, the wielder of the royal prerogative of pardon, assisted by a number of cadis sitting under the palm-trees in Whitehall. The Home Secretary is a slave to the essential principle of any administrator of the aequum et bonum, which is to give no reasons for his decision. His advisers operate in the strictest secrecy. For what it now knows about them the public is partly indebted to an anonymous cadi whose 'serious misjudgment',[1] as the Home Office described it, had consequences which called for an investigation. So we now know that in 1976 there was a special division of the Home Office, dubbed C5, under an assistant secretary with some 17 principals and executive officers fully employed in the task of processing the volume of applications which the Home Secretary receives seeking his intervention after conviction.

It is known to all practitioners that the Home Secretary will not act as a court of appeal; as a rule he acts only when some new factor is brought to his attention. This factor often takes the form of fresh evidence and then he prefers, where it is practicable, to refer the case back to the Court of Appeal. When he does that, the Court of Appeal will consider the fresh evidence notwithstanding that under their own rules they would have rejected it, and may indeed already have done so. While the Home Office methodology, if there is one, is not revealed, it may, I think, be safely assumed that

[1] *Identification Report*, para. 3.88.

they concern themselves with the merits and not with the law; the law they leave to the courts. The Home Secretary is the court of last resort for the meritorious man whom the law has by some mischance condemned, and as such plays an invaluable part in our system of criminal justice.

To return to the Court of Appeal and to the impetus given to the aequum et bonum by the new 'safe and satisfactory' rule. On paper this looks like an unqualified gain. It gives an added protection to the defence and does not seriously harm the prosecution since no one would be happy with the verdict of a jury given on evidence which three judges thought to be unsafe. But it made in 1966 a change in the foundations of the criminal process and any such change may have an unforeseen result on the stability of the structure. The cracks are now appearing. The power and significance of the judges are increasing with the predictable result that the significance of the jury is diminishing. People may begin to ask themselves whether there is any longer a need for a criminal jury. Since the judges now stand ready to use their extensive experience in detecting 'the specious, the irrelevant and that which is intended to deceive',[1] what more can be wanted? Here would be a hard choice for lovers of the aequum et bonum. Would they be willing to desert the jury, which has served the aequum et bonum for so long and so well, and put their trust in judges? This is a thought for another lecture.

So much for what I have called old and traditional crime. Modern crime is a breach of a regulation. The breakers are called offenders rather than criminals. The regulations are without an essential moral content and are made primarily for the convenience of society. A contravention is not punishable because the act is bad in itself but because it is prohibited. In one country it is an offence to drive on the right and in another to drive on the left. A regulation does often have some moral content, though it is never of the essence; it would be, to say the least of it, inconsiderate to drive on the right in a country where everybody else drives on the left. Then there are many regulations whose breach could be made a crime of deception or the like, but it is thought more convenient to have a rule wide enough to catch people who are morally guiltless but deemed to be socially responsible, and under which offenders can be brought to book more easily.[2]

Social regulations can for my purposes be divided into three categories. At the end nearest to the traditional there is the category in which reasonably

---

[1] Per Widgery C.J. in *R.* v. *Turnbull* [1977] Q.B. at 231E.

[2] I have elaborated on this in *The Enforcement of Morals*, Oxford University Press, London, 1965, pp. 25–32.

smooth justice is done. *Mens rea* is accepted as an element in the offence, though it may be that the defendant will have to prove its absence rather than the reverse or that carelessness rather than intent will suffice; the idea of wickedness would be out of place. In the second category, the only question is whether a rule has been broken and whether under the terms of it the defendant has been made responsible for the breach; if so, he is guilty, though he may have done all he could to prevent the breach. In this category, however, the merits or demerits can be, and sometimes are, reflected in the size of the penalty. In the third category the merits are virtually irrelevant: speeding offences and parking offences are penalized according to the tariff. Thus there is in the regulation of modern society a large area in which justice according to law is all that matters; there is no time for the aequum et bonum.

It is indeed a curious contrast. So deep is the chasm that separates the new law from the old that there is a case for saying that jurisprudentially they ought to be treated as two different species, the one in which the law is everything and the aequum et bonum goes for little or nothing, and the other in which the aequum et bonum is ranked equally with the law as a test to be satisfied before conviction.

5

The Judge and the Jury

1. The Power without the Right

THE jury system is the creation of the judges. Statutes have touched it only on the fringe.[1] The first time Parliament made any essential change in the system was in 1966 when the majority verdict of ten out of twelve was introduced.

There have been several accounts of the jury's origin and of the way in which the judges shaped it to their purposes.[2] None of them explained convincingly—perhaps there was no palpable explanation even at the time—how the judges came to permit a body which they instituted for the purpose of furnishing them with the facts to become the judges of what the facts were worth. I doubt if research would now disclose much more about how the change occurred, let alone why. It was a long process. At the beginning, when guilt or innocence depended on what the jury knew and the court had no other evidence, it was perhaps natural to let the jury evaluate their own information, knowledge and belief, and encapsulate them in a verdict. When evidence first began to be received there was a long period, the whole of the sixteenth and seventeenth centuries and maybe more, when the jury both heard evidence (at first only 'to inform their consciences') and used their own knowledge; by the end of it jurymen who wanted to use their own knowledge were being told to notify the court so that they could be sworn as witnesses. By this time the judges had taken a large measure of control over the verdict. They did this by ruling that questions of fact which they thought it best to decide themselves were questions of law. There were specific points which

---

[1] Statutes from the reign of King Henry VIII onwards were concerned about what was to be done with jurors, particularly Welsh jurors, who 'gave an untrue verdict against the King', and also about their property qualifications. The two are connected. A juror who was not more than a freeman, which was the qualification at common law, might not have been able to pay a substantial fine for misbehaviour.

[2] The one with which I am most familiar is *Trial by Jury* by Patrick Devlin, Stevens & Sons, London 1956. Subsequent references are to the revised edition in 1966.

they thought ought for the sake of uniformity to be decided by rule, e.g. what was a reasonable length of notice to give so as to terminate a particular type of contract. But in general what the judges did was to appropriate the extremes at either end of a factual dispute. Whether there was any evidence to sustain a proposition of fact was, they said, a question of law; likewise, whether such a proposition was overwhelmingly sustained so that its rejection would be, as they put it, perverse. On these matters of law they gave directions to juries, and disobedient jurors were punished by fine and imprisonment. Thereby juries were bloodied but in the end, as we know, unbowed. A mighty battle was fought in 1670 when Chief Justice Vaughan released on habeas corpus the jurors who had been imprisoned for acquitting William Penn.

After that all that an affronted judge could do was to set aside a verdict which he deemed to be contrary to law. Nevertheless this left him victorious, even though unable to exact vengeance. He had got rid of the offensive verdict, could order a new trial, and, in theory at least, could go on ordering new trials until he found a jury who would give the verdict he wanted. Except in one case. The rule against double jeopardy was by then so firmly rooted in our law that no judge could shake it and none would wish to. So as Chief Justice Pratt said in 1724, 'it was never yet known that a verdict was set aside by which the defendant was acquitted'.[1] It has not been known since.

Does not this spell anarchy and chaos at the very heart of our legal system? If the jury were to proclaim as they offered their verdict that they were rejecting the law as laid down by the judge, yet he would have to accept the verdict. Lord Chief Justice Mansfield said in 1784 that a judge could tell the jury how to do right, but that they had it 'in *their power* to do wrong, which is a matter entirely between God and their own consciences'.[2] In these words Lord Mansfield recognized the sovereignty of the jury as sovereignty was understood in English law. He was, consciously or not, using the formula which Bracton had applied four centuries earlier to the King: 'the king is bound to obey the law, though if he break it, his punishment must be left to God.'[3] None the less, as applied to a jury, it is a puzzling dictum: if the constitution entrusts the judges and not the jury with the duty of determining what is right, why does it not also confer on them the power to enforce it? So strange a dictum must be examined in its context. It was made in the celebrated trial of the Dean of St. Asaph for seditious libel. The case is celebrated not so much for its place in the law as for the great speech

---

[1] *R.* v. *Jones*, 8 Mod. 201 at 208.

[2] *R.* v. *Shipley* (hereafter referred to as *Shipley*), 9 Douglas 73 at 170.

[3] Quoted in F. W. Maitland, *The Constitutional History of England*, Cambridge University Press, 1920, pp. 100–101.

of Erskine for the defence, which Charles Fox enthusiastically declared to be the finest piece of reasoning in the English language.[1]

In the eighteenth century men who were thought of by the Government as of 'a wicked and turbulent disposition' wrote pamphlets intended, according to them, to promote salutary reform, but intended, according to the Government, to stir up 'discontents, jealousies and suspicions of our Lord the King and his Government',[2] i.e. to amount to a seditious libel. Since jurors were disposed to share the sentiments of the pamphleteers rather than those of the Government, judges had to be very insistent on the common law rule that the question 'libel or no libel' was a question of law for the judge and not of fact for the jury. This meant that the only question to be left to the jury was whether or not the accused had published the pamphlet, and this was usually easily proved.[3]

But insistence on the common law rule might not by itself be enough. Notwithstanding a direction by the judge that the publication was libellous, a jury could, and probably quite frequently would, acquit and then there would be nothing to be done about it. This misfortune could perhaps be avoided by asking the jury for a special verdict. But this was a procedure intended only for use when there was a difficult question of law which the judge could not be expected to solve on the spot. Moreover it was beginning to be established that juries could refuse to give a special verdict and doubtless thought probable that, if they smelt a rat, they would refuse. So the judges exploited the pecularities of the procedure in libel prosecutions to arrive at the same result.

An acquittal means Not Guilty both in law and in fact. The jury take the law from the judge and apply it, but there are not two separate issues, one of law and one of fact, demanding two separate answers. This follows from the accused's right to plead generally Not Guilty; he cannot be made to plead separately to the law or to separate issues of fact. As Erskine was to put it in argument, 'the general plea thus sanctioned by immemorial custom so blends the law and the fact together, as to be inseparable but by

[1] Lord Campbell, *Lives of the Lord Chancellors* (hereafter cited as Campbell), vol. VI, p. 434.

[2] *Shipley*, 74.

[3] The truth of the innuendoes was also a question for the jury, but usually, as in *Shipley*, only a formal one. A legal innuendo is quite different from a popular one. As Erskine put it at 146, 'the judges can presume nothing which the strictest rules of grammar do not warrant them to collect intrinsically from the writing itself'. So the office of the legal innuendo is to make precise for the lawyer what is already precise enough for the layman. Thus a reference in the text to 'the King' must be clarified by the innuendo—'meaning thereby Our Sovereign Lord George III, now King of Great Britain, etc.'—so as to make sure that no suspicion could alight on a foreign potentate.

the voluntary act of the jury in finding a special verdict'.[1] In the ordinary case there was no way round this, as Lord Mansfield was to recognize in his judgment: 'by means of a general verdict they are entrusted with a power of blending law and fact, and following the prejudices of their affections or passions'.[2]

But in cases of libel the procedure required (and still does) that the whole of the libel should be set out on the record. In this way the question of law was separated from the question of fact. There was no need for blending. The question of fact could be decided by the jury upon the evidence, and the question of law by the judge upon the record. The *decantatum*[3] could be literally honoured. The judge need not direct the jury on the law, for it is no business of theirs. The jury need not enter into the province of the law with the opportunity the entry gives of exercising overlordship.

So juries were directed or advised (not instructed; the happy ambiguity of the word 'direct' has for many years oiled the machinery of the judge–jury relationship) on proof of publication to find the accused Guilty. They were only finding him guilty, they were assured, on the record and, if the record disclosed no libel, the accused would be freed on a motion to arrest judgment. True, this might be inconvenient for a legally innocent accused since on the verdict of Guilty he must go to prison and the judge had no power to grant bail pending the hearing of the motion. But with an indulgent prosecution bail could be arranged.[4] True, the question of law might be child's play for the judge to decide on the spot. But since the question arose on the record, 'it was the province of the court out of which the record came, and not of the judge at *Nisi Prius*, to decide that question'.[5]

This was the manner in which the jury was suffered not to enter into temptation.

There was no more of a libel in the pamphlet published by the Dean of St. Asaph than there was of a snail in the *Donoghue* v. *Stevenson* ginger-beer bottle. The pamphlet was the work of Sir William Jones, a man of many parts; there is (or was) a statue to him in Calcutta and a memorial tablet in St. Paul's, his collected works have been published in six volumes, and he has an Epigram in *The Oxford Book of English Verse*. He was called to the Bar comparatively late in life but won early recognition from the practitioners by his *Essay on the Law of Bailment* and from the academics by

---

[1] *Shipley*, 114.   [2] ib. 163.
[3] 'The judges make no answer to the question of fact nor the jury to the question of law'; see p. 132.
[4] As it was for the Dean; *Shipley*, 124–5.   [5] ib. 86.

his translation of Isaeus on the Athenian right of inheiritance. In 1783 he was appointed to the Supreme Court of Bengal and knighted, married the Dean's sister, and found time to compose a little tract illustrating the general principles of government and recommending parliamentary reform, which he entitled 'A Dialogue between a Gentleman and a Farmer'. The contents were as inflammatory as the title suggests.

Sir William sent a copy to his new brother-in-law. The Dean sent it on to what was described in the subsequent proceedings as 'the Flintshire Committee' (evidently a local committee of some society advocating the extension of representation in Parliament) to be translated into Welsh. He did this without reading it. But the pamphlet was not liked by some, including the High Sheriff of the county, Mr. Fitzmaurice, and the Dean was summoned to a committee meeting at which it was said that the pamphlet was treasonable 'and many opprobrious epithets were made use of'.[1] The Dean then read the tract, said that he did not think it so bad a thing, and that it ought to be published 'in vindication'. So he had it printed and published.

The Attorney-General was asked to prosecute, but refused. Proceedings were launched by the High Sheriff, but his resolution faltered 'in consequence of an answer he had received to an application made to the Treasury;'[2] the judge at the trial ruled that the answer was not evidence, but, like so many answers that are not evidence, its terms may be surmised. The prosecution was carried on by another William Jones, an attorney, who presumably got the funds from someone else. All this created quite a stir,[3] and the prosecution, which had been commenced at Sessions, was removed by *certiorari* into the King's Bench and came on at the Shrewsbury Assizes before Mr. Justice Buller and a special jury.

Thomas Erskine, the Dean's counsel, had just taken silk, having practised as a junior for six years. I believe that more of the well-informed would agree upon him than upon any other as the greatest advocate who has ever practised at the English Bar. In this case his respect for Lord Mansfield, a fellow Scot, from whom he had received much kindness, and for Mr. Justice Buller, whose pupil he had been, had somehow to be accommodated with his passionate belief in trial by jury.[4]

---

[1] ib. 84. [2] ibid.
[3] The High Sheriff was the brother of the powerful statesman who had just been created Marquess of Lansdowne. The Dean was the son of the Bishop of St. Asaph (he was Dean, if not quite accidentally, at any rate not by right of primogeniture) and the Bishop was an active member of the House of Lords whose speeches had displeased the King.
[4] When in 1806 he was made a peer on his appointment as Lord Chancellor, he took 'Trial by Jury' as his motto. But, as was pointed out at the time, he could hardly have taken the motto of his family (his father was Earl of Buchan), which was 'Judge nought'; Campbell p. 557.

Although the judge proposed in accordance with precedent to leave to the jury only the question of publiication, he did not seek to prevent counsel on either side from addressing the jury on the contents of the pamphlet. The Crown did not care to rely exclusively on the obedience of the jury to the judge's direction nor did it rashly assume that the jury would not so much as peep at the libel. So it was the practice that prosecuting counsel should, as Lord Mansfield put it,[1] 'expatiate upon the enormity of the libel' so as to 'remove the prejudices of a jury, and to satisfy the bystanders' and also 'to obviate the captivating harangues of the Defendant's counsel'. Erskine's captivating harangue lasted several hours and he concluded by telling the jury boldly 'that if you find the defendant Guilty, not believing the thing published to be a libel, or the intention of the publishers seditious,—your verdict and your opinion will be at variance, and it will then be between God and your own consciences to reconcile the contradiction'.[2]

The judge, after expressing his astonishment at this, told the jury that they were concerned only with the publication and that if they were satisfied of that, they 'ought in point of law to find him Guilty'. The jury took a middle course and returned a verdict of 'Guilty of publishing only'. The judge endeavoured to have the 'only' removed and Erskine fought for its retention. There ensued a furious altercation which, according to Lord Campbell, so confounded the jury that they wished to withdraw, and in which Erskine 'meted out the requisite and justifiable portion of defiance'. But in the end the judge obtained and recorded the verdict, 'Guilty of publishing, but whether a libel or not we do not find'.

Erskine then moved for a new trial and also for arrest of judgment. The motions were heard by Lord Chief Justice Mansfield sitting with his puisnes, Willes and Ashurst. Erskine never thought that the King's Bench would hold the *Dialogue* to be libellous; indeed when the motion for arrest was eventually made, the Bench asked the prosecution to point out any part of it which could be considered criminal and they were unable to do so. Nevertheless Erskine repelled the Chief Justice's suggestion that the two motions should be taken together. He noted privately at the time that he made the motion for a new trial 'from no hope of success, but from a fixed resolution to expose to public contempt the doctrines fastened on the public as law by Lord Chief Justice Mansfield, and to excite, if possible the attention of Parliament to so great an object of national freedom'; so that most of Erskine's speech was concerned with what Mansfield called 'general theory' and 'popular declamation'.[3] 'He treated me,' Erskine recalled eight years

[1] *Shipley*, 166.
[2] This and the following citations are from Campbell, pp. 431 et seqq.   [3] *Shipley*, 169.

later, 'not with contempt indeed, for of that his nature was incapable—but he put me aside with indulgence, as you do a child when it is lisping its prattle out of season.'

In order to succeed, Erskine had to overthrow either a rule of law or a rule of practice. The former, i.e. the rule that 'libel or no libel' was a question for the judge, was so buttressed by authority that it was unshakable outside the House of Lords. Even there it would have been difficult to attack, and when Fox's bill to make it a question for the jury was before the House of Lords, the opinion of the judges, which the House requested and which the judges gave unanimously, was that the bill was inconsistent with the common law. This did not prevent Parliament from showing its contempt for the judiciary by passing the bill as a declaratory Act for the removal of doubts.[1]

The rule of practice, on the other hand, while supported by precedent, was contrary to the logic of the general verdict. Granted that 'libel or no libel' was a question of law, it ought, like any other question of law arising under the general issue, to have been left to the jury with a direction. This was not done. This was the point that Erskine pressed. 'It is easy to show,' he said, 'that the jury could not possibly conceive or believe, from the judge's charge, that they had any jurisdiction to acquit him, however they might have been impressed even with the merit of the publication, or convinced of his meritorious intention in publishing it.'

The three judges were all against Erskine on this point, but they dealt with it in three different ways. Ashurst[2] hardly dealt with it at all: he did not separate it from the rule of law that 'libel or no libel' was for the judge. Mansfield[3] relied upon the peculiarity that the question of law was entirely upon the record and thus could be decided by the judges separately; there was no need, as in the ordinary case, for the judge to give a direction on the law and to leave it to 'the honesty of the jury' to preserve the distinction between the fact and law. The general verdict of Guilty which the jury was told to return on proof of publication was, Mansfield said, 'equivalent to

---

[1] Another question of law which occupied a good deal of the argument at the trial was about whether *mens rea* or an intention to seduce was an ingredient of seditious libel and, if so, whether its existence was a question for the judge or for the jury. The prosecution contended that it would be for the defence to show that the publication was accidental. It is on this sort of point that the legal imagination is always at its liveliest and counsel gave (*Shipley*, 97), as an example of an accidental publication, 'a man having a libel written by another in his pocket' and 'being a clergyman, like the defendant, should mistake it for his sermon, and in a fit of absence deliver it from the pulpit'. As to the argument that the Dean believed the *Dialogue* not to be seditious and published it to demonstrate his belief, this was taken to be destroyed by his comment after reading the pamphlet that it 'was not so bad', for that meant, the judges said, that he was admitting that it *was* bad, though maybe not so bad as all that.

[2] *Shipley*, 122.   [3] ib. 170 and 165.

a special verdict in other cases'. Indeed, the question of law could be left
to the court in the form of a special verdict, 'but the other is simpler and
better'. Willes also treated the verdict as 'in the nature of a special verdict'. [1]
For him the decisive point was that the jury had not been told that they
could not return a general verdict of acquittal. Counsel on both sides had
told them that they could and the judge had not negatived it. Buller in his
report to the King's Bench had strongly denied that he had told the jury
that they had no right to find a general verdict: 'I certainly said no such
thing.'[2]

Thus the two judges who thought about it reached the same conclusion
by two different routes. But it is not immediately apparent why the choice
of route should depend upon whether the action of a jury in rejecting the
law, when it does, is in the exercise of a power or of a right. Let us see
how the point emerged in the argument. The meaning and sense of a general
verdict were most felicitously expressed by Erskine in his first proposition:

When a bill of indictment is found, or an information filed, charging any crime
or misdemeanour known to the law of England, and the party accused puts himself
upon the country by pleading the general issue, not guilty, the jury are *generally*
charged with his deliverance from that *crime*, and not specially from the *fact* or *facts*
in the commission of which the indictment or information charges the crime to consist: much less from any single fact, to the exclusion of others charged upon the
same record.[3]

In discussing this proposition, the leading counsel for the Crown, Mr. Bearcroft, an unsung hero of Westminster Hall ('I honour him for his candour
and integrity of heart,' Willes applauded; 'he would not sacrifice his constitutional principles to the wishes of his client'[4]), conceded 'that it is the
right of the jury, if they please, on the plea of not guilty, to take upon themselves the decision of every question of law necessary to the acquittal of the
defendant'. It was then that Lord Mansfield observed 'that he should call
it the *power*, not the *right*'.[5] The other four counsel who argued for the prosecution accepted Lord Mansfield's amendment, but Bearcroft, as Erskine
later in the argument exulted,[6] stuck to his guns: 'he caught instantly at
your words,' he told Lord Mansfield, 'disavowed your explanation, and declared his adherence to his original admission in its full and obvious extent.'

But Bearcroft was not giving his case away: it did not matter, he went
on, whether it was a right or a power, 'for that the judge had not told the
jury that if they believed the facts of the case, they could not find a verdict

[1] ib. 175.   [2] ib. 82.   [3] ib. 87.
[4] ib. 173.   [5] ib. 94.   [6] ib. 108.

of Not Guilty'. This was the argument that brought Willes round. If the jury, as he declared, 'have a constitutional right, if they think fit, to examine the innocence or criminality of the paper', i.e. to look into what was then a question of law, they must be told about their right and given the opportunity to exercise it. If they choose not to exercise it, well and good, for no one can dispute that a jury can, if they wish, leave the application of the law to the court by means of a special verdict. So for Willes the question was whether the jury were told and whether they voluntarily left the question to the court. Being satisfied that they were and that they did, he could decide against Erskine. Mansfield on the other hand would have been just as happy if nothing had been said about the general verdict. On his view the jury had no business with the law at all. If circumstances place a man who has no right to meddle in a position to do so, you do not have to remind him that you cannot stop him from meddling.

The controversy has not yet been resolved and probably never will be.[1] If a jury acquits when the judge has directed them to convict, it is no easier now than it was two hundred years ago to say whether they are exercising a power or a right. I think myself that Willes has lost the battle but maybe won the war. The claim of 'right' has been tacitly dropped. The practical point is that a jury has to be told of its rights but need not be reminded of its powers. If the judge did not tell the jury that they had the right to disregard a law which they thought was being used unjustly, at any rate he could not stop counsel from telling them so; whereas if there is no right, counsel will be as wrong to invite a jury to disregard what they were told to be the law as he would be to invite them to disregard what they found to be the facts. I have never heard counsel invite the jury, as Erskine did, to disregard the law. The tacit compromise which the years have evolved is that the Bench no longer seeks ways of circumventing what the Bar does not press as a right. What this means is that to be acceptable to the judge, action under the power must spring from an unprompted jury. As it was put in *R*. v. *Shipley*:

This power should only be made use of when the magnitude of the subject and the times require such an exertion of legal and constitutional spirit.[2]

Whether it is a right or a power, what matters is that the jury should be given the room in which to exercise it. The necessary room is the general

[1] Perhaps it will be academically. In the United States the theory has been advanced that a juryman who refuses to apply what he realizes to be the law is nevertheless not acting outside the law. His duty to apply the law is, it is argued, discretionary and not absolute. See M. R. and S. H. Kadish, *Discretion to Disobey*, Stanford University Press, Stanford, 1973, p. 66.
[2] At 171.

verdict. Would that have been preserved if the Mansfield doctrine had been exploited? What the Lord Chief Justice was saying was that, if you could find a procedural way of keeping the law away from the jury, so much the better. The obvious way would be the special verdict. For how long would Mansfield and his successors have sustained the principle that a special verdict could be asked for but not demanded? Would not the time have come when juries were being told that while they had the power (but not the right) to refuse a special verdict, yet in conscience, etc.? Would not other devices, similar to the 'guilty upon the record' device, have been invented? And would not the criminal jury by now have been reduced to a fact-finding tribunal operating within a province whose boundaries were patrolled by the judiciary?

Mr. Justice Willes held the fort. Around it there gathered the forces that eight years later in 1792 supported and enacted Fox's Libel Act. The Act not only by section 1 declared that 'libel or no libel' was for the jury. Also, and as significantly, by section 4 it declared that special verdicts in libel cases, *as in criminal cases generally*,[1] should be at the discretion of the jury. This has remained unchallenged. Moreover, the principle that the judge asks for a special verdict only for an exceptional reason has been accepted and followed. This is how Willes won the war. If there are still at the Bar Erskines and Bearcrofts, his victory will be secure.

There remains the question which I have not yet put. Why do the judges, the guardians of the law, tolerate a body exercising power to which it has no right? Lord Mansfield said that the jury had it in their power to do wrong. But in truth they have no power except what the judges give them. Gaolers listen to judges, not to juries; a verdict has no legal effect until it is embodied in a judge's order.

The source of the jury's power lay, and still lies, in a tradition which by the eighteenth century had gone on for so long as to have grown into a constitutional principle. For five hundred years and more a man charged with a crime had had the right to 'put himself upon his country' by electing to be tried by a jury of his peers. If he was found not guilty, it was as if he had survived trial by ordeal, which trial by jury had replaced. The unanimous verdict was as indispensable as the jury itself. It was treated almost as a sign from Heaven. The judges had tried many ways of getting out of the juries the verdicts they wanted—attainder, fines, and imprisonment. They had bullied and browbeaten, scolded and cajoled. For long after 1784 they continued to shut juries up without meat, drink, fire, or candle until they

[1] Italics mine.

agreed. All this they were ready to do, but not to question the need for a verdict nor even the need for unanimity.[1] Even today the law is that in a criminal case a verdict cannot be dispensed with. If, for example, a judge thinks that the prosecution have not made out their case, he does not simply withdraw it from the jury, he directs the jury to return a verdict of Not Guilty. It used to be the law that even when a prosecution was abandoned, a jury had to be sworn and the accused given in charge, counsel for the prosecution had to say that he was offering no evidence, and the judge to direct that, since the burden of proof was on the prosecution and no evidence was offered, the jury ought to return a verdict of Not Guilty. It was not until 1967 that the judge was authorized to record a verdict of Not Guilty without this ceremony.[2]

So it is strong tradition that is the source of the jury's power. But tradition is naturally a wasting asset. It dwindles as the years go by unless there is within it a life-giving principle. In the case of the jury what lies within is this. In a democracy law is made by the will of the people and obedience is given to it not primarily out of fear but from goodwill. But just as important as the framing of the law is its application. The jury is the means by which the people play a direct part in the application of the law. It is a contributory part. The interrelation between judge and jury, slowly and carefully worried out over several hundred years, secures that the verdict will not be demagogic; it will not be the simple uninhibited popular reaction. But it also secures that the law will not be applied in a way that affronts the conscience of the common man. Constitutionally it is an invaluable achievement that popular consent should be at the root not only of the making but also of the application of the law. It is one of the significant causes of our political stability. It suits especially the British, who have a deeper respect than many for the idea of law but less tolerance than many for the rubs and irritations that its application can cause.

All the judges accept trial by jury as part of the established order of things. I suspect that for many of them tradition plays a greater part in their acceptance than the more elevated thoughts which I have just condensed. But it is truly remarkable that judges should demean their professional talents to popular mediocrity. What other sphere of business or administration is governed by men in the street? Consider how a verdict is made and then consider how difficult it must be for lawyers to swallow the reflection that they could

[1] If there be eleven agreed, and but one dissenting who says he will die in prison, yet the verdict shall not be taken by eleven; *Hale's Pleas of the Crown*, ed. Wilson, 1778, vol. II, p. 297.

[2] Criminal Justice Act 1967 s. 17.

do it much better than a bunch of amateurs. The process requires, first, that all the various pieces of oral evidence should be accepted or rejected; second, that all the proper inferences should be drawn from that which is accepted; third, that these two should be added together and evaluated. Take a case of dangerous driving in which it is alleged that the accused drove at a speed excessive in the circumstances. The evidence on speed will be partly that of direct observation and partly that of inference, e.g. from skid-marks; there will be similar evidence about the nature of the road, the amount of traffic on it, and so on; then there will be the evaluation of the facts—was it dangerous in the circumstances? There are some practitioners who think that judges with their long experience of witnesses would per-form better at the first stage than juries and others who think that a collective opinion is to be preferred. But there are few practitioners who would assert that juries are better at drawing inferences; in a case of any complication they are likely to be worse. On the third point there are some cases in which a judge's and a jury's evaluation of the facts can be so different that each would say that the other was wrong. Why in such cases does the skilled judgment have to give way to average opinion? True, we are now moving into a world in which the standards of the élite are being replaced by the standards of the mass, but it is too early to expect the judges to be in the van of the movement.

Some judges, however, are more forward than others. Broadly, there are two schools of thought as there are, too, in so many sections of the democratic world. There are civil servants, for example, for whom their political masters and the parliamentary question are tribulations of the administrative life; there are others who welcome a popular infusion into bureaucracy. There are politicians as well as administrators for whom freedom of the press is a cross to be borne; there are others who see it as positively valuable. There is no clear division between the schools: the disciples do not stand up to be counted; there is simply a tendency to adopt one attitude rather than the other. So in attitudes to the jury there are two schools of judges. The judges of one school regard the jury as an instrument provided for their use; in the other school there are the judges who recognize it as an indepen-dent power. When I call them—so as to obtain the convenience of a short label—the Mansfield and the Willes schools, I am not representing that the points at issue are just the same as they were in 1784. It is the difference in attitude that is the same.

Not that those judges who gladly accept the jury as the Sovereign have not got a very clear idea of how the Sovereign should behave. Nor are they unready to give him strong advice which they expect him to take. Some of them, like the ministers of inactive monarchs in the past, do not tell the Sovereign more than they think he needs to know and they usually get their way. But they know that there will be times when the jury, like a wayward monarch or a democratic electorate, makes its own choice. So these judges accept that even a virtuous jury will of its nature, that is, because it can do none other, reject law which it cannot stomach; it will dilute law when it thinks that the application at full strength would scorch. On the facts it will not be led by logic or otherwise to results which it intensely dislikes. These judges view the jury's activities sometimes with disapproval but generally with benevolence, accepting that the ways of the jury in the law, like those of the electorate in politics, are often imperfect but on the whole better than anything else we can think of. In short the difference is between those who accept the 'power' because they must and those who accept it believing it on balance to be a good thing.

The core of the difference between the two schools is in their attitude to what is called 'perversity'. This may be of two kinds, omitting the kind in which the word need not be put into inverted commas. No doubt there have been juries who have rejected a law which they disliked without even examining their consciences about it. No doubt too there have been juries (and even judges) of extreme obtuseness. But these are rare nowadays and do not constitute the real problem.

The first kind of jury which the Mansfield school call 'perverse' consists of those who put conscience above the law. For Mansfield this was intolerable; for Willes it was in the last resort right. In the last resort. The power which can make the law submit to conscience when they are irreconcilable is a genie to be kept bottled up. It is a nuclear power which unharnessed could destroy the State. It is like strychnine, a deadly poison which in small doses is a stimulant. There is much to be said about its regulation, but not here. Here it is enough to say that it is the price which justice pays for the use of the jury, a price which cannot, as the Mansfield school would like, be withheld. This school looks at it from the viewpoint of a judge; and a judge is not worried by his conscience as a juryman can be. The judge can make himself aware of the issues in a forthcoming case, and if any of them trouble his conscience, he would not be sitting. He is a professional whose profession has taught him that conformity with principle is the touchstone of justice, a priest accustomed to laying upon the altar the sacrificial offerings of the hard cases. The juryman is an amateur taken off the streets. His conscience can easily be troubled by the consequences of his verdict which he will perceive far more vividly than the principle which the verdict is to serve. Moreover, he can find himself unexpectedly required to participate in the enforcement of a law of which maybe he has never heard but which when he sees it he finds to be repugnant. It would be quite unreasonable to ask of a jury-man that he should leave his conscience behind when he goes into the jury-box. It is reasonable to ask him that he should exercise it in defiance of the law only if, deeply troubled, he feels that he can do none other. That he should have the liberty to exercise it on these terms is one of the guarantees of our freedom. The guarantee was needed during three centuries of our political life and it may be needed again.

But at present it is the other sort of 'perversity' which modern judges have in mind. This other sort is the habit of juries of reaching conclusions which judges consider to be not merely wrong but unreasonable. If this happens in the civil process, the judges can correct it. In the criminal process, where it might lead to a verdict of Guilty, they squash it before it gets there by a direction to the jury. If it leads to an acquittal, a constitu-tional principle so venerable as to be above controversy compels them to acquiesce.

Judges of the Mansfield school acquiesce in it with reluctance and call it 'perversity'. They do not, I think, examine closely enough what they mean by that. Do they mean simply unreasonableness? Yet when they think of a ver-dict as being unreasonable, they do not think of twelve men and women individually as morons or eccentrics, all by fantastic chance collected together at the same time and in the same place.[1] They think of them as persons who have not heeded skilled and experienced advice, who have leant too heavily on their own powers of reasoning and so have come to grief, who must have had regard to what was irrelevant or ignored what was rele-vant.

Judges of the Willes school on the other hand remember that relevance depends upon the angle of view and that the angles of a judge and a jury may sometimes be as far removed as the angles of a parent and a child. They remember too that judges are part of the Establishment. Blackstone called them 'a select body of men'. Their decisions, he wrote, 'in spite of their own natural integrity will have frequently an involuntary bias towards those of their own rank and dignity'.[2] Rank and dignity are no longer what count. But there is still the like divide between the people who settle what is to happen to others and the people who have things settled for them. In our society in the great questions of personal liberty it is the governed who

[1] 'When his Majesty Asked how Twelve Reasonable Persons could Arrive at an Unreasonable Verdict the Regius Professor said that he would Deal with that Topic a little Later.' Theobald Mathew ('O'), op. cit., p. 356.
[2] *Commentaries*, Book 3, p. 378.

decide; this is what the jury system means. It is idle to suppose that there will not be times when the governors think that the governed are foolish and unreasonable.

It is not that the Mansfield school is disloyal to the verdict of acquittal. The difference is that while the Willes school accept an occasional disagreement between judge and jury as in the natural course of things the Mansfield school resents it. Personally I take what may be thought to be an extreme view on perversity. To my mind it is the so-called perversity of juries that justifies their existence. For the rest, they do some things better than judges and some things worse, and there are other reasons for welcoming them, such as the link they forge between the law and the laity. But the favourable balance, if there be one, is not large enough to pay for the elaboration of the jury. What makes them worth while is that they see things differently from the judges, that they can water the law, and that the function which they filled two centuries ago as a corrective to the corruption and partiality of the judges requires essentially the same qualities as the function they perform today as an organ of the Disestablishment. In our society today we are looking for ways of melding managers and men. The jury system is the oldest and still the most successful of the ways in which so far this has been achieved.

What I have been saying is no more than what Chief Justice Vaughan said three centuries ago. I would have said it simply in his words were it not that the change of setting makes literal transposition impossible. Vaughan was dealing with the punishment of jurors who delivered 'perverse' verdicts, to which punishment indeed he put an end.[1] But when he says that it is absurd for judges to punish jurors for disagreeing with them, is it not— except that hard words break no bones—as absurd, no less pernicious, to call them perverse? It is true that at the time when Vaughan was speaking, it was theoretically possible, though the practice was dying out, for juries to act on their own knowledge, and theoretically their knowledge might have contradicted the evidence. But for at least a century before Bushell's case in 1670 not much attention had been paid to theory. During the sixteenth and seventeenth centuries juries were often punished simply for acting contrary to the evidence—*contra plenam et manifestam evidentiam*, as the indictment went.

[1] In Bushell's Case (1670) Vaughan 135. There is a recent study of this case in a fine article by Professor John H. Langbein, in the *University of Chicago Law Review*, Winter 1978, vol. 45, p. 263. In 1668 Vaughan, then in the House of Commons, was chairman of a committee to which there was referred a Bill against Menaces, Fines, and Imprisonments of Juries and Jurors. It did not become law.

It was for acquitting William Penn at the Old Bailey in 1670 of unlawful
and tumultous assembly *contra plenam et manifestam evidentiam et contra
directionem Curiae in materia legis*[1] that Bushell and his fellow jurors were
imprisoned, and the return to the writ of habeas corpus so stated. Since
it did not set out the full and manifest evidence, the Chief Justice held the
return to be insufficient, but he went on to explain why the return would
not have been good anyway. First, he asked what was meant by saying
that the jury acquitted 'contrary to the direction of the Court in a matter
of law', and he disposed of the argument (not for ever, for it is heard today)
that if the facts are clear, what is left can only be a question of law:

> If the meaning of these words, finding against the direction of the Court in a matter
> of law, be, that if the Judge having heard the evidence given in Court (for he knows
> no other) shall tell the jury, upon this evidence, the law is for the plaintiff, or for
> the defendant, and you are under the pain of fine and imprisonment to find accord-
> ingly, then the jury ought of duty so to do; every man sees that the jury is but a
> troublesome delay, great charge, and of no use in determining right and wrong, and
> therefore the tryals by them may be better abolish'd than continued; which were
> a strange new-found conclusion, after a tryal so celebrated for many hundreds of
> years. For if the Judge, from the evidence, shall by his own judgment first resolve
> upon any tryal what the fact is, and so knowing the fact, shall then resolve what the
> law is, and order the jury penally to find accordingly, what either necessary or con-
> venient use can be fancied of juries, or to continue tryals by them at all?[2]

Later he explained the working of the 'decantatum' which comes at or near
the beginning of every judge's charge to the jury—'the facts are for you
and the law is for me':

> That decantatum in our books, *ad quaestionem facti non respondent judices, ad quaes-
> tionem legis non respondent juratores*, literally taken is true: for if it be demanded,
> what is the fact? the Judge cannot answer it: if it be asked, what is the law in the case,
> the jury cannot answer it. . . . In special verdicts the jury inform the naked fact,
> and the Court deliver the law. . . . But upon all general issues . . . the jury . . . resolve
> both law and fact complicately . . . so as though they answer not singly to the question
> what is the law, yet they determine the law in all matters where issue is joyn'd, and
> tryed in the principal case, but where the verdict is special.[3]

As to *contra plenam et manifestam evidentiam*, he is not disturbed by the
thought that judges and juries are bound to reach different conclusions on
the facts:

> I would know whether anything be more common, than for two men students, bar-
> risters, or Judges, to deduce contrary and opposite conclusions out of the same case
> in law? And is there any difference that two men should inferr distinct conclusions
> from the same testimony: . . . How then comes it to pass that two persons may

[1] Vaughan 136.   [2] ib. 143.   [3] ib. 149.

not apprehend with reason and honesty, what a witness, or many, say, to prove in the understanding of one plainly one thing, but in the apprehension of the other, clearly the contrary thing: must therefore one of these merit fine and imprisonment, because he doth that which he cannot otherwise do, preserving his oath and integrity? And this often is the case of the Judge and jury.[1]

And lastly there are these words of warning to judges who consider that juries should look at the facts in the same way as they do themselves:

A man cannot see by anothers eye, nor hear by anothers ear, no more can a man conclude or inferr the thing to be resolv'd by anothers understanding or reasoning.[2]

In 1974 three distinguished judges expressed themselves differently:

If the court has no reasonable doubt about the verdict, it follows that the court does not think that the jury could have one; and, conversely, if the court says that the jury might in the light of the new evidence have a reasonable doubt, that means that the court has a reasonable doubt [per Viscount Dilhorne].[3]

It is, of course, true that two equally reasonable men may differ as to whether there is a reasonable doubt as to the guilt of the accused. But if I feel sure that he is guilty and you feel a doubt on the point I must regard your doubt on that point as unreasonable, however reasonable a person I consider you in general to be. Conversely, if I regard your doubt as reasonable I cannot feel sure that the accused is guilty [per Lord Cross].[4]

To concede that a reasonable doubt is open is to admit that one has a reasonable doubt oneself [per Lord Kilbrandon].[5]

If these dicta are followed and extended, it will soon be judges and not juries who make verdicts. So I should not quote them without putting alongside three dicta delivered in 1976 by three equally distinguished judges. These latter were considering the reasonableness of decisions given not within the jury-room but within the curtilage of administrative discretion, wherein likewise judges are not supposed to trespass.

The very concept of administrative discretion involves the right to choose between more than one possible course of action upon which there is room for reasonable people to hold differing opinions as to which is to be preferred [per Lord Diplock].

---

[1] ib. 141.　　　　　　　　　　　　　　　　　　[2] ib. 148.

[3] In *Stafford* v *D.P.P.* [1974] A.C. 878 at 893F. Students of genetics may wish to know that Lord Dilhorne, whose name before ennoblement was Manningham-Buller, is the sixth descendant in the direct line from Mr. Justice Buller.

[4] ib. at 907C.

[5] ib. at 912F. Do these three dicta clothe with a posthumous respectability the summing-up recalled—without approval—by Mr. Justice Hawkins in his memoirs and quoted in the *Criminal Law Revision Committee Eleventh Report*, H.M.S.O., London, 1972 (Cmnd. 4991), at p. 11? Its entire content was: 'Gentlemen, I suppose you have no doubt? I have none.'

Two reasonable persons can perfectly reasonably come to opposite conclusions on the same set of facts without forfeiting their title to be regarded as reasonable [this is Lord Salmon adopting a dictum of Lord Hailsham].

History is replete with genuine accusations of unreasonableness when all that is involved is disagreement, perhaps passionate, between reasonable people [per Lord Russell of Killowen].[1]

The last set of dicta are surely closer to the traditional. Indeed, I would venture with great respect the opinion that the first will not be perpetuated. The point which the law lords were making in the earlier case was that it was *their* reasonable doubts which mattered in that case and not those of a hypothetical jury, and they allowed their words to overflow the channel of their thought. This would not, however, have been possible without the ambiguity that lies in the word 'reasonable'. In one sense the word describes the proper use of the reasoning power, and in another it is no more than a word of assessment. Reasoning does not help much in fixing a reasonable or fair price or a reasonable or moderate length of time, or in estimating the size of a doubt. Lawyers say a reasonable doubt, meaning a substantial one; the Court of Appeal has frowned upon the description of a reasonable doubt as one for which reasons could be given.[2]

In the other sense, the reason is, to use a dictionary definition, the guiding principle of the mind in the process of thinking. If we think that a decision has been reached without reasoning at all, purely emotionally, we say that it is irrational. If we think that the reasoning power has been used wrongly, has, for example, failed to detect what is relevant, we use the softer word unreasonable. The reasonable man, beloved of the law, is a man who both uses his reason sensibly and arrives at fair and moderate results.

There can surely be no difficulty about saying that while you have no reasonable doubt, you can see that another man might have. You need not mean more than that he puts a greater weight on the dubious factors than you do. It is only when you can see nothing which you think could induce a doubt in any rational mind that you are bound to hold the doubt unreasonable.

If I am wrong to derogate from the dicta in 1974, if they are to be taken at their face value, they amount to much more than a muting of the *decantatum*. Pushed to their logical extreme they would shake the foundations of the relationship between judge and jury as it has been understood from time

---

[1] These three dicta were made in *Secretary of State* v. *Tameside Borough Council* [1977] A.C. 1014 at 1064F, 1070H, and 1075B.

[2] *R.* v. *Stafford* [1968] 3 All E.R. 752.

immemorial. Trial by jury would be preserved no longer by the *decantatum* but solely by the procedural barrier which prevents appellate judges from getting at the facts of an acquittal. Since there is no appeal from an acquittal, they are denied the opportunity of substituting, under cover of the fiction that juries think as they do, their own reasonable convictions for the reasonable doubts of the jury. But woe betide the man who is wrongly convicted. He must go to the judges for his remedy and they will give it to him only on their own terms. To measure the consequences of this would require another lecture. In this lecture I am dealing not with upheavals but with the comparatively minor divergences between two schools, both of which accept the *decantatum* and differ only about where the line is to be drawn. I shall resume my inspection of the divergence with a quick look at a manifestation of it in the civil process.

In a civil case in which a jury goes beyond the judicial bounds of reasonableness, the appellate judges are not as powerless as they are in the case of an acquittal. They do not have to accept the situation; they can set aside the verdict. But are they then bound to order a new trial by jury with a possibility of getting a string of similar verdicts, or can they tidy things up themselves? On this point the two schools differed.

One type of case in which the question arose was when a jury awarded damages that the appellate judges regarded as so excessive as to be unreasonable, with the result that the verdict was set aside. No one was so daring as to propose that the judges should then fix the sum themselves. But a practice grew up in the Court of Appeal whereunder the court would state the sum which it thought to be appropriate and make an order for a new trial unless the plaintiff agreed to accept the lower sum. This was convenient for the plaintiff since he was given an option, but the defendant was thereby deprived of the chance of getting a new jury to award a sum even lower than that thought appropriate by the Court of Appeal. The practice was formally challenged in the Court of Appeal in 1884 and approved. But in 1905 the House of Lords, led by Lord Halsbury, condemned the practice as unconstitutional in that it deprived the defendant without his consent of his right to have damages assessed by a jury.[1]

There was another type of case in which the difference of opinion went deeper. If the verdict of a jury on the merits is set aside as perverse, it is usually because there is in the opinion of the appellate court only one conclusion which could reasonably be reached on the facts. What then, it was asked, is the point of ordering a new trial: why not let the court enter forth-

[1] R.S.C. Order 58 rule 10 (4) now embodies the rule.

with the verdict that they consider to be the only possible one? This question
has never been finally answered and, because of the demise of the civil jury,
it probably never will be. While some judges favoured the short cut, the
greater names—Halsbury, Atkin, and Wright—were against it. It would,
Lord Wright said in 1935, amount, not to 'controlling, but to superseding
the jury and exercising the function of affirmatively finding the facts'. Lord
Atkin in the same case reaffirmed the *decantatum*.

Once it has been decided that a civil case has to be tried by a jury, that tribunal,
and that tribunal alone, is the judge of fact, and no appellate court can substitute
its own findings for those of the lawful tribunal.[1]

A similar sort of divergence could not arise in criminal cases until after the
creation of the Court of Criminal Appeal in 1907. To show how then it did
arise I must give some of the background to the criminal appeal.

An appellate court must have some formula for distinguishing between
big and little error. If judgments were to be reversed for the tiniest of errors,
justice would not be done. The crucial question is: would it have made a
difference to the result? In civil appeals the rule was that the court was not
bound to order a new trial unless in its opinion, 'some substantial wrong
or miscarriage has been thereby occasioned'.[2] When the Court of Criminal
Appeal was set up in 1907 the same rule was adopted by means of the famous
'proviso'. The enumeration of the grounds of appeal was followed by the
proviso that the court might dismiss the appeal if they considered that no
substantial miscarriage of justice had actually occurred.

The general terms of the proviso were good enough as an assurance to
Parliament that criminals would not go free on technicalities, but the courts
looked for a more precise formula. They did not interpret the Act as authorizing them to do justice on their own. It was the jury which had convicted,
the jury whose verdict was historically the condition precedent to punishment; accordingly it was the effect upon the jury of the error or irregularity
which had to be considered. If it was thought that it might have made a
difference to the verdict, the trial by jury was flawed and the verdict could
not stand. It might be that if the judges themselves examined the evidence
in the light of truth and not of error, they would themselves be satisfied
of the accused's guilt. But that was not the point. That would be trial by
judge and not trial by jury. The accused was constitutionally entitled to trial
by jury and, if that process was flawed, there would be a miscarriage of justice
and so the proviso could not be applied. Thus the *Stirland* formula[3] eventu-

[1] *Mechanical & General Inventions* v. *Austin* [1935] A.C. 346 at 369 and 379.
[2] R.S.C. Order 59 rule 11 (2).
[3] *Stirland* v. *D.P.P.* [1944] A.C. 315.

ally took shape as permitting a conviction, once a good ground of appeal had been established, only if a reasonable jury, properly directed, could not have failed to convict.

Suppose that a piece of evidence has been wrongly excluded. It might be so trivial that one could tell at a glance that the exclusion could not have mattered. But usually it is necessary to study the excluded evidence in the light of the whole story before one can say whether or not it really mattered to the verdict. The appropriate question then becomes: on the whole of the admissible evidence could a reasonable jury have failed to convict?

A reasonable jury. Does this mean that appellate judges ought to review the case from their own standpoint of reasonableness, or ought they to make allowance for what their experience will tell them would in some cases be the different standpoint of a jury? It was soon made clear that an appellate court ought not to speculate about what the particular jury who tried the case would have thought. But should the standard applied be a judge's standard or a judge's appreciation of a jury's standard? The difference is not perhaps so large as to demand a corporate choice; it has so far been left to the individual judge to follow his own preference.

The danger in the first approach, the judge's own standard (which doubtless judges of the Mansfield school would favour), is that judges will simply make their own assessment of the whole story. This is not the *Stirland* formula. If the House of Lords in *Stirland* had thought that there was no difference between a judge and a jury assessment—or, thinking that there was a difference, had thought that the judge assessment ought to prevail—the formula would have expressed that thought. There would have been no point in the reference to a jury, properly directed. The formula would have been a simple instruction to a court of appeal to dismiss the appeal whenever they thought, on the evidence as they themselves assessed it, that the conviction was right. The danger in the other approach is that judges may follow a will-o'-the-wisp, for they can never lay their minds alongside the mind of a jury and see things just as a jury would. They can only concern themselves to see that an accused has not because of judicial error lost a fair chance of acquittal.

A reconciliation can perhaps be sought through Lord Wright's description, in the case to which I have already referred, of what was necessary to set aside the verdict of a civil jury. First he went back to the phrase 'miscarriage of juries' used in 1655. Then he quoted Lord Halsbury as saying: 'I think the test of reasonableness in considering the verdict of a jury is right enough, in order to understand whether the jury have really done their duty.'[1] Then Lord Wright himself put the question as being whether the verdict 'is such as to show that the jury have failed to perform their duty'. So a judge, considering whether or not to apply the proviso, might ask himself: 'Would a jury, properly directed, have been failing in its judicial duty if it acquitted the appellant? Would such a verdict have been a miscarriage?' This takes the beam off the narrow point of reasonableness, evades the enquiry into precisely what standards should be applied, and lights up the broader question of judicial duty.

In whatever way the point is put, however, it is inevitable that the needs of the appellate process should place upon the judges some of the burden of deciding fact, actual or hypothetical, which under the *decantatum* does not belong to them. An evaluation of fact, although it is only on a hypothesis, i.e. a conclusion which a jury might be supposed to have reached, is made by a judge and not by a jury. This is the price the accused pays for the right of appeal. Before 1907 an innocent convict would have had only the dubious hope of a pardon; now he has the substantial hope that any error which a judge thinks to be material will set him free. Even the least favourable use of the proviso leaves him better off.

But the line between judge and jury is so delicately balanced that any disturbance of it may start a commotion. Under the *Stirland* formula judges were constantly asking themselves whether there was more than one conclusion on the facts that a jury could reach, and answering themselves that there was only one, namely, guilt. Sooner or later some judge of the Mansfield school, about to sum up to a jury, was bound to say to himself: 'If from a given set of facts a reasonable jury can draw only one conclusion, why should I not draw it for them and so make sure that they get it right?' I have collected elsewhere a number of cases in which the judge has, intentionally or unintentionally, either told the jury what to conclude or else failed to place an issue of fact before them because he thought the answer too obvious, and in which the course of action he took was approved on appeal.[2] I collected also the various descriptions of the exceptional circumstances which are held to justify such a course—where the facts are proved in such a way that there can be no question about them, where the evidence is all one way, where there is no other possible conclusion, where the matter

[1] *Metropolitan Railway Co.* v. *Wright* (1886) 11 App. Cas. 152 at 156.

[2] *Trial by Jury*, p. 187. Since then the principle has been expressed rather differently. Widgery L.J. said in *R.* v. *Kelly* (1970) 54 Crim. L.R. 334 that where there was no dispute as to the primary facts, what was left was a matter of law. This dictum was modified in *R.* v. *Martin* (1972) 57 Cr. App. R. 279 where Orr L.J. said that it did not apply where there was an inference to be drawn from the primary facts. But what if the inference was 'beyond argument'? The *Stonehouse* case (see below) has doubtless called off the search for an answer to that.

is beyond argument. They are all, are they not, renderings in the vernacular of the *contra plenam et manifestam evidentiam* of the sixteenth and seventeenth centuries?

The House of Lords has now settled the point by a vote of three to two in favour of what I have labelled (though by now the label is becoming rather blurred) the Willes school of thought.[1] It arose in this way. Mr. Stonehouse, a politician turned financier, had by November 1974 got himself into financial difficulties which he felt could only be solved by artificial death and re-birth into another identity. So he faked death by drowning in Florida and surfaced in Australia under another name. A few months before he did this, namely, in July and September 1974, he took out insurance policies on his life in his wife's name. She was not a party to the deception: the case for the prosecution was that he intended and expected that, when his supposed death became known, she would claim under the policies and that in this way he could make some provision for her. But before any claim was made, the trick was discovered. Consequently all that he could be charged with was the attempt to enable his wife to obtain money by deception.

The law on an attempt to commit a crime is clear. There are three elements in it—intention, conduct, and proximity. The matters to be proved are, first, the intention to commit the crime, second, the commission of an act or acts leading up to the crime, third, proximity between those acts and the crime contemplated. Proximity means that 'acts remotely leading towards the commission of the offence are not to be considered as attempts to commit it; but acts immediately connected with it are'.[2]

Mr. Stonehouse was charged not only with the fraudulent attempt to make provision for his wife, but also with a number of other offences arising out of the difficulties which had stimulated his disappearance. They were the major matters for which he was put on trial. The trial lasted seventy days, during most of which Mr. Stonehouse defended himself with verbosity rather than relevance. Mr. Justice Eveleigh appears to have displayed every imaginable judicial virtue. Towards the end of what Lord Salmon in the House of Lords described as 'a most fair, accurate and lucid summing up',[3] he came to the attempt counts and he dealt with them briefly and in what the Lord Chief Justice described in the Court of Appeal as 'a novel form of direction'. He did not state for the jury the relevant principle of law and leave them to apply it to the facts, giving them on that the benefit of such views as he had under the reservation that they were not bound to adopt

---

[1] *Stonehouse* v. *D.P.P.* [1978] A.C. 55.
[2] *R.* v. *Eagleton* (1855) 6 Cox 559.
[3] [1978] A.C. at 79E.

his views if they did not like them. He told them simply that if the case on intention and conduct was proved to their satisfaction, there was an attempt within the legal meaning of that word.

So he omitted the requirement of proximity. Proximity is a question of degree and therefore essentially one to be settled by a jury. But on the facts of this case all the judges were agreed that the connection was so clear and close that no reasonable jury, once satisfied on conduct and intention, could have failed to convict, as the jury in the case actually did. So the appeal was bound to be dismissed, the point of dissension being whether it should be dismissed because there was no misdirection, or because, there being a misdirection, it was one which caused no miscarriage of justice. This was one of those academic points which strip from principle the barnacles of practice. The Crown conceded that there was a misdirection. But the House of Lords, realizing the significance of the principle at stake, debated it in full. The argument did not break new ground. Lords Salmon, Edmund-Davies, and Keith of Kinkel in the majority rested their decision in effect on the *decantatum*, citing *Joshua* v. *Rex*[1] as the leading case in which the withdrawal of an issue of fact from the jury had been condemned; the fullest treatment is in the speech of Lord Edmund-Davies. Lords Diplock and Dilhorne in the minority did not rely upon any of the numerous decisions in the Court of Appeal supporting their conclusion; they would not of course have been binding on the House. They simply declared that in those exceptional cases in which there was room for only one conclusion, that is, in which any other conclusion would be perverse, the judge was entitled to tell the jury what their conclusion should be. This was not quite how they put it; whether there is any substantial difference between this and the way they put it is a point in the case of real though secondary interest which I shall examine later. What they said was that in this exceptional case the judge was entitled to tell the jury that, if they were satisfied on intention and conduct, there was an attempt in law, the nature of the exception presumably being that on proximity the jury could not be other than satisfied.

The minority conclusion has an obvious appeal to the practical man. Why manufacture an error, he will ask, out of something which, as soon as the proviso is applied to it, will be shown to be immaterial? Why should not a judge be allowed to tell a jury that any other conclusion would be perverse, if that is what it would be? True, if the jury insist on being perverse, he can do nothing about it, but why object to his telling them how not to be perverse? True also that by telling the jury how not to be perverse he may deprive the accused of his chance of a perverse acquittal, but to say that

[1] [1955] A.C. 21.

the accused is entitled to that chance is to take, said Lord Diplock, a 'cynical view of justice and the jury system'.[1]

It is the use of the word 'perversity', I must apologize for repeating, that illuminates the difference between the two schools. There is the school which would like to treat the jury as a subordinate body to find only such facts as are in dispute within the bounds of reasonableness as set by the judge; to wander outside the bounds is to be perverse. Opposite, there is the school which respects the jury as an equal. Perverse has come to be a lawyer's word for a jury which applies its own standards instead of those recommended by lawyers. It is an inappropriate, even an impertinent, word to use about an equal when all that you are saying is that you disagree with the conclusions which it is his job to reach and not yours. Looked at dispassionately, it is as impertinent as if the foreman of the jury were to criticize a direction on law as narrow, pedantic, and out of touch with the world.

The smear of perversity is applied by judges but erased by time. It is not the disobedient jurors whom history has reprobated, but the judges who called them perverse. It has been said that the future is the judge of the past. We may not all go as far as Mr. Justice Willes, who said that the jury who acquitted the seven bishops 'by their solemn verdict upon that occasion, became one of the happy instruments, under Providence, of the salvation of this country',[2] but none of us now would say that the jury in that case was perverse. Not even the severest critic of the press now wishes to restore to the judges their power of determining as a question of law what is libellous. Yet listen to Lord Mansfield, one of the greatest of judges:

The *licentiousness* of the press is Pandora's box, the source of every evil. Miserable is the condition of individuals, dangerous is the condition of the state, if there is no certain law, or, which is the same thing, no certain administration of law, to protect individuals, or to guard the state. Jealousy of leaving the law to the Court, as in other cases, so in the case of libels, is now, in the present state of things, puerile rant and declamation.[3]

It is not a perverse acquittal that an innocent man is looking for when he asks for trial by jury, but a trial by men and women of his own sort. A professional man accused of a professional offence is not said to be seeking a perverse acquittal when he demands to be tried by men of his own profession. He is invoking the obverse of the right which enables the ordinary man charged with an ordinary offence to demand trial by ordinary men and not by a professional. Each is seeking the application to his case of a set of standards which he believes will be better understood and applied

[1] [1978] A.C. at 70D.
[2] *Shipley*, 172.
[3] ib. 170.

by the one tribunal than by the other. Jury standards are just as applicable to the question of whether a matter is obvious or beyond argument or open to only one answer, or whatever other like expression is used, as they are to the question of whether there is or is not a reasonable doubt. It would be different if there were only one standard that could conceivably be applied, something as universal as the rule that $2+2=4$. But what are the limits of reasonableness? This is a question that often provokes dispute and judges are often among those provoked. As I have ventured to say elsewhere, writing of the concept of reasonableness in the doctrine of judicial review of administrative acts,

> The law of defamation is studded with cases in which one judge has held words not to be reasonably capable of meaning what another judge was quite convinced that they did mean. Exceptions clauses in a contract are said to be ineffective unless they are clear and unambiguous, but the fact that two judicial bodies differ completely about the meaning is never regarded by the body ultimately triumphant as proof of ambiguity.[1]

If there were a bench of nine considering whether a decision was perverse or merely wrong, no practitioner would be surprised by a lack of unanimity in their judgment. Perversity is a matter of opinion.

Looked at in this way, it does not at all follow that the propriety of a summing-up is to be tested in the same way as the application of the proviso. The latter, as I have said, necessarily involves some invasion of the jury's province. When the necessity is lacking, there can be no justification for the invasion. If a point depends upon the decision of a particular tribunal and the tribunal is still open, it must be better, however obvious the answer is thought to be, to get the tribunal itself to give it. It is only when the tribunal is closed, when the jury that decided the case is *functus officio*, and there is no way of getting another one, that the judges are forced themselves to determine what a jury might think.[2]

Nor does it follow that the proviso would invariably be applied. In *Stonehouse* v. *D.P.P.* the misdirection was probably a slip. It related to only one of the three issues of fact, and that a minor issue in the sense that it was an overflow from the main issues of intention and conduct. It could not be said that the whole question of innocence or guilt was taken out of the jury's hands. If it had been, would it have made a difference? Logically it

---

[1] *The Times*, 27 Oct. 1976.
[2] I think now that my criticism of *R.* v. *Beeby* (1911) 6 Cr. App. R. 138 in *Trial by Jury*, p. 197, is ill-founded. This case was a precursor of *Stonehouse* v. *D.P.P.* In it the Court of Criminal Appeal held that the question whether certain fires (the charge was arson) were started deliberately or accidentally ought to have been left to the jury, notwithstanding that no fair-minded person could conclude that they were accidental; but they then applied the proviso.

AND THE JURY I: THE POWER WITHOUT THE RIGHT

should not. If a single issue can be withdrawn from the jury on the ground that the facts relating to it lead in the eyes of the judge to one conclusion only, then, if the same thing can be said of all the other issues, they too should be withdrawn. But suppose that at the end of the evidence in such a case the judge was, without summing up at all, simply to direct the verdict of Guilty in the same way as he directs a verdict of Not Guilty when the prosecution has failed to make out a case. This would mean that there had not been even the semblance of a trial by jury. Whatever formula may be devised to facilitate the application of the proviso, the statutory requirement is that there should be no miscarriage of justice. It would be going very far to say that there was no miscarriage in a process which deprived an accused entirely of his constitutional right to trial by jury. In some of the cases in the Court of Criminal Appeal the judge did go so far as to direct a verdict of Guilty. But these cases get no endorsement from the dissentient law lords, who both stress that the course they were approving was for very exceptional use.

But when you are considering something so fundamental as the division between the provinces of judge and jury, it is better to draw a clean line. All clean lines are open to the criticism that the distinction between a case that falls just on one side of the line and a case that falls just on the other is inevitably narrow and often in appearance purely technical. So sometimes it is better for the courts to wobble a bit as they thread their way through the very exceptional cases that always lurk around a border and that beg for justice and not law. It all depends on what is at stake. When there is at stake the principle that no man is guilty unless he is so found, not upon this or that issue but of the *whole crime*, as Erskine put it, I believe in the clean line. An assurance, however eminent the guarantors, that incursions will be made only in very exceptional cases is not to my mind good enough.

I have said that logically, if a single issue can be withdrawn from the jury, then the whole case can. But logic does not stop there. I know that English lawyers are warned to beware of logic. But even in the law it is not a good thing to make an enemy of it. Its rivals are common sense, which is change-able, and sound sentiment, which crumbles with time. Logic is indestruc-tible. When it sees the sentiment on which you are relying weakening, it will emerge and offer itself to your opponent as a powerful ally. The logical end of the dissenting view is the curtailment of the power of the criminal jury to the same extent as that of the civil jury. There the question whether a reasonable jury can convict is established as a question of law for the judge; let the question whether it can acquit be treated likewise and the criminal jury will be left, as is the civil jury, with only the middle ground for its domain.

For the practice of withdrawing an issue or a case from the jury because only one conclusion is possible is not one which, once initiated, can be left to the discretion of the trial judge. It could be if there was power in an appellate court to set aside an acquittal judged to be perverse, for uniformity in practice would be obtained in that way. Thus in a civil case the judge does not direct the jury that it would be perverse to find against the plaintiff; he lets them do it, if they are so minded, and leaves the correction to the Court of Appeal. But in crime there is no court with such a power of correction.

So if there is to be uniformity, the giving of the direction must not be optional. The trial judge must not only be permitted to tell the jury in a proper case that there is only one conclusion that they can draw, it must be his duty to do so. Otherwise, some accused may escape because the jury has not been warned not to be perverse, while others will be convicted because the jury has accepted the judge's direction. Put in another way, the justification for judicial interference with suspected perversity is that the question whether a verdict is so unreasonable as to be perverse is as much a question of law as the question whether there is any evidence to support a verdict. The judge is under a duty to direct the jury on all questions of law; he cannot pick and choose.

But then what will come next? There will be an appreciable number of cases in which the facts are clear and the conclusion so obvious to the judge that he will consider no other to be within the limits of reasonableness. What does the judge do? He cannot for the reasons I have just given gamble upon the jury taking the same view. He must direct them to convict. If the jury accept the direction, it will be said, quite rightly, that the accused has been convicted by the judge and not by the jury. The constitutional principle that no man is imprisoned for serious crime unless he is found guilty by his fellows would be destroyed. Quite often it would be unnecessarily destroyed, for the direction would be given in many cases in which the jury would have returned a verdict of guilty anyway. It is far from certain that on balance the practice of giving such a direction would result in the conviction of more guilty men. For if the judge tells the jury that an acquittal would be perverse and an appeal court considers that at worst it would only have been wrong, the conviction must be quashed.

If juries habitually disobey the direction and acquit, there will be a running battle between judges and juries in which the former declare men to be guilty and the latter let them go free. This could not be allowed to continue. Sympathies will be divided as they were in the eighteenth century. The Establishment will say that juries must be kept under firm control. The Disestablishment will ask why juries which are composed of representative and reasonable men and women are not better judges of the limits of reasonableness than the elderly and unrepresentative, whose learning in the law is no guarantee of their reasonableness. This will re-open the same sort of question as the one settled by Fox's Libel Act in 1792. There the question was whether the judges could rob the jury of any significant part in the trial of seditious libel by saying that what was libellous and what was not must be settled by them. Here it would be whether the limits of resonableness are to be settled by judges or jurymen. If the issue goes against the judges, it will not be good. The tacit compromise upon which the power of the jury rests will be impaired, if not destroyed; the power of the jury formalized and strengthened; and the influence exercised by a judicious use of the summing-up diminished.

If on the other hand the judges win, they will not remain content with hectoring recalcitrant juries. They will want to consolidate their victory by seeking from Parliament a statutory power to convict *non obstante veredicto*. That would be the end of the sovereign power of acquittal and—after a time—of trial by jury. For it is this sovereign power which gives to the jury its place in the constitution. Bereft of it, it will become an expensive and unwieldy fact-finding tribunal which sooner or later will go the way of the civil jury. Not of course that this is what anyone intends. All that is intended is a light flick of the whip to discipline the jury into greater conformity with judicial thought. Mr. Justice Humphreys, who administered the first flick in one of those cases in which there could be no question about the facts,[1] was to end his life an ardent believer in trial by jury, subscribing to the doctrine that a jury was always right.

I have noted that there was a point of secondary interest in *Stonehouse* v. *D.P.P.*—something in the nature of a sub-plot, but not independent of the main. It concerns the form of the summing-up which the Lord Chief Justice described as novel.

A charge to the jury can proceed either from the law to the facts or from the facts to the law. The former is the usual course. The judge states the principles of law which the jury are to apply. Thus in *Stonehouse* v. *D.P.P.* he would direct the jury as a matter of law (though maybe not with the ample circumlocution which for the sake of example I use here) that the acts particularized in the indictment would, if the object alleged had been

[1] *R.* v. *Larkin* [1943] 1 All E.R. 217.

achieved, amount to the offence of obtaining property by deception. He
would then tell them that the accused was charged with the attempt only
and that—again as a matter of law—before they could convict of the attempt
the three elements of intention, conduct, and proximity must be proved to
their satisfaction; and he would explain the meaning of these terms. Then
he would discuss the evidence on each of these three issues. In this way
he keeps distinct his direction on the law which the jury must follow, and
his observations on the facts, to which the jury can have such regard as they
think is merited. This method has also the advantage that it leaves it to the
jury to apply the law, as it is their right to do.

If on the other hand he proceeds from the facts to the law, he will discuss
the facts first and then tell the jury the legal consequences of the various
findings of fact which he conceives to be open to them. He can then, if he
wishes, proceed to the extremity of saying nothing about the law except just
to mention it. This is what Mr. Justice Eveleigh did. As Lord Keith put
it, he directed the jury 'that if they were satisfied that the appellant falsely
staged his death by drowning, dishonestly intending that a claim should be
made and the policy monies obtained in due course, then in law there had
been an attempt to commit the offence'.[1] But for the omission of proximity
this would not have been erroneous. This type of summing-up was indeed
authorized by Chief Justice Vaughan:

> Therefore alwaies in discreet and lawful assistance of the jury, the Judge his direction
> is hypothetical, and upon supposition, and not positive, and upon coercion, viz. if
> you find the fact thus (leaving it to them what to find) then you are to find for the
> plaintiff; but if you find the fact thus, then it is for the defendant.[2]

These two patterns of summing-up were considered by Lord Diplock and
Lord Keith. The former recommended the pattern chosen by the trial judge
and the latter did not. Lord Diplock said:

> A summing up is not meant to incorporate abstract disquisitions on the general law
> relating to the offence with which the accused is charged. It ought to be tailored
> to the evidence that has been adduced in the particular case. It should explain to
> the jury what facts they must find to be established by the evidence and, where appro-
> priate, what opinion they must form about those facts, in order to justify in law their
> bringing in a verdict of guilty or not guilty.[3]

Lord Keith said:

> It is the function of the jury, not only to find the facts and to draw inferences from
> the facts, but in modern practice also to apply the law, as they are directed upon
> it, to the facts as they find them to be. I regard this division of function as being

---

[1] [1978] A.C. at 94B.   [2] Vaughan 144.   [3] [1978] A.C. at 69A.

of fundamental importance, and I should regret very much any tendency on the part of presiding judges to direct juries that, if they find certain facts to have been established, they must necessarily convict.[1]

The preference for one method over the other is perhaps another reflection of the difference of outlook between the narrow and the broad schools. The judges who prefer the novel and the bold pattern are likely to be those who see the jury as an instrument for judicial use rather than as a partner in the doing of justice. On this view it is the jury's function, with some help from the judge, to package the facts and to stick on the package the correct legal label, black or white according to the contents, as directed by the judge. They are not to be told, even as a matter of interest, why it is to be a black label rather than a white; to go into that question would be unnecessary and distracting.

For myself I think that there are exceptional occasions in which the novel and bold is to be preferred. These are occasions on which, while the facts shape themselves to a black or white solution without variations, the law is complicated and difficult to explain. But as a general rule I should with respect follow the practice of Lord Keith. I should agree of course that when a judge is summing up he is not holding a seminar for students; his charge to the jury is not the sort of bedside lecture that eminent surgeons are said to deliver to their pupils before deciding on an operation. But I should not regard the sort of summing-up which I suggested above as an abstract disquisition. I would be happy to call it tailor-made, provided that it is the tailor's object to clothe the body more or less completely and not only certain parts scantily.

The jury now is very different from what I take it to have been in Vaughan's day, or indeed what it was half a century ago. Education has made it more capable of thinking for itself, less respectful of authority, and less amenable to direction. It is not likely to be dumbfounded by statements of the law on particular topics; one of the worthwhile by-products of the jury system is that the criminal law has to be such as can be understood by the average citizen; if it were such as to confuse the modern jury, there would be something wrong with the law.

So Vaughan's 'discreet and lawful assistance' should now take a different form. To withhold the law because it is 'theirs not to reason why' may lead to obduracy or incomprehension, either of which may spoil the verdict. There may be, as Lord Keith observed, nuances apparent to the collective lay mind but unperceived by the lawyer. It is the jury's right to apply the

[1] ib. at 94D.

law unless they choose to offer a special verdict, and in applying it they should not be constrained. Indeed, the novel and bold form of summing-up smacks a little of seeking a special verdict by stealth. The jury are not being told to apply the law; instead they are told in what form to find the facts almost as they would be for a special verdict; the difference is that instead of the judge telling the jury, after they have stated the facts to him, what their verdict should be, he tells them the verdict in advance and hypothetically. To my mind the novel and bold form of summing-up should be used only a little less rarely than the special verdict. The freedom of thought given by the general verdict is of the essence of the jury system.

11. Sapping and Undermining

TODAY is the feast of the great Saint Athanasius, the scourge of heretics, who died this day sixteen hundred and five years ago after much wielding of the anathema. So it is a day on which a man may pluck up his courage and challenge even a unanimous decision of the House of Lords. The decision against which I am levelling a charge of heresy is one that has affected, albeit unobtrusively, the constitutional right to trial by jury in a criminal case. Until a few years ago it was true to say that there was not in any English prison any person serving a sentence of more than a year who had not been found guilty by a jury which had heard substantially all the relevant evidence. I say 'substantially' because it is always possible that after conviction a piece of fresh evidence may turn up. The question on appeal then used to be whether the fresh evidence would have made any difference to the verdict. Unless it was thought that it could not have made any difference, the conviction was quashed.

It is no longer true to say that there are no persons serving long sentences who have not been convicted by a jury in the sense I have stated. How many such persons there are I do not know. But I shall name two, Mr. Cooper and Mr. McMahon, and I shall examine their case, which has indeed already aroused widespread anxiety. I am not asserting their innocence; in fact, in the opinion of three very able and experienced appellate judges they are guilty. What I am saying is that they have not been convicted by a jury which has heard substantially the whole of the relevant evidence. I say also that just as they have been tried by a jury in form only and not in substance, so their appeal has been only in form. What the appellate judges were really doing was trying the case for the first time on the whole of the evidence which they were ready to admit. The function of an appellate court is not to try but to review; and the review must be a separate and independent process conducted by a body other than that which has reached the conclusion at first instance. In the case of these men there has been no such review.

This state of affairs has been brought about by the construction which the House of Lords, sitting judicially, put upon s. 2(1)(a) of the Criminal Appeal Act 1968 in *Stafford* v. *D.P.P.*[1] In this case the law lords held that the words of the section compelled them willy-nilly—they sounded more willy than nilly—to decide for themselves whether in the light of the fresh evidence that had arisen since the trial, the accused were guilty or not. Ever since criminal appeals were instituted, the basic rule has been that where fresh evidence is admitted, the appellate court must ask itself whether, notwithstanding the fresh evidence, a reasonable jury would inevitably have convicted. The House destroyed this rule; the words of the section, they said, had made this a question of fact for them; it was for them to decide whether the new evidence made the conviction unsafe.

The Criminal Appeal Act 1964 had modified the rule by giving the appellate court power to order a new trial by jury. This also got short shrift. They could not order a new trial, the House said (or appeared to say; I shall examine the appearance later), unless they allowed the appeal; they could not allow the appeal unless they decided that the conviction was unsafe; so in effect they had to conduct the new trial themselves.

If without the supposed intervention of an Act of Parliament the House had been asked to say that it would be much better if in future new trials in fresh evidence cases were conducted by judges instead of by juries, its members, sitting judicially, would have been horrified. They would have declared that so great a reform was a matter for legislation. Yet if any of their lordships had looked back (which under our system they are forbidden to do)[2] at the Parliamentary debates in which some of them had themselves participated, they would have seen that Parliament had not the slightest intention of making this great change. No one in the debates in either House so much as mentioned it as a possibility. What then caused the enactment of a section which compelled the House to effect a reform which nobody had ever asked for?

[1] [1974] A.C. 878.
[2] A prohibition decisively re-affirmed by the House of Lords in *David* v. *Johnson* [1978] 1 All E.R. 1132.

The first cause was an accident of the system. When the construction of an Act of Parliament depends almost entirely on the words used a slight adjustment of the text can have unintended consequences. In other countries a reference to the 'legislative history' would strangle the consequences at birth. In England they can survive to create at the very least troublesome ambiguities. In *Stafford* v. *D.P.P.* an amendment to a key section of the original Criminal Appeal Act of 1907, an amendment that appeared to be so innocuous that it was characterized in both Houses as merely endorsing the current interpretation of the section, turned out to offer an alternative construction of it to the one which was time-honoured. The House surprisingly, for it is not often disinclined to the time-honoured, chose the alternative. I shall consider first how the accident arose and secondly how it was that the law lords were disposed to make the most of it.

As to the first, the root of the trouble lay in the fact that while the 1907 Act gave to the court which it created the power to receive new evidence not adduced at the trial, it made no procedural provision for how it was to be treated when received. The natural procedure, provided that the new evidence was influential (a word I shall use to mean that it might have influenced the result of the trial), would of course be, as in a civil court, to order a new trial, but it was not until 1964 that Parliament partially overcame its dislike of the idea of a second trial in a criminal case. Yet something had to be done with it. What the new court did was to treat influential evidence as if it constituted a good ground of appeal. This meant that a fresh evidence case had to be plugged into one of three sockets, none of which was really shaped to take it. For there was not in the 1907 Act any residual power to allow an appeal. On the contrary the court was explicitly enjoined to dismiss the appeal unless it could be brought within one of the three grounds set out in s. 9. The first ground was if the court thought 'that the verdict of the jury should be set aside on the ground that it is unreasonable or cannot be supported having regard to the evidence'. The second was if there had been at the trial a wrong decision of any question of law. The third was if on any ground there had been any miscarriage of justice.

As to which of these three sockets gave the best fit I have not found any serious discussion by the court. The only one that could not be used was the second. The first could be made to fit, provided that the word 'evidence' was not restricted to evidence at the trial but taken to include evidence thereafter made available. The third ground was perhaps the most appropriate. The fact that at the trial there was missing evidence which might have affected the result would be a miscarriage of justice. Miscarriage need not be confined to error. It may just as easily be caused by an accident for which neither the judge nor the parties are responsible.

This, as I say, was the beginning of the trouble. A ground of appeal normally arises when something has gone wrong at the trial. The discovery of fresh evidence creates a new ground outside the trial. There was nothing to remind a draftsman, when he came to tinker with s. 9, that he must not alter the structure in such a manner as to destroy the habitat therein of fresh evidence cases. As we shall see, he did destroy the third ground as a dwelling-place and made the first a good deal less comfortable. But this was sixty years later. For a long time the system worked well on the practical footing that fresh evidence once received—of course not all the post-trial evidence discovered and tendered was received—was treated exactly as if it were evidence wrongly excluded at the trial. The proviso was applied to it in the same way. Under the *Stirland* formula the court quashed the conviction unless they were satisfied that on the whole of the evidence, old and new, a reasonable jury would inevitably have convicted.

I shall now discuss the provenance of s. 4 of the amending Act of 1966 which became in due course s. 2 of the 1968 Act (which was a consolidating Act) and so the focus of attention in *Stafford* v. *D.P.P.* I shall not deal with the provenance as briefly as I could because it makes a striking example of the way in which we in England ignore legislative history or the absence thereof. At several points in this book I have touched on our methods of law reform and this is a good opportunity to see them at work.

The amending Act, as is customary, followed upon the report of a committee. This one was under the Chairmanship of Lord Donovan, a law lord.[1] His committee was really set up to consider questions of organization. It was thought by some to be unseemly that criminal appeals should be determined by ordinary justices in the Court of Criminal Appeal, while civil appeals were heard by persons of superior rank, to wit, lords justices. The solution found was to abolish the existing court and create a new division of the Court of Appeal in which lords justices mingled with justices.

In addition to its main labours the committee considered some minor points. Some people had questioned whether the first ground of appeal, as phrased in s. 9 of the 1907 Act, gave the Court enough power to interfere with a verdict about which they were unhappy or, in Lord Widgery's celebrated formula yet to come, had 'a lurking doubt'. In cases of disputed identity where the evidence was clear but slight, it might be difficult to say that the jury's acceptance of it was either unreasonable or unsupported, but

[1] (1965) Cmnd. 2755.

nevertheless the conviction might be felt to be unsafe. So the committee suggested substituting for a verdict that was 'unreasonable or cannot be supported having regard to the evidence' one that was 'under all the circumstances of the case unsafe or unsatisfactory'. The committee thought that by the change of wording 'the safeguards for an innocent person wrongly identified and wrongly convicted are sensibly increased'; it might operate also in other cases such as rape.[1] It was with these modest hopes that the new section was launched.

Its prospects of an interesting life were not improved when the bill to implement the Report was discussed in the Lords.[2] Nobody objected to the change, but there was an argument about whether it made any difference at all. Lord Pearson thought that it did, Lord Parker, then Chief Justice, supported by Lord Morris, thought that it did not; he said that it only gave legislative sanction to the existing practice. Lord Conesford revealed that the new wording had in 1907 been proposed unsuccessfully by the future Lord Chancellor Birkenhead.[3]

Two other minor changes to s. 9 had been inserted into the bill. One followed a recommendation in the Donovan Report to drop the adjective 'substantial' which qualified 'miscarriage of justice' in the proviso. The other, not in the Report, wanted to change the third ground of appeal from 'miscarriage of justice' to 'material irregularity'. This was not so smoothly received. A fierce debate broke out in committee. What was the object, Lord Conesford asked: the amendment had not been proposed in the Donovan report; he moved to strike it out. When the object was unveiled, it was seen to be one of those skeletons which hang in every draftsman's cupboard. As things stood, the combination in the 1907 Act of the third ground and the proviso read as follows:

The Court ... shall allow the appeal if they think that on any ground there was a miscarriage of justice ... provided that the Court may ... dismiss the appeal if they consider that no *substantial*[4] miscarriage of justice has actually occurred.

From this it will easily be seen that the Act, now an elderly gentleman reaching his sixties, could preserve his respectability only by clutching 'substantial' close to his form. Remove the fig-leaf, as the new bill proposed so brutally to do, and the clause becomes one in which the court is enjoined to allow the appeal if there was a miscarriage but to dismiss it if the miscarriage had not actually occurred. Rather than to expose its nakedness to the jeers of the legal profession, was it not best to hustle the old clause off the stage

[1] ib. para 150.   [2] Hansard H.L. vol. 274 c. 808 and vol. 275 c. 243.
[3] ib. vol. 275 c. 253.   [4] Italics mine.

and bring on in its place a youthful, robust, and well-clothed phrase like 'material irregularity in the course of the trial'? But what did that mean, several lords asked. Lord Parker thought that it might cover the sort of case he had had the other day in which the prison authorities, having to provide for the accused's transport from the prison to the court for a three-day trial, had engaged a taxi driven by the foreman of the jury. After this revelation the debate shifted back to 'substantial'. Why was the word being dropped? Lord Pearson thought it a significant word and moved an amendment to have it restored; what harm was it doing? Lord Donovan defended the removal, Lord Dilhorne found it a very difficult question, and Lord Parker could not care less.

In these debates it is usual for many more spirits to be raised from the vasty deep than there is time to lay to rest. There were many other clauses to be considered and the great river of legislation must flow on. By 7.51 p.m. the House had grappled with the details of the bill for almost two hours, it was time for dinner, and Lord Parker had still to introduce his bill to empower local authorities to require the registration of buildings used by clubs and kindred bodies for purposes of entertainment, dancing, and the playing of games. All controversial amendments to the Criminal Appeal bill were courteously withdrawn, suggestions then and later that the whole section might be reorganized (how could a verdict be satisfactory if it was based on a wrong decision of law or a material irregularity, and *per contra*, if a verdict was safe, why should an irregularity matter?) were courteously ignored: after all, Parliament has enough to do passing new laws without trying to clarify old ones. The section which was later to become s. 2 of the 1968 Act and as such to be the hinge of the decision in *Stafford* v. *D.P.P.* became law in the form proposed. It is now usual for bills whose object is to reform legal procedure to be debated first in the Lords. When the bill got to the Commons no new point was taken on the amendment.[1]

The change of wording meant that fresh evidence cases had to be accommodated within the first ground, for it could hardly be said that unadduced evidence constituted a material irregularity. At first this caused no difficulty. The appeal was to be allowed if the verdict was not satisfactory. On a narrow interpretation it could be argued that there was nothing wrong with the verdict considered in relation to the material before the court of trial. But such a narrow interpretation would exclude fresh evidence from ever taking effect and it has in fact never been advanced. If the verdict continued to be judged, as in the past, in relation to the new evidence added to the old, the test

[1] Hansard H.C. vol. 731 c. 1107.

remained the same as in the past—could the addition have made a difference? If it could, the verdict was unsatisfactory because it was not given upon the whole of the evidence. True, it was nobody's fault that it was not so given. But just as in the case of a miscarriage it does not matter whether the cause of it is deliberate or accidental, so it does not matter whether the unsatisfactoriness is anybody's fault. An accident can make a verdict unsatisfactory; the section does not demand that a culprit be found.

So, after 1966 cases of fresh evidence continued to be dealt with in the same old way. When in such cases the appeal was allowed, whether or not a new trial was ordered under the recent Act of 1964, the verdict was declared, in conformity with the new wording, to be unsafe or unsatisfactory. But in determining whether the verdict was so, the old test, the proviso test, was still applied. In 1971 Lord Chief Justice Parker said in relation to new evidence tendered,

The Court is quite unable to say that their evidence is incapable of belief; the sole question is what weight should be given to it. For that purpose one has to imagine a jury who heard their evidence together with all the other evidence in the case, and ask oneself whether nevertheless the jury must have come to the same conclusion. It may well be that any jury would come to the same conclusion.

But, the court said, since they could not in all strictness say that the jury would have come to the same conclusion, they would allow the appeal and direct a re-trial.[1]

During the same period the same words, 'safe and satisfactory', were being applied to the ordinary appeal in which what was being asked for was not the admission of fresh evidence but a review of the existing evidence. In relation to such appeals the new wording was being used to work a powerful change in appellate practice.[2] This statement needs a little elaboration.

Until 1907 it was broadly true to say that the verdict of the jury sealed the accused's fate. The Criminal Appeal Act of that year led to three qualifications of this simple concept.

First, it introduced the idea of a 'properly directed' jury. It was no longer to be *any* verdict that was to be final and conclusive. If there had been a wrong decision of law (the second ground of appeal), the verdict was vitiated; then, there being no true verdict, no *veredictum*, the conviction dependent on it must be quashed. Thus if the jury was given the wrong law to apply, if evidence was wrongly excluded, and so on, there was no true verdict.

Second, the requirement of proper direction was extended to cover fact

[1] *R.* v. *Barker* (unreported), 12 Jan. 1971.
[2] See p. 112.

as well as law. If the judge failed to present the facts clearly and fairly, if he overstressed the case for the prosecution or did not put adequately the case for the defence, if he muddled the issues, there was a misdirection of fact which came under the third head 'on any other ground a miscarriage of justice'. Then also the verdict was vitiated.

Third, there was the first ground of appeal. On the narrowest interpretation of the text a verdict was vitiated if it was perverse, but perverse convictions are almost non-existent. On its widest interpretation, it is arguable that it would have permitted the court to quash any verdict with which on the facts it disagreed. This would have meant the court setting itself up as an independent tribunal of fact, which no appellate court had ever done, even in relation to the civil jury. It would have refused to pass any verdict that it did not consider safe and satisfactory. How far it had got towards this position by 1966 was, as we have seen, one of the points discussed in the Parliamentary debates. I think that all through the century the court was extending its interventions but doing it by widening the boundaries of misdirection of fact. It was not difficult for it in a case about which it had serious doubts to find in the presentation of the facts to the jury flaws which in stronger cases it would have overlooked. But we did not in my time, which ended in 1959, consciously review the evidence with the object of coming to a conclusion ourselves about guilt or innocence.

The function of the proviso within this framework is to give the answer to a question which crops up constantly in every legal process – when does an error or irregularity annul? There are irregularities which chip the surface and others which flaw the centre; the very big are easily distinguishable from the very little, but where in the middle is the line to be drawn? One starts from the point that to authorize judgment and sentence there must be a verdict. But a verdict means more than an utterance by the foreman of the jury; it is the utterance made by him at the end of a process which has throughout been properly conducted. What errors or omissions in the conduct of a trial are big enough to constitute a fatal flaw? The answer which the proviso gives is that they are such errors or omissions as are big enough to cause appellate judges to think that a reasonable jury might have reached a different conclusion. When there are such errors or omissions, there is no true verdict; what is masquerading as such is to be formally quashed. No matter that the appellate judges may think that there is ample evidence to justify a conviction. It is not they who are the judges of that.

What was done in 1966 was to complete the liberation of all the forces which had been held in check either by the text of the first ground in the 1907 Act or by the practice which had restricted its interpretation. Lord

Justice Widgery's celebrated judgment in 1969 gave the keynote and released 'the lurking doubt'.[1] No matter that the jury was properly directed and no matter that they showed by their verdict that they had no reasonable doubt. The judges would not only study the evidence themselves, they would also get the feel of the case; and if they saw lurking in it a reasonable doubt, they would quash the conviction. Thus the judges set themselves up as an independent tribunal to review the facts. There must still of course be a verdict of a jury. But henceforth there would be two tribunals which the prosecution had to satisfy on the facts, the jury first and the Court of Appeal thereafter.

Fresh evidence cases are only a small minority of those coming before a court of appeal. In the great majority the question which the court is daily asking itself and answering is not 'Might a jury have acquitted?' but 'Do we think it safe to convict?' In the rare fresh evidence case, has this second question tended to replace the first? It would be a laborious work—and perhaps not very rewarding since on this sort of point extempore judgments are not always indicative—to trace the course of change. There was never in the Criminal Appeal Division any formal declaration. But when in 1973 in *Stafford* v. *D.P.P.* the Court, dismissing an appeal based on a large body of fresh evidence, more remarkable perhaps for its size than for its weight, used language which suggested that the Court was no longer applying the proviso test, counsel asked the Court to certify a point of law for the House of Lords and the request was granted. The question framed was whether

the correct approach of the Court of Appeal is to evaluate the fresh evidence, to endeavour to set it into the framework provided by the whole of the evidence called at the trial, and in the end to ask itself whether the verdict has become unsafe or unsatisfactory by the impact of the fresh evidence.[2]

In the House counsel for the appellant opened his argument with the assertion that

the Court of Appeal asked the wrong question in that they took as the test the effect of the fresh evidence on their minds and not the effect that that evidence would have had on the mind of the jury.[3]

At the beginning of his argument counsel for the respondent retorted with

There is nothing in the Act or in the cases which support the view that the Court of Appeal should allow the appeal when they do not themselves think that the verdict

[1] *R.* v. *Cooper* [1969] 1 Q.B. 267. In June 1972 the *C.L.R.C. Eleventh Report*, p. 11, was still treating as occasional the quashing of convictions where no fault could be found with the conduct of the trial. But now unsafety or dissatisfaction on the facts is the usual ground given.

[2] [1974] A.C. 891A.   [3] ib. 880F.

was unsafe or unsatisfactory, or when they are themselves convinced of the guilt of the appellant but consider that some hypothetical jury might have thought otherwise.[1]

Thus was issue joined and the House unanimously decided in favour of the respondent.

Lord Dilhorne's was the leading speech. Two of the speeches, those of Lords Pearson and Diplock, were concurrent and no more. Lord Cross followed a rather different line from that taken by Lords Dilhorne and Kilbrandon, so that it is best to look at these two for the kernel of the case. It is contained in the words 'they think'. Under the section the court shall allow the appeal only 'if they think that the verdict of the jury should be set aside on the ground that under all the circumstances of the case it is unsafe or unsatisfactory'. They could not, they said, quash the conviction unless they themselves thought on the evidence, new and old, that it was unsafe or unsatisfactory.

It is certainly true that it is what *they think* that counts. The question is what have *they* to think about. They have to think about whether the verdict of a jury is satisfactory, not about how they themselves would decide the case. The cardinal point was put for the defence by junior counsel:

A verdict of a jury must be unsatisfactory if reliable and cogent evidence exists which was reasonably not before the jury at the trial. If a jury has considered only part of the evidence in a case, that in itself shows that the verdict was unsatisfactory.[2]

Whether one regards, as I do, this point as unanswerable or, as the law lords did, as unworthy of comment depends, as such deep divisions usually do, upon a fundamental difference between two ideas. In my idea no conviction can stand that is not based on the verdict of a jury given after a full and proper trial. No matter that the guilt of the accused cries out to the heavens through the voices of all the judges of England. This is the first and traditional protection that the law gives to an accused. The second and more recent protection, given in the way I have chronicled, is that even such a verdict will not be enough if on the evidence the appellate judges find the lurking doubt which they consider that the jury has missed. But the second is an addition to the first and not a substitute for it. The profound mistake which I respectfully believe the House made was to go straight to the second and ignore the first. If they had not made that mistake, their judgment would have run as follows:

Since trial by jury is the constitutional right of every person accused of crime to whom Parliament has not expressly denied it, a verdict is unsatisfactory, whether

[1] ib. 886E. [2] ib. 884C.

or not in the opinion of the Court it is sustained by the evidence, if it has not been reached by a jury properly directed on the whole of the relevant evidence. If the verdict has not been so reached, there is a miscarriage of justice unless the Court is satisfied that if the jury had been so directed, it must have reached the same verdict.

Certainly, when there is no miscarriage in this sense, this is not the end of it. The judges must then go on to inquire whether on the evidence they think the conviction to be safe. The phrase 'unsafe or unsatisfactory' is usually interpreted as if the words were joint and not several. It may be that one or the other is tautologous. But if I was using them separately, I would say that the verdict of a jury which has not been properly directed or which has not considered the whole of the influential evidence, is unsatisfactory; if in these respects it is satisfactory but is based upon evidence which does not convince the appellate judges, it is unsafe. However this may be and if the words are indivisible, I see no reason why as a matter of construction they should not perform a double duty—first, to test the verdict as a verdict, and second, to test the evidence. The result of both tests will depend upon what the appellate judges think. But in the first test they will be thinking about whether the fresh evidence would have made any difference to the jury's verdict; and in the second about whether the evidence is so formidable as to satisfy them as judges that a conviction would not be safe.

It is not in my view tenable to say that Stafford and his fellow accused were convicted after a trial by jury. They might have been; if the courts had applied the right test, they might well have concluded that the fresh evidence *could* have made no difference; Lord Cross practically says so.[1] But since the proviso test was not applied either in the Court of Appeal or in the House of Lords it is not possible to uphold the verdict on the traditional ground. Certainly the accused had a trial on all the evidence, but it was not a trial by jury, it was conducted in accordance with the new mode invented to conform with the new interpretation.

Since the mode is now likely to be generally used, its main features should be noticed. It is a mixed trial by judges and jury, the jury inevitably, since they have not heard or read the whole of the evidence, playing a subordinate part. In this new trial witnesses have to be accepted or rejected, inferences drawn, and the resulting mass weighed to see if it turns the scales. As to the witnesses, it is the judges who finally pass judgment on the reliability of all of them, new and old. They did not hear the old witnesses and there are no specific findings about them to be found in the general verdict. So the judges have to decide upon their reliability on the record, fortified by conjectures from the verdict; to reach their verdict, the judges would say,

[1] ib. 911B.

the jury must have believed this or that. In assessing the reliability of the new witnesses whom they may hear in the box, the judges are on their own.[1]

There follows the main task of drawing inferences and of assessing the weight of the whole. This task, normally within the exclusive province of the jury, now falls exclusively on the judges. They know of course that the jury in the old trial thought that $A+B+C$ for the prosecution minus $(X+Y)$ for the defence was enough to prove guilt. But that is no help when you have to add Z to the defence; you have then to start the weighing process all over again.

We may take it for granted that the evidence, old and new, is most thoroughly examined and dissected. In Stafford's case in the Court of Appeal, where the point of law was not discussed at all, the Lord Chief Justice's judgment was one of more than ten thousand words. The law lords also treated the facts at length; they account for about three-quarters of Lord Dilhorne's speech. So certainly there is a re-trial, albeit one conducted at a disadvantage, as Lord Dilhorne said.[2] But it is not a re-trial in the only form authorized by law, i.e. before a jury. Sometimes at the end of such a process the judges pray the old verdict in aid of their new conclusions and talk as if all they were doing was to affirm it. But the jury missed all the new evidence. It is as if the court was affirming the verdict at a trial at which the jury had left the box for an hour or so to seek some light refreshment. Or it recalls the legend of the judge who at the end of his judgment said that 'My brother Snodgrass, before he went off to sleep during the last half of the argument, authorized me to say that he fully agrees with what I have just said.'

The correctness of *Stafford* v. *D.P.P.* depends upon which construction of s. 2(1)(a) of the 1968 Act is the right one—the one that requires the Court of Appeal to consider only whether the verdict on the old evidence has in their judgment been rendered unsafe by the impact of the new, or the one that requires them to consider first whether there has been in any meaningful sense a verdict of a jury at all. In opting for the latter I do not myself need to go beyond the language of the section itself coupled with the consideration that on the other interpretation the constitutional right to trial by jury is denied to an accused whose fresh evidence the Court has decided to receive; I think that only clear and express words should be allowed to do that. If the jury had heard only 10% of all the relevant evidence and the other 90% had been heard by a judge, no one would be likely to say that there had

---

[1] Often when the new evidence is lengthy the court will have it taken before an examiner, as they did in *Stafford* v. *D.P.P.*, and then all that they will have of it is the record.

[2] [1974] A.C. 894C.

been trial by jury. But it does not matter whether it is 10% or 90% that the jury hears. It cannot be put into percentages. The letters A, B, C and X, Y, Z which I used just now stand for unknown quantities. It is only when Z is found to equal zero, i.e. when the new evidence could make no difference, that the old verdict can safely be allowed to stand. This is the test that has served for half a century and it is, I believe, beyond the wit of man to devise any other.

What follows now is a more searching look at the reasoning in the *Stafford* speeches.[1] I begin with a puzzle. Did the House regard their decision as reconcilable with the existing authorities, both before and after 1966, which had apparently settled the law? Or were they breaking with the past? And, if so, was the break made by choice or because they considered that the wording of the new section in the 1968 Act left them with no alternative? I cannot from the text of the speeches give an absolutely confident reply.

At first sight it certainly looks as if their lordships were saying that it was the new section which prevented them from following the earlier authorities. Certainly much emphasis is placed on the language of the section. But it is not contrasted with the language in the 1907 Act. If it had been, it would have been seen that the same reasoning would have applied in 1907 as in 1968. The original Act also required the Court to allow the appeal only 'if they think' that the verdict was unreasonable or could not be supported having regard to the evidence or that there was a miscarriage of justice. If the reasoning in *Stafford* v. *D.P.P.* had been applied to the 1907 Act the Court of Appeal would have had to judge for itself whether, when the new evidence was added to the old, it made the verdict unreasonable or unsupported or a miscarriage. It is clear from the authorities that under the old wording the Court never did. Yet, even apart from the legislative history, it is hard to suppose that the few verbal alterations which Parliament made in 1966 were intended to transfer from juries to judges the decision of a question of fact on which guilt depended.

This leads to the second hypothesis. Was the House saying that the approach to the problem, whether the problem was contained in the Act of 1907 or the Act of 1968, was the wrong one? This would mean overruling a large number of decisions given at the level of the Court of Appeal which were cited for the appellants. Only one was referred to in the speeches, and this was distinguished, rightly or wrongly, by Lord Dilhorne on the ground that it was given under another section of the 1907 Act.[2] It seems

[1] Which the unlearned in the law may wish to skip, resuming at p. 165.
[2] [1974] A.C. 892E.

unlikely that their Lordships intended by implication to overrule all the others.

So one is left with the first hypothesis. Surprising though it may seem, I think that what the House was saying was that there was nothing to reconcile; you could look at the problem either way, they said; it did not matter. Lord Dilhorne said:

Mr Hawser in the course of his argument drew attention to the many cases in which, since 1908, and since the amendment made in 1966, the Court has quashed a conviction saying that in the light of the fresh evidence the jury might have come to a different conclusion, but I do not think that it is established as a rule of law that, in every fresh evidence case, the Court must decide what they think the jury might or would have done if they had heard that evidence. That it is a convenient approach and a reasonable one to make, I do not deny.[1]

Lords Cross and Kilbrandon said the same thing.[2]

But if, as the latter put it, they were just alternative routes, what factors in a particular case are to dictate the choice between them? If the accused had the option, he would almost certainly prefer to have his fresh evidence assessed on the basis of what a reasonable jury might think about it than upon the basis of what three judges did think.

Here again all three law lords were unanimous and emphatic. What a jury might think if they heard the evidence was just the same as what judges actually thought when they did hear it. If a judge had a reasonable doubt, so would the jury; if he had none, neither would the jury.

I have set out in an earlier chapter the dicta in which the three law lords expressed this thought.[3] I there suggested that they were contrary to the principles on which the courts act when they are engaged in judicial review. I think also that they do not conform with reality. It is true that judges and properly directed juries do not frequently disagree; this is not because all reasonable human beings always agree, but because juries reach their conclusions with the aid (but not under the coercion) of judicial guidance which they are usually happy to accept. But surely any judge who has presided over an appreciable number of jury trials will remember cases in which he had no reasonable doubt but the jury had. In *R. v. Cooper*, which Lord Dilhorne cited with approval,[4] Lord Justice Widgery said that what was significant was the reaction of the court which could 'be produced by the general feel of the case as the Court experiences it'. Surely no one will contend that a jury, taking part for the first time maybe in the legal process, will always have the same feel as an experienced judge. Indeed *R. v. Cooper* supposes that they will not, since it instructs the appellate judges to search

[1] ib. 893B. [2] ib. 907C and 912E.
[3] See p. 133. [4] [1974] A.C. 892B.

for reasonable doubts which the jury must have thought to be non-existent. It must be remembered too that the difference between a judge and a jury is not just the difference between a judge and a juryman. It is also the difference between the situation where a single man, be he a judge or a juryman, has no doubt and one where ten out of twelve men chosen at random have no doubt. Anyone who disputes this distinction should make the experiment of getting an unhesitating opinion from one judge and then trying it out on the next eleven he meets.

I say therefore that the dicta I have cited do not conform with reality. They are fictitious. This is not necessarily a term of reproach. Historically the judges' use of legal fictions is to reform the law without obvious innovation. If in 1974 the law lords had off their own bat said that in future judges and not juries would assess the weight of fresh evidence, they would have been accused of legislating. The seventeenth-century judge would not have minded that, but his successors do. So the signposts to the old route are left standing. It is still open to a judge—it is not 'a wrong approach', Lord Dilhorne says[1]—for a judge to ask himself what the jury might have thought, so long as he appreciates that the jury will think what he thinks. The judge who follows the old route will first ask himself what a jury would think and then, because a jury must think the same as he does, he will inevitably find out by this means what he thinks himself; it seems rather a cumbersome way of going about it and is perhaps unlikely to survive longer than is necessary to maintain a link with old times. Behind the bland words the intent is clear. 'The ultimate responsibility,' Lord Dilhorne says, 'rests with them'—the judges—'and them alone.'[2]

But legal fictions are dangerous because they have a tendency to spread. It will be difficult to keep this one confined to the small category of fresh evidence cases. Already Lord Cross has given a hint[3]—not acceptable perhaps to Lord Dilhorne[4]—that the existing proviso test will be the next thing to go. Is not this logically correct? The fresh evidence test is simply the proviso test adapted, the omission of relevant evidence being substituted for the misdirection as the defect to which the proviso is to be applied. It is only when there is a miscarriage of justice that the appeal is to be allowed. But how can there be a miscarriage of justice, it must now be asked, if the

---

[1] ib. 906B. Nevertheless the Court of Appeal in R. v. King (unreported; 320/O/74) treated Lord Dilhorne as offering an option to a court either to decide the matter itself or to order a new trial, and it chose the latter. This is consistent with what Lord Dilhorne says at 893B and G, but is not easy to reconcile with the passage here cited or with his view as expressed at 893F.

[2] ib. 906B.

[3] ib. 907H.   [4] ib. 893H.

appellate judges find the conviction to be safe and satisfactory? If there is no miscarriage, the grossness of the misdirection cannot matter. If, instead of summing up, the judge, telling the jury that since he is of the opinion that there is no reasonable doubt about guilt and since, if he has no doubt, the jury cannot have one either, directs them to convict, the only question on appeal can be the question whether on the evidence the judge was right to have no doubt.

Or take a broader view still. In a criminal trial the terminal question of fact is whether there is a reasonable doubt about guilt. If judge and jury are bound to give the same answer to this question, why bother with a jury? Their deliberations take more time and they cost more. Chief Justice Vaughan asked this question 308 years ago.[1] It is of course unlikely that the new doctrine released in *Stafford* v. *D.P.P.* will spread as far as this. In the common law new doctrine dries up and evaporates on ground that is trodden down by custom and tradition. Nevertheless theoretical projections of this sort are a common and useful way of testing the nature of the doctrine. Logic has a part to play in the growth of the law as well as custom and tradition.

The broad conclusion which I have set out above can be fortified by arguments of a more technical character designed to show that the construction of s. 2 of the 1968 Act adopted by the House causes that section to fall foul of other provisions in the Act. The first of them is that it would seem to be the logical consequence of the majority view in the House that there can never be an order for a re-trial; this makes s. 7 of the Act of 1968 (which re-enacts the Act of 1964) a dead letter.[2] That follows inescapably from the fact that the Court of Appeal, before it can take any action at all, must make up its mind about the facts. Lord Kilbrandon put that point most firmly:

The setting aside of a conviction depends on what the Appellate Court thinks of it—that is what the statute says. . . . being convinced, as the Court of Appeal was in the present case, that 'the inference of guilt is irresistible', they could not think that the conviction was unsafe or unsatisfactory, and therefore had no statutory power to interfere with the verdict. . . . It is the opinion of this House on the safety of the verdict that is in debate.[3]

So the logic runs: the court cannot order a new trial unless they allow the appeal; they cannot allow the appeal unless they think on the evidence that the conviction was unsafe. But if they think that, it must follow that any

---

[1] See p. 132.
[2] I am not saying that there *will* never be an order for a new trial; in fact there have been several since 1974. It may take some time to work *Stafford* v. *D.P.P.* into the fabric of the law.
[3] [1974] A.C. 912B and F and 913E.

jury, which on the same evidence considered that it would be safe to convict, would be wrong. So the only point of the new trial would be to give the prosecution the chance of launching a second attack. Since that would amount to double jeopardy and would be contrary to the spirit of the criminal law, a new trial should never be ordered.

It is difficult in any event to reconcile the text of s. 7 with the majority view. The section lays down the condition of a new trial as being 'where the Court of Appeal allow an appeal ... and do so only by reason of evidence received or available to be received'. The alternative of 'availability' should make it possible for the court in a suitable case to do no more than look at the written evidence and decide on paper that it is enough to justify a new trial. This alternative is unusable if before the Court can act at all, it has itself to receive the evidence, to allow cross-examination on it if appropriate, and itself to decide the issue. So the majority view makes a dead letter of the alternative.

Lord Cross's line of argument escapes these criticisms. It rests entirely on the doctrine of the conclusive presumption that a new reasonable jury will not have a reasonable doubt if the Court of Appeal (or, I suppose, if need be, the majority of the Court) have not got one. So he is able to make room for the 'available evidence' case in which the Court does not commit itself to any view of its own and in which therefore there can be a re-trial. His argument does not depend upon an interpretation of s. 2 which requires the Court to decide on the evidence whether the conviction is safe and satisfactory.

Lord Cross's willingness to accept the death of the *Stirland* test as applied to the proviso escapes also, though at the price of creating a much greater upheaval of the authorities, a criticism that can be levelled against another feature of Lord Dilhorne's speech in which he said:

Mr Hawser argued that in a 'fresh evidence' case the Court should follow the same principle as that applicable to the proviso and only hold that a conviction was safe and satisfactory if they thought that the jury which heard the fresh evidence would inevitably have come to the conclusion that the accused was guilty. I cannot accept this argument. When the application of the proviso is under consideration, something has gone wrong in the conduct of the trial. In a 'fresh evidence' case nothing has gone wrong in the conduct of the trial and I see no warrant for importing the principles applicable to the proviso into the determination of whether the verdict is or is not safe and satisfactory. The words of s. 2(1)(a) are clear and unambiguous and they are the words which have to be applied.[1]

Mr. Hawser's argument seems to be securely based on *R.* v. *Collins*[2] and until 1966 Lord Dilhorne could not have spoken as he did without overruling that authority. The distinction supposedly introduced in 1966 does not to my mind produce a sensible result. Suppose that a piece of relevant evidence is not considered by the trial jury, in one case because it was wrongly excluded by the trial judge, and in another because it was not discovered until after the trial. They are both misfortunes affecting the verdict. If an omission can be timed like an occurrence, then they were both operative in the course of the trial. But why should it matter when they occurred? Except in the rare case when the omission is the personal responsibility of the accused (when it is far from certain that the fresh evidence would be admitted), it is no more his fault than judicial error. Why should he be put in a worse position in the one event than in the other?

I say 'in a worse position' because this is what every practitioner would think and what Lord Dilhorne seems in this passage to be accepting. But to say that may be inconsistent with the passages in all the speeches which maintain that what judges think juries think also, so that one test can be no worse for the accused than the other. Here again Lord Cross seems to me to have put himself logically in the stronger position.

I come now to another puzzling feature of *Stafford* v. *D.P.P.* which will lead me eventually to *R.* v. *Cooper and McMahon.* What is the effect of the former case on the credibility of fresh evidence? Before 1974 the question for the appellate court was whether the evidence was capable of belief, not whether it ought in fact to be believed. Before 1964 the latter question could not be answered at all and after 1964 it could be answered only by a jury at a new trial. Is it now a question of fact for the appellate judges? This depends on whether the general dicta in the *Stafford* case about the ultimate responsibility for the decision being with the judges cover the question of whether or not a witness is telling the truth.

Looked at in one way, it seems unlikely that the law lords intended their reasoning to apply to belief; the proposition that if I believe a witness, then so in my view must every other reasonable person, does not readily command assent. Looked at in another way, it is difficult to see how an appellate court can decide for itself on the evidence, old and new, that a conviction is safe or unsafe without also deciding for itself, when there is a conflict of evidence, whether the new evidence is to be accepted or rejected.

The Criminal Appeal Division is not obsequious to authority. I have noticed only one of its members[1] who has troubled in this connection to refer to *Stafford* v. *D.P.P.* The others have continued without reference

[1] Roskill L. J., who was brought up in the Commercial Court.

to *Stafford* to order new trials whenever the question was whether or not a fresh witness was to be believed.[1] But one cannot be sure that this means that credibility is to be treated officially as the only exception to the rule. It may mean no more than that the *Stafford* doctrine has not yet been fully absorbed; there has been at least one case since 1974 in which the Court of Appeal have quashed a conviction in the old style because they could not say that if the fresh evidence had been added to the totality of the evidence at the trial, the jury would certainly have convicted.[2] It seems at any rate to be clear that, until *R. v. Cooper and McMahon*, the question of belief continued in practice to be treated as a question for a jury.

Cooper and McMahon, in sharp contrast with *Stafford*, turned entirely on credibility. In *Stafford* the facts do not matter; in *Cooper* they do. In *Stafford* I think that if the appellate court had applied the old proviso test, they would probably have reached the same result. The verdict at the trial was based on the inability of the accused to deflect the conclusion against them to which all the circumstantial evidence pointed. In such a case it is possible to call innumerable witnesses whose evidence, if accepted, will cause the exact shape of the circumstances to be pinched here and to bulge there, but evidence of this sort is not influential unless the change of shape is sufficient to bend the conclusion. As Lord Cross put it, if at the trial the prosecution's evidence weighed 100 lb. and the defence 5 lb. another 3 lb. of fresh evidence cannot matter.[3] The case is one for lawyers to worry about on the law, but on the facts it has not, I believe, caused public anxiety.

R. v. Cooper and McMahon on the other hand has—I quote from the Minister of State speaking in the House of Commons on 14 December 1977, eight years after the crime—'resulted in a great deal of criticism in the Press, among the public and elsewhere'.[4] It is a case of identification and alibi; a chief witness for the prosecution, upon whom admittedly their case depended, who was a professional criminal, who had turned Queen's evidence, and who was conceded to be lying on many points; an officer in charge of the case who is at present serving a sentence of five years' imprisonment for taking small bribes from a dealer in pornography; unprecedented interventions by the Home Secretary. The story must be told as briefly as possible. On 10 September 1969 the chief prosecution witness, Mr. Matthews, set out with three other men from London in three cars, one of which belonged to Matthews, to rob a post office in Luton. They failed, but in

---

[1] Examples, all unreported, are *Atkinson* (3330/A/73), *Benjamin* (1198/R/76), *Frieze* (5230/R/76), and *Simmonds* (6419/R/76).

[2] *R. v. McGuirk* (unreported, 3930/B/75).

[3] [1974] A.C. 911B.   [4] Hansard H.C. c. 874.

the attempt one of them shot and killed the sub-postmaster. Police inquiries eventually led to Matthews, whose car had been identified. He was arrested on 22 October 1969 and interrogated. He told a false story about getting rid of the car before 10 September and set up a false alibi for the time of the murder. When these lies were exposed, he made on 25 October a written statement which is a partial confession. He said that he had been persuaded by a man whom he knew only as 'John' to take his car in the convoy of three that went to Luton; the two other men who joined them he said that he had never seen before. At Luton two of the cars, including his, parked in the station car park; the other car and the other three men went off. Sometime later they returned in a panic saying that a man had been shot.

The police do not have to disclose the details of their investigation nor the methods which they use. With some exceptions, which are gradually being increased, they do not have to disclose the results save in so far as they form part of the prosecution's case. Clearly they should not be made to furnish the defence with a detailed report on every aspect of the inquiry, but there are some aspects where a knowledge of just how the police proceeded would be very relevant. One of these is when an accused turns Queen's evidence and incriminates others. Who takes the initiative, he or the officer in charge; what passes between them? In this case we know that the Post Office offered a reward of £5,000 and that after the trial the distribution of it among the various police helpers and informers was apparently left to the officer in charge, the one who has since been sentenced for corruption. We know that Matthews received the lion's share of £2,000, that he paid that sum into his bank on 22 May 1970, and on the same day withdrew £700 in cash. The last of the four courts of appeal found unconvincing his explanation of what he did with the cash. But the allegation that he had paid it over to the officer was denied by the officer and not pursued in the appeal. We do not know whether the prospect of a reward played any part in Matthews's decision to turn Queen's evidence; in fact we do not know anything at all about that decision. The bare facts are as follows. On the evening of the day of his confession, i.e. 25 October, Matthews was charged with being concerned in the murder. He was also shown a series of police photographs from which he picked out Cooper as 'John' and McMahon and Murphy as the other two men. On 29 October and succeeding days these three men were arrested and subsequently picked out by Matthews on identification parades. On 15 December the charge against Matthews was dropped and he was released.

The three accused were tried for murder at the Old Bailey in February

and March 1970. Matthews's evidence consisted substantially of the story
in his statement, coupled with an insistence that, so far as he was concerned,
the purpose of the journey to Luton was the innocent one of picking up
some parcels. The accused all denied that they were in Luton and called
alibi evidence, mainly of relations and friends. The judge told the jury that
the case really turned on Matthews and gave them a strong warning against
the danger of relying on his evidence, whether or not they found him to
be an accomplice. On 19 March the jury convicted all three accused and
they were all sentenced to life imprisonment.

In the four appeals that followed, much fresh evidence was tendered, some
of it with the object of discrediting Matthews. If the old law on credibility
is untouched by *Stafford* v. *D.P.P.* there is no doubt about how such evidence should be dealt with. The Court would ask itself whether the addition
of this new evidence to the other discrediting factors might have caused the
jury to disbelieve Matthews; if it might, they would quash the conviction,
ordering a new trial if they thought fit. In *Baksh* v. *R.* the Privy Council
quashed the conviction in a case in which fresh evidence showed the honesty
of the prosecution witnesses to be open to question.[1] In *R.* v. *Knudson* an
important witness for the prosecution, who was at the trial put forward
as a man of good character, was found afterwards to have a number of
convictions. The Court of Appeal said that if the jury had known of
this, they might have come to a different conclusion; they quashed the
conviction.[2]

I shall address myself to only one piece of the fresh evidence, probably
the most important, which arose in the following way. Mr. Murphy's
advisers discovered a Mr. Edwards whose evidence, if true, provided
Murphy with a complete alibi. On a reference back by the Home Secretary
the Court of Appeal accepted Edwards as an independent witness of good
character, impressive and honest; on 13 November 1973 they quashed the
conviction of Murphy. This decision raised an issue, the Home Secretary
rightly thought, 'about the credibility of Mr. Matthews' evidence against
Mr. Cooper and Mr. McMahon', and consequently referred that issue back
to the court.

When the reference reached the court, *Stafford* v. *D.P.P.* had not long
been decided and it was not noticed by the court. The court had to start
from the presumption that there was a reasonable doubt about the identification of Murphy. Mattthews might of course be able to explain why he could
have been mistaken about Murphy and yet remain certain about the other
two. The defence applied for him to be recalled for further cross-examina-

[1] [1958] A.C. 167.   [2] (1974) unreported; 2883/B/73.

AND THE JURY II: SAPPING AND UNDERMINING

tion. The court refused the application, doubting whether they had the power to grant it. (Of course they had!) They dismissed the appeal, saying simply that a jury could well have acquitted Murphy and found the others guilty. Of course a jury could have done that, though it would hardly be sensible for them to do so without first hearing what Matthews had to say. But the court put the question the wrong way round, thereby transferring to the defence the burden which all the pre-1974 authorities put upon the prosecution. The test is not whether the jury 'could well' have acquitted Cooper and McMahon, but whether they would inevitably have convicted them.

The appellants later applied to a court of appeal, differently constituted, to certify a question of law of public importance so that they might take the case to the Lords. They framed two questions, the first being whether the court had applied the right test, and the second being whether it had power to recall a witness for further cross-examination. It could, I suppose, be argued that questions which can be answered as easily as these two cannot be questions of public importance. It can hardly, however, have been on this ground that the court decided that there was no point of law fit for certification. As is the custom they gave no reasons, but the Lord Chief Justice alluded to *Stafford* v. *D.P.P.* and observed that that case decided that it was 'not a necessary function of this court when considering fresh evidence to evaluate the effect which it would have had on the jury at the trial'.[1] This observation would have been pertinent if the earlier court had applied *Stafford* v. *D.P.P.* and evaluated the fresh evidence themselves. As it was, the court applied correctly neither the old law nor the new.

The Home Secretary did not weary of well-doing and in April 1976 he referred the case back to the court again, an unprecedented step. The new court of appeal, the fourth, extracted itself with skill and suavity from the worst blunders of its predecessor. Matthews was recalled for cross-examination and was in the box for two days. He did not admit to any mistake about Murphy; he remained as positive about him as he was about the others. The court applied *Stafford* v. *D.P.P.* Without discussing its scope they treated the case as authorizing them to determine the issue for themselves even when it depended entirely on the credit of the witness. They said:

Each of us watched him closely while he was giving evidence. The conclusion which each of us independently has reached in this Court on the vital part of his story is that he was clearly telling the truth.... There is nothing in the new evidence to which

[1] (1975) 61 Cr. App. R. 215.

we have listened which makes the verdict against either of the appellants unsafe or unsatisfactory.

They dismissed the appeal.[1]

As I have said, there are two forts to be captured by the prosecution before a man can be deprived of his liberty. First they must secure the verdict of a jury and then they must obtain the endorsement of it on the facts by the judges on appeal.[2] Here there was no verdict of a jury, only the semblance of one given on a portion of the evidence. But there was also only the semblance of an appeal.

It is not the business of a court of criminal appeal to hear the witnesses again; it does not descend into the arena; it takes as convincing all the evidence which the jury must have accepted; it does not suppose that by its superior gifts of observation it will detect physical signs of falsehood which a jury has missed; on demeanour the jury is final. What an appellate court does is to stand back and to look at the case immobilized on paper. Before the jury the case is unwound as on a revolving cylinder; before the judges it is spread out. The jury sees the whole performance, but cannot except in memory move from one incident to another; the judges can freeze the significant points, study, and correlate them. It is the examination of the case on paper that gives to appellate judges the detachment which is the essential quality of a court of review.

So in *R. v. Cooper and McMahon* what was wanted from the Court of Appeal was not confirmation that Matthews appeared from his demeanour to be a truthful witness, whether on essentials or on the whole. What was wanted was an answer, based on a more comprehensive view of the case than the jury could have as well as a more detached one, to the question whether, however convincing Matthews might sound, it was safe to act upon the evidence of an habitual liar, who even at the trial had not come clean, who was an accomplice almost uncorroborated,[3] and who had turned

---

[1] This was on 22 July 1976. On 13 November 1973 the court had doubted Matthews's identification of Murphy. To a layman it might then have seemed obvious that the next question—and an immediate one—would be to inquire whether Matthews was still sure of his identification of the other two and, if so, on what grounds. Under the system which the Court of Appeal is content to operate it took two years and eight months to get an answer to that.

[2] One is reminded slightly of the functions of the heralds at a medieval battle. In 1415 the English and the French heralds watched the battle together from a high place. When the French had fled the field, King Henry waited anxiously until the principal French herald confirmed that the English were the victors. That disposed of the 'lurking doubt'. It was for the French herald to name the battle, which he called Agincourt. John Keegan, *The Face of Battle*, Jonathan Cape, London, 1976, p. 112.

[3] The third Court of Appeal thought that if the credibility of Matthews was in doubt, the conviction could not be saved by the rest of the evidence. (Transcript p. 11E.) The fourth Court

Queen's evidence in the hands of a police officer who was not above suspicion. This is a question for three appellate judges who will have known of angels in the witness-box later proved to be perjurers, as well as of devils who have on rare occasions told the truth. To give to Matthews as the chief witness on one side an opportunity of exhibiting to them his persuasive quality was not only unnecessary since it could be taken for granted, but might, especially since a similar opportunity to carry conviction to the ears and eyes of the same judges was not given to the accused, distort the balance. If in fact it does not distort it, it will appear to do so. It would be difficult for a court to say: 'We observed him to be truthful but it is unsafe for us to act upon the truth'.

It seems to me that even those judges who are in favour of extending the domain of the judges over the facts must accept that the position which has now been reached is not a satisfactory one. Instead of the re-trial by jury for which Parliament provided in 1964, there is an imperfect re-trial by judges, in which the normal appellate review has been swallowed up. This has happened because the House of Lords, sitting judicially, is not, as it has often itself emphasized, the right body to effect reforms of this magnitude; they need more detailed planning than can be given in speeches whose function it is to state the reasons for a decision in a particular case. But, one may ask, in principle, and if one could get rid of the imperfections, is there anything wrong with the idea of allowing fresh evidence cases to be decided by judges? Fresh evidence cases are not easy to handle and the accused cannot be given all the advantages that he has when first he is charged. He does not then have to submit his proposed defence to the scrutiny of a judge who will decide whether or not his witnesses are capable of belief and, if they are, whether what they have to say is likely to be influential. Yet everyone will admit that in fresh evidence cases there must be a preliminary test of this sort; a convicted person cannot be allowed to re-open his case simply by stating that he has something to add. If there is a preliminary test, it must be the judges who administer it. If they are entrusted with the preliminary test, might they not be entrusted with the whole thing? Would it be wrong for us to say to a petitioner with fresh evidence: 'You have had your chance before a jury: you have used up the right which the constitution gives you: the best we can offer you now—and it is as much as you would get anyway in most countries—is a trial by three judges'? In other words, trial by jury is the soft option which can be had once but not twice.

said that while their decision depended on the veracity of Matthews, there was some supporting evidence. (Transcript pp. 32C and 42G.)

If such a proposal had been made to Parliament in 1968 I wonder how it would have been received. Many would have opposed it in principle. We should also have pressed some practical points. Ought we not, we should have asked, to take much greater care than we do to search for all the evidence before the trial, even if it means some sacrifice of speed and some modification of the adversary system? What proposals are there for a form of trial that will improve upon the hybrid procedures used in the *Stafford* and *Cooper* cases? Why is it assumed apparently that a new trial cannot be ordered if more than two or three years have elapsed; is this just an arbitrary assumption or is it based on a proper study of re-trial processes in other countries? If in Cooper's case witnesses could be heard by the second, third, and fourth Courts of Appeal four, six, and seven years respectively after the event, why could they not also be heard by a jury? Prosecutions are not stifled because the witnesses have to speak of events which occurred seven years before; such prosecutions are rare, but so are re-trials with fresh evidence.

I do not think that in 1964 Parliament would have taken kindly to a trial by judges alone in fresh evidence cases. The Act of 1964 was based on the Tucker Report,[1] which was clear that the new trial must be by jury; Lord Dilhorne said the same when he spoke on the second reading of the bill.[2] The Donovan Report said that the Court of Appeal could not re-try cases.[3] What to me is beyond question objectionable is that the courts have un-obtrusively effected a constitutional change which Parliament has not even been asked to consider. On the authority of *Stafford* v. *D.P.P.* it is now for the judges to say whether evidence leaves a reasonable doubt, and, if *R.* v. *Cooper and McMahon* is right, to say also whether a witness is speaking the truth. Blackstone, thou should'st be living at this hour.

So that the liberties of England cannot but subsist so long as this Palladium remains sacred and inviolate; not only from all open attacks (which none will be so hardy as to make), but also from all secret machinations, which may sap and undermine it.... Though begun in trifles, the precedent may gradually increase and spread, to the utter disuse of juries in questions of the most momentous concern.[4]

The open attack, if anyone had had the hardihood to make it, would have left me less unhappy. If Parliament decreed that re-trials should be by judge alone, there would be nothing worse to fear. But when judges are seemingly indifferent to whether a jury has heard all the evidence or not, when they act as if all that matters is that they alone should be satisfied of the safety

[1] (1954) Cmd. 9150 para. 30.
[3] (1965) Cmnd. 2755 para. 140.
[2] Hansard H.L. vol. 254 c. 523.
[4] *Commentaries*, Book IV, pp. 349–50.

of the conviction, when they declare that if they have no doubt then neither should a jury, is there not then the sapping and the undermining of which Blackstone wrote? Is it fanciful to fear a time when a verdict, though doubtless tradition will keep it as a ticket to imprisonment, is no more than the certificate by a jury that the judge who summed up to them told them that he had no reasonable doubt?

We may avoid such a catastrophe if we perceive clearly where we have got to and how we got there.

At the beginning of this century the common law judges sincerely believed in the virtues of the jury. They appreciated that some cases were unsuited to trial by jury. But they believed that in the ordinary civil case (of which the majority were then still being tried by jury) and in all criminal cases the verdict of a jury gave to the litigants and to the public at large a greater degree of satisfaction than their own judgments could give. I have shown how this belief was reflected in their attitude to the Criminal Appeal Act of 1907. The new criminal appeal judges disliked intensely the idea of substituting their own conclusions for the verdict of a jury and interpreted the Act so as to avoid it. On questions of fact the jury remained supreme and alone. The amendment of 1966 formally declared the end of the sole supremacy and at the same time offered the temptation to the judges to spread their wings. It was the words 'safe and satisfactory' that began it all.

To say this is not inconsistent with the statement that the amendment made no real difference to the text of the 1907 Act. The point is not what the text meant but what it was treated as meaning. Until the 1960s the text was never allowed openly to interfere with the conclusiveness of the verdict. It is true that a verdict could be set aside where there was no evidence to support it. But the court's power to do this was reconciled with the jury's exclusive domain over the facts by means of the fiction that whether or not there is evidence to support a verdict is a question of law. It is true also that the Court of Criminal Appeal did interfere with unsatisfactory verdicts, but they did so usually on the ground that the jury had not been properly directed. It was in 1966 that it was first recognized that judges as well as juries must on the facts be satisfied of guilt. The demarcation treaty enshrined in the *decantatum* was formally at an end.

In retrospect one can see that its doom was sealed in 1907. This is not because the words of the Act encompassed its doom. It would have been easy then to forecast that the words would be given a restricted interpretation and that such an interpretation, once given, would be hard to dislodge. It was not the words of the Act but the bare fact that a verdict became appealable which made the end inevitable. For when it involves a matter of life or liberty an appellate court will not give satisfaction if its power to do justice over the whole of the case is circumscribed.[1]

The ending of the *decantatum* deposed the jury as monarch of the facts and created a diarchy. Diarchy is an unstable form of government and sooner or later one of the two rulers tries to get the upper hand. Then the battle of propaganda begins. If three judges have looked thoroughly into the facts and are satisfied of guilt, what more do you want? What is now the use in the amended section of the second and third grounds of appeal, i.e. the error of law and the material irregularity: if the judges are satisfied of guilt, why should errors or irregularities matter? What is now the point of the proviso?

This is how the amendment led to the decision in *Stafford* v. *D.P.P.* It played a dual role. It occasioned the decision because it was the change in wording that was the lever used to upset the old law. But it was also the inspiration of the decision itself. The law lords took it for granted that if on the whole of the evidence, old and new, they were satisfied of guilt, the fact that on that evidence there was no verdict simply did not matter. The consequence of this decision, unless checked on the familiar ground that logic in law is not exact, cannot be limited to particular categories. The presumption of common thinking by judges and juries about fresh evidence will inevitably be extended to cover all evidence.

The continued existence of the jury within the framework now created by *Stafford* v. *D.P.P.* depends upon whether some function can be found for it which of its nature cannot be discharged by judges. If there is no such function, the jury will atrophy. Not of course immediately: legal institutions do not just vanish. The reduction of the civil jury to its present state, where its use is confined to an annual handful of unusual cases, began in 1854 with the Common Law Procedure Act of that year (one of those trifles of which Blackstone wrote, comparable to the present trifling with fresh evidence) and concluded with the sentence of restriction passed by *Ward* v. *James*[2] in 1965. The reduction of a venerable institution has to be spread over three or four generations so that each may grow up without the attachments of its forerunner.

So there is no need to fear the immediate demise of the jury. On the con-

---

[1] Thus the House of Lords, while it cannot entertain an appeal unless a point of law is certified, once a certificate is granted will take possession of the whole case.

[2] [1966] 2 Q.B. 273.

trary, the desirability of calming the traditionalists is likely to stimulate a search for a function for it which can be reconciled with *Stafford* v. *D.P.P.* If, as can plausibly be argued, the scope of that authority is limited to cases of inference and evaluation, it will leave something for a jury to do which could be hailed as significant. The function has recently been expressed by Lord Chief Justice Widgery as follows:

It is for the jury in each case to decide which witnesses should be believed. On matters of credibility this Court will only interfere in three circumstances: first, if the jury has been misdirected as to how to assess the evidence; secondly, if there has been no direction at all when there should have been one; and thirdly, if on the whole of the evidence the jury must have taken a perverse view of a witness but this is rare.[1]

If this line is adopted, *R.* v. *Cooper and McMahon*, which has not been reported, can either be forgotten or sent to limbo as a wholly exceptional case decided in wholly exceptional circumstances, and any future cases where the new testimony is in conflict with the old can be sent to a jury for re-trial.

This will be a sign that the jury has another half-century or so of life to be spent in the sort of comfortable reservation which conquerors, bringing with them a new civilization, assign to the natives whom they are displacing. It is true that many people believe that juries are better judges of truthfulness in a witness than are judges themselves. But there is not enough difference in this to make it worth while to preserve juries solely for this purpose. Moreover, the difference is likely to be diminished as psychology brings to light more sophisticated methods of determining truthfulness and reliability than we have at present. Finally, it is not practicable to divide fact-finding between two tribunals, one of which speaks only through a verdict. The jury cannot in a verdict say which witnesses they believe or which parts of their evidence. Even if they were told not to bother about a verdict but just to state what they believed and what they did not, this is not a task that they could discharge with unanimity. It would soon be found preferable to give the job to a judge who can state exactly what evidence he believes and why. In fact the rule stated by the Chief Justice is, if one reads the references to misdirection as applicable to a judge directing or misdirecting himself, and if one finds a suitable replacement for the word 'perverse', which is not officially applicable to judges, the same as that which prescribes the way in which an appellate court should treat the findings of a trial judge based on the demeanour of the witness; the Chief Justice does not allow the jury any greater immunity than is allowed to the judge.

[1] *R.* v. *Turnbull* [1977] 1 Q.B. 231D.

In my opinion there is only one really great function which a jury can discharge and which a judge cannot, and that is, as I have now said so often, the application of a popular instead of a professional standard. To do that they must have charge of the whole crime, as Erskine put it, not of the facts only, and certainly not only over the selection of the witnesses to be believed. They must have control of the verdict. If they lose that, they lose their *raison d'être*.

There are two reasons why they should retain it. The first is for the sake of freedom. A jury cannot fight tyranny outside the law, but it ensures that within the law liberty cannot be crushed. It was the political conditions in the eighteenth century that gave to men like Erskine their devotion to trial by jury and their suspicions of judges. We are right to ask ourselves whether we still need to man eighteenth-century ramparts. But if the twentieth century is not the eighteenth, neither will the twenty-second century be the twentieth. We must listen to our fears as well as to our hopes, knowing that there is only one thing certain and that is that if we lose the jury in the twentieth century we shall not be given it back in the twenty-second. If allowed to crumble, it can never be rebuilt.

The other reason is for the sake of contentment. People who before were content to be governed are now demanding a greater say in the management of their affairs. Through the jury the governed have a voice not only in the making of the laws which govern them but in their application. It is good for a nation when its people feel that in the gravest matters justice belongs in part to them.

6

The Judge and Case Law

I TAKE as my text for this lecture a dictum by Lord Widgery in *R*. v. *Turnbull* in 1976.[1]

Case law of this kind is likely to be a fetter on the administration of justice when much depends upon the quality of the evidence in each case. Quality is what matters in the end.

But it is case law that makes up the common law, is it not? And are not all British students brought up to believe that the common law is vastly to be preferred to those codes with which other legal systems fetter their judges? And is not the common law made by the judges themselves? So is it not a great shock to read of a Lord Chief Justice of England, speaking for a court of appeal of five, and saying, as it seems, that the common law fetters the administration of justice?

Let us begin by examining what it is that constitutes modern case law. Historically, it is made quite differently from the Continental code. The code precedes judgments; the common law follows them. The code articulates in chapters, sections, and paragraphs the rules in accordance with which judgments are given. The common law on the other hand is inarticulate until it is expressed in a judgment. Where the code governs, it is the judge's duty to ascertain the law from the words which the code uses. Where the common law governs, the judge, in what is now the forgotten past, decided the case in accordance with morality and custom and later judges followed his decision. They did not do so by construing the words of his judgment. They looked for the reason which had made him decide the case the way he did, the *ratio decidendi* as it came to be called. Thus it was the principle of the case, not the words, which went into the common law. So historically the common law is much less fettering than a code. Case law does still create

[1] [1977] Q.B. 224 at 231A.

new principles, but only very rarely. The bulk of English law is now enacted by Parliament in the form of statutes. Sometimes the statute is a codification of the old common law on the subject. The common law does not now reach out into new fields, and even in the old fields it tends more and more to leave new husbandry to Parliament. But the judges have to apply the law to particular cases and application has often to be helped out by development. Modern case law is the development of principle which results from application.

In this respect it is not very different from case law in other systems. To illustrate this, I shall compare it with a 'betwixt and between' system with which I am familiar. This is the system of law which governs the conditions of employment of the international civil service. I call it 'betwixt and between' because the law is partly codified and partly at large. International government is conducted by bodies such as U.N.O., the I.L.O., the F.A.O. and so on, the O always standing for Organization. Each Organization has its own Constitution and Rules and also, though they all follow the same pattern, its own Staff Regulations. These are by our standards extremely elaborate providing not only for appointment, rates of pay, pension rights, disciplinary measures, and so on, but also for classification of posts, promotions and transfers, and working conditions generally. This is the codified part. But each official has also a contract of employment; this is interpreted and applied according to principles of contract law which the judges of the two tribunals (there are for historical reasons two tribunals and an Organization makes its own choice of the one to which it adheres), who are of different nationalities, take to be generally acceptable. This may be called the common law, because it is uncodified. It is not, however, drawn especially from the substance of the English common law. The procedural law of the tribunals, on the other hand, is taken from European administrative law.

In the last thirty years these tribunals have produced a small corpus of law. The one on which I serve has now given between 300 and 400 judgments. They are all reasoned judgments, as is required by our Statute, but in comparison with an English judgment they are brief. There have been studies both in French and in English, the two languages of the tribunals, commenting on the jurisprudence that is emerging; and a digest of cases is being prepared. This is the way in which case law begins, stemming from the desire of practitioners to learn how best to present their cases.

The case law of these tribunals differs in two respects—apart from size, of course—from case law as we know it in England. The more important of the two is that it is much looser. The tightness and coherence of English case law is to be explained by its origins. A typical English judgment today is an exegesis either of a section of a statute or of a principle of the common law which age has made almost immutable; there is now little difference between a decision applying such a principle and one applying the section of a code. But originally an English judgment was not just an exposition of the law, it *was* the law itself, the very fabric. It was formulated as a rule— the rule in Shelley's case and so on—and judges had to obey it just as they would have to obey a code. 'Authorities established', said Lord Chancellor Hardwicke in 1754, 'are so many laws.'[1] This is the doctrine of precedent. Decisions of a superior court are binding. Other decisions have what is called 'persuasive authority' and the same status is conferred on *obiter dicta*, i.e. passages in the judgments outside the *ratio decidendi*, and on the great works of learned authors.

The chief distinction between English and foreign case law, or jurisprudence as it is usually called on the Continent, is that the latter is never more than persuasive. In the I.L.O. tribunal our previous decisions are frequently cited in the arguments addressed to us. It is supposed, quite rightly, that we wish to be consistent; indeed, whether they are cited or not, we do look back at earlier decisions. But the fetters hang looser than they do in England. An English judge must in his judgment deal with every case which is cited to him as a binding precedent and say whether he follows or distinguishes it. Indeed he does not usually differentiate between the binding and the persuasive and he is much more concerned to obtain support from authority than he is to evade it. So in the discursive style that is usual in the English judgment, the introductory 'I must now deal with the cases' presages a lengthy and sometimes tedious meander.

In the I.L.O. tribunal, and I imagine in foreign courts generally, there is nothing like that. Authorities are digested in silence and unmentioned in the judgment. In some ways this is an inconvenience. A rule of general import—for example, the rule enumerating the circumstances in which the tribunal will interfere with an act of administrative discretion—can never be referred to with brevity, as the rule in Smith's case. It must be set out each time, albeit in the selfsame words. The judge cannot express himself as starting from what Lord Jones said in Robinson's case. It has, however, the advantage, particularly for laymen, that the judgment is self-contained.

The secondary distinction between English and foreign case law is in the manner of its making. In the I.L.O. tribunal it emerges almost ready-made from the judges' pens. The judgment is contained in a short document made available to anyone interested. All that is necessary to make it fit for use is the digest, and ultimately perhaps the textbook. The digest is especially

[1] *Ellis* v. *Smith*, 1 Ves. Jun. at 17.

needed since there is no clue in the judgment itself to other decisions on similar points. In this process there is no call for the services of that most important functionary in English case law, the law reporter.

In England until little more than a century ago law reporting was a private venture; even now it is only semi-official. When a judgment was delivered extempore—as most are still, even in the Court of Appeal—the reporter was the only channel through which it could reach the legal public. There is now a transcript made of most judgments in the High Court as they are delivered, but it is still the reporters, individually or collectively, who decide what is to go into the law reports.

So in England case law is not something which is made by judges alone. Judges spin and others weave. Each time a judge gives a reasoned judgment he spins a thread. It is for the law reporters to decide in the first instance whether the thread can be woven into the law. They have a vital and under-estimated part to play in the making of law, for it is their reports which provide the material for the textbooks and in the lower courts it is the law in the textbooks that is usually applied.

But if it is true to say that an unreported judge makes no law, it is also true to say that a reported judge may make law whether he wants to or not. The only way in which he can make quite sure that one of his decisions does not get used as a precedent is to give no reasons for it. It is the *ratio decidendi* that makes the precedent; a case without a *ratio* is as harmless as a wasp without a sting; it can only buzz. Lists of cases which have been decided one way followed by lists of those decided the other way are like lists of irregular verbs: they make no grammar.

I turn now to consider the uses of case law. First, it achieves the uniformity in judicial decisions which society demands; otherwise, as Lord Camden said, 'each judge would have a distinct tribunal in his own breast, the decisions of which would be as irregular and uncertain and various as the minds and tempers of mankind'.[1] Secondly, since it is manufactured in the higher reaches of the judiciary, it provides rules for the rank and file, who in the judiciary itself are numerous (on 1 January 1975 there were 266 Circuit Judges and 338 Recorders)[2] and stretch down to the deputy-recorder and the clerk to the justices. It is easy to tell three lords justices, who can confer and gather strength from each other, to do justice off their own bat; but

---

[1] *Donaldson* v. *Beckett* (1774) 2 Brown 129; quoted in C. H. S. Fifoot, *Lord Mansfield*, Oxford University Press, Oxford, 1936, p. 226.
[2] Figures given by Lord Justice James, who discussed also the volume of work; Brian W. Harvey (ed.), *The Lawyer and Justice*, Sweet & Maxwell, London, 1978, p. 172.

a situation which would for a lord justice hold all the pleasures of intellectual freedom, might for the young deputy-recorder create a plight. Outside the judicial world there is the administrative. There are solicitors who have to decide whether or not to prosecute and policemen whether or not to act. The needs of all these have now to be met by occasional pronouncements described as 'offering guidance'. The description sounds permissive. But those who do not wear fetters themselves sometimes find them useful for others; so 'a failure to follow these guide-lines is likely to result in a conviction being quashed'.[1]

Thirdly, case law, being made out of the reasons which judges give in their judgments, necessarily contains the judiciary's account to the nation of the way in which they are using their vast powers. It makes possible criticism, amendment, or curtailment. It is more than an account; it is also, because of the doctrine of precedent, a broad description of the way in which, unless Parliament intervenes, the judges intend to continue using their powers. Respect for precedent is exacted, not only to keep the law in good shape, but primarily as a safeguard against arbitrary and autocratic decision-making.[2]

Fourthly, case law is a source of judicial strength. For a judge to decide fairly and convincingly every case that comes before him in the light only of his own sense of justice, he would have to be a superman. I doubt if there have ever been more than a handful of men on the Bench who could do it, though doubtless there are slightly more who think that they could. Without the law a judge would be an autocrat, a role in which he should be unhappy. While every judge must be ready to act on his own and with no other guide than his own sense of justice, judges are not by nature autocratic and need the protection and support of the law.

What is it then that makes case law 'fettering'? Not, surely, the fact that it is promulgated by the courts themselves rather than by the legislator. Many of our criminal statutes are not much more than the codification of the common law and no one would suggest that by the act of codification fetters are struck off. The objection must, I think, be based on the supposition that the legislature puts into the statute or the code all that is necessary and anything that it omits should be left to the discretion of the judge or judges concerned with each particular case.

I believe on the contrary that between the territory which is best regulated by precise statutory language and the territory which is best left to the sense

[1] [1977] Q.B. at 231B.
[2] Sixteen years ago (in *Samples of Lawmaking*, Oxford University Press, London, 1962, p. 20) I made the point that the doctrine of precedent was 'one of the pillars of the constitution; without it a man's future would be at the mercy of the individual mind uncontrolled by due process of law'.

of justice of the individual judge, there is an area fit for occupation by a controlled discretion. It is not desirable to move straight out of obedience to statute into freedom for every judge to 'do his own thing'. There is room in between for a rule, not absolute but general. This is the way in which in all walks of life the theoretical is merged with the practical: 'as a general rule', the man on the spot will say, 'I do it this way, but there are cases in which I use my discretion.'

This intermediate area can be covered either by statute law or by case law. It is common enough to find it filled by statute when our legislators are feeling either meticulous or a little distrustful of the judiciary. The control may be severe, as when a judge is enjoined not to pass a sentence of imprisonment on certain categories of offender unless he is satisfied that the circumstances of the case leave him with no alternative. Or it may be very light, as when he is given what appears to be a complete discretion but told that when he is exercising it he must have regard to this, that, or the other factor. In between there are numerous ways in which statute can lay down a general rule.

But the traditional way of filling the intermediate area is with case law. When new fields are being opened up, e.g. when new crimes are being created, the essential purpose of a statute is to lay down the new principles. The lawmakers need concern themselves with detail only to the extent that they wish to make sure that the principles will be applied in the way they want. But someone has to see, not only that the statute is applied in a way that carries out its purpose, but also that the law which results from its development is coherent. This is work for judges. They are the architects of case law and they should construct it to achieve the objects I have listed— especially uniformity, clarity, and accountability.

There are two advantages that case law has over statute in the development of a statutory purpose. First, the development need not be minutely planned in advance; when it comes, it can be shaped to meet real problems that have arisen and not possible problems forecasted. Second, it is elastic, not having to be exactly expressed in words. There is on the other hand the disadvantage from the lawmakers' point of view that the judges may not develop the statutory purpose in the way that they hoped and expected. This is the importance of what I have called accountability, constitutionally the most significant function of case law. If Parliament knows just what is going on, it can, if it disapproves the trend, interfere. As it can also, of course, interfere for the purpose of clarification, for elasticity sometimes leads to conflicting decisions which end up in a muddle. But that case law is looser and therefore less fettering than statute seems to me to be beyond dispute.

So Lord Widgery is not, I think, asking for planned development to be put into the statute rather than into the cases; what he would like to see is no formal development at all; what appeals to him is the free hand to the man in charge of the case or, if not to him, to the appellate court when the case reaches it. To understand the nature of the appeal I must say something about the nature of the case in which the dictum was made and, before that and more generally, about authority and precedent in the criminal law.

In English civil law there has always been an abundance of case law and I do not know of anybody who has spoken disparagingly of it in general. The appellate courts are the natural sources of case law and one of the innovations of the Judicature Act 1875 was the creation of an appellate court to cover the whole of the civil law and to be manned by regular appellate judges, the Master of the Rolls and the lords justices. Not every judge has what may be called an appellate outlook.

There is all the difference in the world between disposing of a case as though it were a discreet instance and recognizing it as part of the process of judgment, taking its place in relation to what went before and further cutting the channel for what is to come.[1]

All judges should of course be primarily concerned with the case they are deciding. But while some have an eye on the effect of their decision on the law in general, others prefer to stick to the book and decide the case in accordance with precedent or its own facts, anxious that there should be no other and perhaps dangerous emanations arising from it. It is the former class that naturally levitates to the courts of appeal.

Between 1875 and 1907, a period which was very prolific of precedent in civil cases, there was no regular court of criminal appeal.[2] When this was created, it sat for a day or two in the week; and apart from the Lord Chief Justice, who presided over it when not otherwise engaged, there were no regular members. The channel from it to the House of Lords was so severely filtered that very little got through. The would-be appellant required the certificate of the Attorney-General that the decision of the Court of Criminal

---

[1] Justice Frankfurter in *Irvine* v. *California* (1954) 347 U.S. at 147.

[2] There was always a way—for example by a motion to arrest judgment—of getting before the whole court a point of law which had been decided by a single judge. Statutory provision was made for it in the Crown Cases Act 1848. But 'point of law' was narrowly interpreted. It did not, for example, extend to the propriety of allowing the uncorroborated evidence of an accomplice to go to the jury; *R*. v. *Stubbs* (1855) Dears 555. The facts raising the point had to be stated briefly—the annexing of shorthand notes of evidence was disapproved in *R*. v. *Gray* (1903) 68 J.P. 40—and the court would not consider any point other than the one reserved for it by the judge stating the case; *R*. v. *Tyree* (1869) L.R. 1 C.C.R. 177.

Appeal involved a point of law of exceptional public importance and that it was desirable in the public interest that a further appeal should be brought.[1] The best appellate minds in the common law were naturally in the House of Lords and the Court of Appeal, so the criminal law saw very little of them.

This—the fact that its craftsmen were not the most talented and moreover had no great affection for what they were producing—is the chief of several factors which have combined to make criminal case law the starved relation of the civil. Case law has to be very skilfully made and maintained if its great asset, its elasticity, is to be properly used. The danger is that a precedent, once created, will be treated as if it was as impregnable to a judge as is statute law. It gets forgotten that a judge-made rule should always be designed to fit the circumstances. The circumstances are general and not special; the latter must be left for the trial judge. They are expected to last for some time, else there would be no place for a general rule, but they are not expected to last for ever. An example, which I have given before,[2] taken from the civil law, is that of the c.i.f. contract. This was designed by commercial lawyers to effectuate trading custom. In the days of sail, when voyages were long and goods exported from one country to another could be out of circulation for weeks, it was not unreasonable to ask the buyer to pay before he got the goods provided he was given documentary proof that they had been consigned to him at a named port, that the freight had been paid, and that they had been insured for the voyage. The document which satisfied the last of these requirements was the policy of insurance. At the start shippers insured cargo separately for each voyage. Then it became the custom for shippers on a large scale to take out a master policy against which they made declarations of named cargo for named voyages and received in return a certificate or letter of insurance. Of course if a statute calls for a policy, it may be difficult for a court to hold that the demand is satisfied by the tender of its commercial equivalent in the form of a certificate. Under case law there should have been no such difficulty, but there was.

There is a comparable example of obtuseness in the criminal law. It is an ancient common law rule that a reasonable but erroneous belief in the death of a spouse is a good defence to a charge of bigamy. The Court of Criminal Appeal refused to admit as a defence a like belief in the validity

---

[1] Criminal Appeal Act 1907 s. 1(6).

[2] *Samples of Lawmaking*, pp. 48–50. By contrast, in *Nordenfelt* [1894] A.C. 535 the House of Lords held that the established rule that a covenant in restraint of trade must not be world-wide must yield to the growth and development of world trade.

of a decree of divorce. This is throwing away all the advantage that case law has over statute. 'Death' in a statute cannot be interpreted to include 'divorce', but case law could surely recognize that, since both events end the legal marriage, they are for the purposes of bigamy just the same.

One of the commonest sources in modern times of a stream of case law is the conferment on the courts of a new statutory power in general terms. In its usual form it is a wide discretionary power and the only clue which the legislature gives as to when or how it should be exercised is expressed in some such encompassing phrase as 'if the interest of justice so requires'. If Parliament is to be credited with any knowledge of human nature, it does not seriously intend that individual judges should pursue the interests of justice, each in his own way. Then the stretch between the timid and the bold would cover results so different as to cause injustices. What are wanted are general rules for standard cases with the proviso that they can be departed from in exceptional circumstances.

The judiciary is often, and I think justifiably, criticized for its lack of eagerness to explore such new domains. Certainly there is little fervour when the statute is planting innovations in the judges' own garden of legal pro- cedure. Then the judicial response is usually negative. The judges cannot affront Parliament by saying that they will never exercise the new power in any circumstances, but they do the next best thing by saying that it should be exercised only in exceptional circumstances. Thereafter the formulation of one or two exceptional categories seems to exhaust their creative power; unless it is revived by a new statute, nothing more gets done.

I have already recorded[1] the judicial reaction in 1907 to the idea of crimi- nal appeal in general and fresh evidence in particular. The reaction to the latter illustrates what I have just been saying. S. 9 of the Criminal Appeal Act 1907 gave the court power to admit fresh evidence whenever 'they think it necessary or expedient in the interests of justice'. I have not found any report of its use before 1920. In 1925 the court laid it down that it should be used only in very special circumstances.[2] In 1961 the court formulated what special circumstances were.[3] Thereafter it left any modification to Par- liament, which made one in 1966.[4]

This reluctance on the part of criminal judges to make case law goes back a long way. At the root of it there is, I think, the idea that criminal justice ought to be made to measure. One of the speakers in the Commons debate on the 1966 bill, Mr. Petre Crowder, an eminent barrister, said that, if he had his way, the bill would have but one clause saying 'the Court shall have

---

[1] See pp. 111–14.   [2] R. v. Thorne, 18 Cr. App. R. 186.
[3] R. v. Parks, 46 Cr. App. R. 29.   [4] Now in the Criminal Appeal Act 1968 s. 23.

complete power to deal with any appeal as it thinks fit, having regard to all the circumstances of the case'.[1] He said in parenthesis that he was never likely to have his own way. Perhaps he was being too pessimistic. When we come to examine *R. v. Turnbull*, we shall find that in the intervening decade the judges have made considerable strides towards this Utopia; they cannot resist the commands of statute but at least they can rid themselves of self-imposed restraints. Lord Justice Lawton too, writing extra-judicially, has contrasted the comparative freedom in our criminal appeals with the 'tyranny of precedent under which American judges work'.[2]

There is, however, the countervailing consideration that the criminal law should be clear, comprehensive, and precise. These last-named virtues have frequently been forced upon the judiciary from outside. Thus the celebrated Judges' Rules, which govern the use of admissions made to the police by an accused and which are akin to case law in that they are judge-made, originated in response to a demand by the police that the judges should clear up the confusion caused by some judges refusing to admit confessions which had not been preceded by a caution and others saying that a caution was unnecessary. Likewise, the identification parade, which is now regarded as an almost essential procedural step in any case in which identity is in dispute, was evolved by the police. True, it had judicial encouragement, but the first general set of regulations, issued after the Beck case,[3] was in the form of instructions to the police approved by the Home Secretary. They are still in the form of a Home Office Circular 'prepared in consultation with the Lord Chief Justice'.[4] If a question arises at the trial as to whether a parade was properly conducted, the judges are virtually in the position of having to decide it in accordance with a code for which they are only in part responsible.

Doubtless it is the judicial unwillingness to make any case law at all which accounts for the sloppiness with which it is made, when it is. What I have said about fresh evidence as a ground of appeal serves as an example: since obviously it must be fitted in somewhere, why bother to find it a niche?[5] Discussion of general principle is not encouraged. Cases relating to *mens rea* as an element in crime live in a shambles from which academic writers try to rescue them. It was not until the publication in 1953 of Professor Glanville Williams's work on 'The General Part'[6] that there was any textbook which got below the surface of the criminal law.

[1] Hansard H.C. vol. 731 c. 1131.
[2] (1973) 89 L.Q.R., at pp. 565–6.   [3] See p. 188.
[4] *Identification Report*, p. 158.   [5] cf. p. 150.
[6] *Criminal Law, The General Part*, Stevens, London, 1953. The sub-title is the description given by Continental lawyers to the general principles of a subject.

The old Court of Criminal Appeal had the air of a place where regimental officers foregathered and staff wallahs were not highly thought of. Unless the change over to lords justices and the Court of Appeal proper was intended to be only cosmetic,[1] one must suppose that an object was to introduce a lawmaking element into the determination of criminal appeals. Yet, if it was, it has failed. The atmosphere of the orderly-room has proved too potent for the newcomers. Most new points are tersely rejected, tersely because any elaboration might disclose a reason which ill-natured persons might try to turn into a *ratio decidendi*. An unfriendly law reporter might publish it; hey presto, there is a precedent. 'Wholly exceptional' is the catchword: 'it could only be in a most exceptional case that we should exercise this power' (this power being any power that has not been exercised before) 'and this is not an exceptional case:' finis. Occasionally, the case *is* found to be 'wholly exceptional' and then the power is exercised with as strong an intimation as possible that no one must expect that it will ever be exercised again. There are of course cases in which it is genuinely impossible to say more than that on the facts the conviction is safe or unsafe as the case may be. But there are also cases in which to abstain from giving a reason in the judgment is to exhibit an attitude of *sic volo, sic jubeo*, which is very unbecoming in a court of justice. Witness the reception given by the third and fourth Courts of Appeal[2] to the application to recall Mr. Matthews for cross-examination. This was a novel application. The reasons for its acceptance or rejection would inevitably assist practitioners in gauging the prospects of similar applications in the future. But would there not for that very reason be a danger that the case might be reported and used as a precedent? Both Courts avoided this by the use of the phrase 'wholly exceptional'. The third Court doubted, without pressing the doubt to the point of any analysis of the language of the Act, whether the Act would allow such a thing at all. The Act permits the Court to 'order any witness', whether or not he had been called at the trial, 'to attend for examination'. So it could only be by restricting 'examination' to examination-in-chief—an almost impossibly narrow interpretation when there is nothing in the context to support the restriction—that the power could be denied. But anyway, the Court said, if there were such a power, it should be used only in 'a wholly exceptional case'. Why? The Act says nothing about exceptional cases; it says that the power may be exercised if 'expedient in the interests of justice'. In the case of a vital witness whose credibility must on any view be regarded as marginal when a fact comes to light which suggests that he must either have been lying or mistaken, how can it be against the interests of justice to ask for his explanation? The Court, however, said no more than that the case with which it was dealing was not an exceptional case. They gave no reasons. If they had, they might have given a clue to the nature of the exception, which might even have led to a description of it being put into words and so resulted in 'the build-up of case law',[1] which, as Lord Widgery was to say in *R*. v. *Turnbull*, was the thing to be avoided.

In the fourth appeal the recall of Mr. Matthews was allowed. The Court considered that it had power to do so under the Act. But it was taking what it described as 'a wholly exceptional course in a wholly exceptional case'. The present case, the Court said, was 'plainly wholly exceptional, particularly for the reason that this is the first occasion upon which the Secretary of State has ordered a second reference to this Court'. Here at last is a reason, but one to baffle rather than to enlighten. If the recall is in the interests of justice, why does justice have to wait outside a court of law until a Secretary of State has blown his trumpet twice?

It is no longer possible to find out from the law reports what the Criminal Appeal Division is doing. This is not the fault of the law reporters. When a judgment contains little or no reasoning, it is difficult for a reporter to assess its significance. Fortunately, the transcript of every judgment is preserved and filed in the Registry.[2] On the civil side it is very unusual for a case to be cited which is not in the law reports. In *Stafford* v. *D.P.P.* in the House of Lords the list of authorities shows that out of thirty-six English cases, twelve were unreported.[3]

I now come to the case in 1976 in which the Lord Chief Justice made the dictum which I have taken as my text. *R*. v. *Turnbull* was preceded by a long history, beginning with the case of Adolf Beck. Beck was twice wrongly convicted, having been identified in 1896 by eleven witnesses and in 1904 by four. This miscarriage of justice was the goad which finally pricked Parliament into setting up the Court of Criminal Appeal. But no speedy solution was adopted for the problem of eye-witness identification.[4]

There is a well-established precedent for handling this type of situation

---

[1] [1977] Q.B. at 231A.
[2] In common with many practitioners I am enormously indebted to the Registrar, Master Thompson, and his assistants, who place their knowledge and experience at the disposal of any enquirer. The reader may have noted a number of unreported judgments, existing only in transcript, cited in the last chapter, which without such assistance I should never have found.
[3] [1974] A.C. 879.
[4] The material which follows is taken from the *Identification Report*, chapter 4. Specific references are given only for passages quoted.

in which appearances are deceptive and in consequence the reliability of the witness is exceptionally difficult to assess. This is the rule that the jury must be warned that it is dangerous to act on such evidence unless it is corroborated. A type of case in which a warning is required is that in which a charge of a sexual offence is made by a woman; these are sometimes due to sexual neuroses which can produce phantasies in which the woman half or even wholly believes. There are not as yet any satisfactory forensic methods for the detection of make-believe in an honest witness.

But the Court of Criminal Appeal was born and had died (or more correctly had been assumed into the heaven where dwell the lords justices) before the appellate judges were ready to apply this palliative to cases of eye-witness identification. They said it should be left to each judge to decide whether or not the jury should be warned and they offered him no criteria to help him in his decision. In 1912 a man on a charge of murder was identified by no less than seventeen witnesses, but fortunately was able to establish an irrefutable alibi. In 1928 Oscar Slater, after he had spent nineteen years in prison and after a public agitation in which many distinguished people joined, had his conviction for murder quashed; he had been identified by fourteen witnesses. Nevertheless, cases continued to be left to the jury as if they raised only a simple issue between the identifier and the accused as to which was telling the truth. A submission that in such cases a warning should be given was rejected by the Court of Criminal Appeal in 1956. Six years later in 1962 the Supreme Court of the Republic of Ireland held that a warning should be given; the House of Lords, however, in a case from Northern Ireland indicated that it was better to leave such matters to 'the discerning guidance'[1] of the trial judge. In 1966 the Donovan Committee recommended the widening of the powers of the Court of Appeal to quash convictions which they thought to be unsafe and unsatisfactory; the primary reason they gave for this was the danger of unsafe convictions in cases of disputed identity. In 1972 the Criminal Law Revision Committee under the chairmanship of Lord Edmund-Davies recommended that a warning to the jury should be required by statute. Also in 1972 there was another much publicized case of disputed identity in which George Ince was charged with murder; fortunately the jury at the first trial disagreed and at the second acquitted, for subsequently another man was convicted of the murder. All this left the judiciary unmoved. In *R. v. Long* in 1973 the Court of Appeal once again refused to require the trial judge to give a warning. They did, however, certify the question as a point of law of public importance for the House of Lords to consider, but the House refused leave to appeal.

[1] ib. 4.47.

In 1974 two shattering cases of mistaken identity came to light within four weeks of each other. In the first of them Mr. Dougherty was convicted of shop-lifting, having been identified by two witnesses, at a time when he was on an excursion with some twenty other persons. The accidents and blunders which led to his conviction, and to his appeal from it being dismissed, are not relevant here. What is relevant is that it affords another example of a situation which needs a general rule but which the courts prefer to leave to discerning guidance. This is the situation created by what is called 'dock identification'. In it the identifier, when he is in the witness-box, is told to look around the court and asked if he sees anywhere the man he has come to identify. Naturally, unless the two figures are totally dissimilar in his mind, he identifies the man in the dock. This was the situation which the identification parade was designed to avoid. But it is no use providing for a parade if it is not going to be held. There is need for a general rule which makes an identification on parade an essential preliminary to identification in the dock. There must be exceptions to it, since there are situations in which the holding of a parade is unnecessary or impracticable. So what is needed is a general rule with exceptions. It is arguable that the exceptions should be left, undefined, to the trial judge's discretion. But that the judge should disallow a dock identification, when he is given no reason why a parade was not held, is a matter which I should have thought to be beyond debate. There is then nothing for him to exercise his discretion upon except the question whether dock identifications are desirable or not, and surely that is a matter for a general rule. For at least half a century, however, the courts have held that it is a matter for the discretion of the trial judge. In Mr. Dougherty's case there was no parade and no satisfactory reason given for not holding one. The trial judge permitted what turned out to be tantamount to a dock identification and the Court of Appeal said that this was a matter for his discretion.

After he had served most of his sentence in prison and on a reference back to the Court of Appeal by the Home Secretary, Mr. Dougherty got his alibi evidence before the Court and the prosecution threw up the sponge. Here was an opportunity to review the law and practice on a subject which the Lord Chief Justice was later to describe as 'perhaps the most serious chink in our armour'.[1] But in conformity with the policy of giving decisions without reasons the Court said no more than that the conviction was unsafe and that 'it disclosed a number of matters which we must look after in our own way and in our own time'.[2] This type of answer is more common in administrative than in judicial circles.

[1] ib. 4.21.   [2] ib. 2.60.

This was on 14 March 1974. On 5 April the Home Secretary discharged with the grant of a free pardon a Mr. Virag from the prison in which he had been for five years. As was conclusively proved in the subsequent inquiry, he had been wrongly identified by eight witnesses, four of them police officers, on six different occasions. The Home Secretary did me the honour of inviting me to be chairman of a committee which he set up on 1 May to consider the serious questions raised by these two cases about the law and procedure relating to identification.

The Committee's *Report* was published on 26 April 1976. Most of it was taken up with procedural questions, such as the conduct of identification parades, rather than the law. On the points with which this lecture is concerned, the *Report* made three recommendations. The Committee could not of course recommend the creation of case law; it was not within its province nor within that of the Home Secretary to advise the judges what to do, nor in the light of *R. v. Long* did there seem to be much likelihood that the judges would take any advice. So the recommendations had perforce to be for statutory enactment, though I for one would always have welcomed the use of case law instead. The first recommendation was for an absolute and unconditional rule that the jury should be directed or warned about the dangers of identification evidence. The second was for a general rule that the jury should not be allowed to convict on eye-witness evidence alone. This rule had to be general and not absolute because admittedly there would be exceptions, e.g. when the witness was identifying someone he knew well or who had been under frequent or prolonged observation. The Committee refused to codify a list of exceptions, holding that they were better left to be developed by case law; this was the case law whose introduction the Lord Chief Justice deplored. Thirdly, the Committee recommended that dock identifications should not be permitted save in circumstances in which the holding of a parade was impracticable or unnecessary, e.g. when the accused refused to attend or was already well known to the witness.

The Court of Appeal decided to forestall legislation by giving in July 1976 in three pending identification cases a comprehensive judgment laying down a new approach consisting of two sets of guide-lines. In the first the Court accepted at last the need for a warning and imposed the requirement in terms which make the description 'guide-line' sound rather mild. In the second the Court laid it down that cases in which the identification evidence was of poor quality should not, unless supported by other evidence, be left to the jury.

As to the first, for the moment I need say no more. As to the second, if it is true to say that to make law demands precision, it would appear to be equally true that to avoid making law demands obscurity. On the face of it what the Court is saying is only an unremarkable truism: it must be unsafe to convict on evidence of poor quality, whether it is evidence of identification or of any other sort. If the Court meant more than this, as I am sure that they must have done, one must search for a special meaning for 'quality'. Quality is not a word commonly used in legal language in relation to evidence. Reliability or weight are the expressions commonly used. Is 'quality' intended only to mean 'reliability'? In assessing reliability a jury is usually told to have regard to the reputation of the witness, his demeanour, the coherence and probability or otherwise of his story, and, where he is deposing to what he has seen, his opportunities for accurate observation, etc. This applies to evidence of every sort. The problem peculiar to evidence of visual identification is that this evidence, because of its type and not because of its quality, has a latent defect that may not be detected by the usual tests. The highly reputable, absolutely sincere, perfectly coherent, and apparently convincing witness may, as experience has quite often shown, be mistaken. Is then 'quality', when it is used in the judgment, referring to the character of a witness and to the way in which he gives his evidence, or to the nature of the evidence? The enquirer will find an indication both ways in the facts of the cases considered in the judgment. In one case the judgment refers to the quality as being 'meagre in the extreme' and follows this immediately with personal criticisms of a witness who 'had made up his mind'.[1] In another case the Court says:

It is conceded that Miss Kennedy in particular was an impressive witness. But the quality of the identification was not good.[2]

But I think that the better view, although it involves a rather artificial and restricted use of the word, is that quality refers only to the circumstances in which identification is made, and that the key sentence in the judgment is:

When, in the judgment of the trial judge, the quality of the identifying evidence is poor, as for example when it depends solely on a fleeting glance or on a longer observation made in difficult conditions, ... the judge should then withdraw the case from the jury and direct an acquittal unless there is other evidence which goes to support the correctness of the identification.[3]

This is the sentence on which trial judges are likely to fasten. They cannot really be expected to assess evidence as if it were a piece of cloth to be rubbed between finger and thumb and pronounced as shoddy or good stuff, and the results would vary widely if they did. They will take the two cate-

[1] [1977] Q.B. at 238B.   [2] ib. at 236C.   [3] ib. at 229H.

gories given as examples in the judgment, the 'fleeting glance' and 'the difficult conditions' (difficult in the ways suggested in the judgment, e.g. poor
lighting or obstructed view), and disallow such cases. The adventurous may
disallow some others, and so may the Court of Appeal. If the Court of Appeal
gives reasons for the disallowance and the case is reported, a third category
will be created. If the Court gives no reasons, there will be no addition to
the categories. But quite likely zealous counsel will with the aid of the
Registrar search among the transcripts for cases 'on all fours' with the one
he is going to argue.

In short, while the rule proposed by the Committee is a general rule that
unsupported evidence of identification should be left to the jury only in
exceptional circumstances, such as repeated and prolonged observation, the
Turnbull guide-lines will be operated as a general rule that such evidence
should be left to the jury unless the identification was only a fleeting glimpse
or was made under poor conditions. Recognition of familiar faces will be
treated as a special category common to both systems. The *Turnbull* rule
imposes a lighter burden on the prosecution; an unsupported case, instead
of being left to the jury as exceptional, will be left as one in which the evidence is not of poor quality. The object in both cases is the purely pragmatic
one of devising a test which will result in the acquittal of as many as possible
of the innocent and the conviction of as many as possible of the guilty. The
Turnbull judges, who embody collectively much greater experience than the
members of the Committee, may well be right in lightening the burden;
time will show. But there is nothing to be gained by veiling the inevitable
categorization with nebulous distinctions between good and bad quality,
unless—and to this I must return later—the Court of Appeal means to deliver
empty judgments amounting only to declarations of good or bad quality.

The *Turnbull* judgment incorporated some general reflections intended
to allay public disquiet about miscarriages of justice in identification cases.
It did not refer in this connection to the beneficial effect of the warning
to be given to the jury. The public, it seems, are to place their faith in the
judges 'released from the limitations which the Criminal Appeal Act 1907
and the case law based upon it had put upon the old Court of Criminal
Appeal'.

We do not hesitate to use our extended jurisdiction whenever the evidence in a case
justifies our doing so. In assessing a case, however, it is our duty to use our experience
of the administration of justice. In every division of this Court that experience is
likely to be extensive and helps us to detect the specious, the irrelevant and that which
is intended to deceive.[1]

[1] ib. at 231E.

To return now to the fetters of case law. All law is meant to restrain, and to restrain the rulers as well as the ruled. The description 'fettering' is a convenient way of saying that the restraint is excessive, but restraint there must be. As I have sought to demonstrate already,[1] without restraint the perfect judge, if he exists on earth, could do justice in a particular case, but unless he tried every case he could not do justice in general. That is one side of the coin. The obverse is when the judge has to restrain himself from doing justice in a particular case because he has to apply a law which does not truly fit the circumstances; this is when case law, or any other law, becomes fettering. It is quite easy in theory, though of course there will be difficulties in practice, to distinguish fettering law from necessary law. The principle is that whenever in the course of the application of the law there is found to be room for a subsidiary rule, then for the sake of uniformity there should be one. What can be ordered should be ordered: this is only the principle of law as opposed to anarchy, of order as opposed to chaos. There is room for a general rule whenever it is possible to define a category of cases which ought to be decided in the same way. If the category is large, the rule will be a major one; if it is small, the rule will be minor. It may be a category with exceptions and then each exception will form, as it were, a sub-category with its own definition or description. But as soon as you reach the point where you can envisage a number of cases which come within the description but which ought not to be treated in the same way, you must give up; to go on will be to impose fetters.

I regard case law as the best tool for the creation of categories of this sort. It is, however, a tool which can be and has been badly used. To the extent to which it has been badly used it is the fault of the judges themselves. To throw the tool away is a confession of failure. It is as if the judges as lawmakers were to say that since they cannot trust themselves to make good law, they must try to get on without any law at all.

To my mind English case law is subject to three main defects. First, though this is not, I suppose, what most of its critics like to complain of, it is not used when it ought to be. For an example of that I need only refer to what I have already said about identification evidence. The weakness in eye-witness evidence of this sort is inherent in the type; it does not depend on the particular case. It is simply that, as is known to all judges from their experience but may be unknown to juries because they have not the experience, identification evidence is not always what it seems. It has taken the judges at least three-quarters of a century to accept this fact.

The second defect is that rules are made absolute when they ought only

[1] See p. 84.

to be general; there should be no limit to the exceptions which can be created to the letter of every general rule, which is perhaps only another way of saying that it is the spirit and not the letter that should be applied.

The third defect is that a rule of case law, once made, is seldom adapted and never unmade. Of this also I have given examples. It may well have been the fear that a rule once made was there for ever that discouraged the courts from applying to identification evidence the rules already laid down for the evidence of accomplices and in sexual cases. No doubt the rule about accomplices was desirable when it was laid down in the eighteenth century, but for a long time past, the weakness of such evidence has been obvious to any jury.[1] There is, you may say, no harm in an unnecessary warning, but the danger is that it may be accidentally omitted and a safe conviction quashed in consequence. It may not be long before the ordinary juryman's and jurywoman's knowledge of sexual cases is sufficient to make a warning unnecessary there. Sooner or later the weakness of identification evidence will become common knowledge. But I cannot recall a single instance of an obsolete judge-made rule being abrogated by the judiciary.

There is much to criticize in English case law and in the way in which it has been and is still being made. It is not the charge of 'fettering' which I think to be objectionable; the fear that the Committee's proposals might have led to fetters is, in the light of the way in which the judiciary has handled case law, an understandable one. I would sympathize greatly with a proposal to soften its rigidities; I would even, if no other solvent was found, entertain a proposal to reduce its status to that which it holds in European law. What I disagree with is the implication in *R. v. Turnbull*, itself only a reflection of much that has gone before, that there is nothing to be done with case law except to scrap it. 'Scrap' is too bold a word. If I may say so without disrespect, it is timidity and not boldness that has warped the attitude of the criminal appeal judges. They have no ambition to tackle the defects of case law. Their policy seems to be to put up, with as good a grace as they can, with those they have got and to try not to create any more.

To my mind this attitude involves a number of misconceptions grouped together in such a way that one leads to another. The first of them that I shall consider is the misconception that all that the judges have to do to dissipate case law is, so to speak, to turn off the gas. This is not so. That will just create a vacuum which other gases will rush in to fill, for it is unnatural for the exercise of power to be left unregulated. Even when power is concentrated in an autocrat, he will have neither the time nor the inclina-

---

[1] Its abolition was recommended by the Criminal Law Revision Committee in 1972 (Cmnd. 4991, para 185), but the rule remains.

tion to think out every case afresh; he will make his own rules. When power is diffused, even when the diffusion is only among the servants of the auto-crat, rules become essential to efficiency, if not to justice; a system has to be created. When Parliament grants what seems to be absolute power to a minister, it is only a matter of months before a system is created for its exercise, and rules and precedents laid down. Government departments work in secrecy and need not disclose their system or publish their rules. Judges work in the open and must publish. Those who have to obey the law have a right, and those who administer it have a need, to demand that judges should in similar cases say similar things and say them publicly. Wit-ness the Judges' Rules.

You may have noticed that *R.* v. *Turnbull* said nothing at all about the third recommendation of the Committee, the one designed to end the prac-tice of leaving the admissibility of dock identifications entirely to the trial judge. On 27 May 1976 the Attorney-General announced in the House of Commons[1] that a Crown witness would not normally be asked to make a dock identification unless he had previously identified the accused at a parade. While formally this applied only to cases conducted by the Director of Public Prosecutions, the Attorney was in effect setting the practice for all prosecutions. So when in the future objection is taken at the trial to a dock identification, the judge may be asked to uphold the objection on the ground that rules made by the Attorney-General have not been complied with. Likewise a judge may be asked to uphold an objection on the ground that they were yielding against their better judgment to the implied threat by the Home Secretary in the form of advice to the police, have not been followed. The judges are losing control. They seem to prefer—I think re-grettably—to have procedural rules settled by anybody rather than by them-selves, and if not by the legislature, then by the executive. They do not by refusing to make case law escape fetters. They simply leave the forging to others in the hope—presumably, but without any guarantee—that they will be consulted about their size and shape.

It is not only those who have to administer justice who need rules to follow. Those who are subject to the law, though they may complain of its quirks—and even in the agony of defeat of its asininity—want, I believe, in their heart of hearts to be governed by laws and not by men. Am I right? For to the contrary of this belief there can be traced from *Cooper* in 1969 through *Dougherty* in 1974 to *Turnbull* in 1976 the sentiment that what the public really wants is to look to judges rather than to juries for their protection, for the judges to get away as far as possible from the constraints of the law

[1] Hansard H.C. vol. 912 c. 115; also printed in Archbold under para. 1350.

and to try cases by 'feel' and by 'quality' and to do things in their own
way and in their own time which the public is not necessarily to hear
about. If judges are to try cases on quality and feel rather than by analysis and the application of a rule, the public will have to rely on the judges
as individuals being men of quality and men to be trusted accordingly.
Judgment by feel is quintessentially government by men and not by
laws.

I do believe that our judges are men of high quality and that they deserve
a high measure of trust. This is my fundamental belief, and because it can
be briefly stated, because I am going to introduce two qualifications of it,
and because to qualify takes longer than to state, it should not be taken to
be diminished.

The first qualification is that the judges themselves are too complacent
about their qualities and about the esteem in which they are held. Quality
equal to theirs is not exceptional in British life. My own experience equips
me to give as much praise to the higher ranks in the civil service and in
journalism, and no doubt there are others. Whether these others are all as
complacent I do not know; probably not, for, as I have already suggested,
self-confidence is a judicial necessity. But it is necessary to mention here
judicial complacence, since the *Turnbull* judgment displays such an astonish-
ing amount of it. Consider its history.

Long after everyone else had been convinced that identification evidence,
and dock identification in particular, demanded special treatment and the
imposition of a uniform rule, the judges persisted in thinking that it did
not. When in 1976 they abandoned the position which they had affirmed
only three years before in *R.* v. *Long*, they did not even trouble to overrule
formally their earlier decision,[1] let alone to explain to the public why they
had changed their minds. Inevitably they left the public with the impression
that they were yielding against their better judgement to the implied threat
of a statutory rule which they would find even more irksome than case law.
No doubt this is the sort of tactical misfortune that can occur in the development of any form of institutional life and it would not be sensible to suppose
that the English judiciary is exempt from it. What marks it as an excess
of complacency is, first, that they should assume that an *ipse dixit*—a thing
done in their own way and in their own time—says all that needs to be said;
and secondly, their apparent belief that *R.* v. *Turnbull* was a case in which
they could appropriately proclaim their own sagacity and their conviction
that the future handling of a problem which they had ignored for so long

---

[1] This is the only case I know of an appellate court overruling one of its own decisions without
mentioning it, except for the purpose of a complimentary reference to another aspect of it.

could now be left exclusively in their hands. It is with this sort of utterance that the judiciary gives hostages to its critics.[1]

The second qualification is that the respect is for the judiciary as an institution and not, with rare exceptions, for judges individually. It depends therefore upon the continued acceptance by the judges of the traditions which characterize the judiciary as an institution. There is nothing uncommon about this. The reverence for the British Navy, for example, at its highest in the early part of the century, was never personally attributable to the Lords of the Admiralty. We listen to a bishop because he expounds a doctrine or a morality in which we believe or at the least respect; when he takes to expounding his personal views, he loses authority. So we respect judges as expositors of the law and practice of justice and not primarily as assessors of quality; we respect them as men who work by precedent and not by the pricking of their thumbs.

Another profound misconception is to think that judges can do things in their own way and present the consequences to a public which accepts that it is theirs not to reason why. I have said that if judges 'turn off the tap' of case law, they will create a vacuum which will be filled from other sources. But I have also said that they have only one effective way of turning off the tap and that is by ceasing to give reasons for their judgments. If they take this course they will, in a broad sense of the word, be acting unconstitutionally. The powers which are entrusted to them are given to them on the condition that they use them judicially, which means among other things that, where possible, they give their reasons. This is one of the vital distinctions between administrative and judicial decisions. The courts themselves, exercising their power of judicial review, are beginning to hold that when administrators have a duty to act quasi-judicially, as when they are interfering with the rights of the subject, they must give their reasons. It is impossible for the judges themselves not to do likewise.

The judicial function is not just to render a decision. It is also to explain it, wherever explanation is possible, in words which will carry the conviction of its rightness to the reasonable man whom in his mind the judge should always be addressing. In its purest form, which inevitably is rare, it should lack the personal element; it should be simply an exposition of how the law affects the facts of a particular case. Such an exposition cannot help being case law. A judiciary which fails to make case law in this sense sentences

---

[1] One of Junius's criticisms of the King's Bench under Lord Mansfield was that 'the judge, instead of consulting strictly the law of the land, refers only to the wisdom of the court, and to the purity of his own conscience'. See Sir W. Holdsworth, *A History of English Law*, Oxford University Press, Oxford, 7th edn. 1956, vol. 1, p. 467.

itself to extinction. For the failure would destroy the claim that judges must be lawyers. Men and women are not made judges simply because they can 'detect the specious, the irrelevant and that which is intended to deceive'. There are many disciplines which train men to do that. There are many types who can administer orderly-room justice in a minimum of words. It is comparatively easy to decide what is just in the particular circumstances of a case and to say Guilty or Not Guilty as jurymen do, according to whether the stuff is quality or shoddy. This is justice, but without the lawyer it is not justice according to law. What the lawyer is uniquely trained to do is to produce the just decision out of the law and to expound the reasons for it in terms that conform with the law and add to it. This is justice according to law and, if it is not what is wanted, lawyers are not needed. There are always plenty of people who would like to get rid of them.

In an earlier lecture I have tried to show the effect which the formula 'safe and satisfactory' has had on judicial consideration of the jury's verdict. It has had an effect also on the judicial attitude to case law. It is under its auspices that the movement for judging cases by the feel has prospered: in their search for quality judges are not to be tripped up by case law.

I agree that there has been an excess of case law and that some of it can with the judicious use of the 'safe and satisfactory' formula be got rid of. Trial by jury requires the procedural law to be more elaborate and detailed than is necessary for trial by judge alone. The semi-finality of a verdict which can be subjected to only a limited review makes it necessary to guard against the danger of a jury being misled. The material that reaches them must be strictly controlled and their deliberations must be directed into the right channels. They must, for example, be accurately directed on what evidence is capable of amounting to corroboration and what is not. The inflexibilities and technicalities of this section of the law have been criticized recently in two reports.[1] Had the Act of 1907 been interpreted to permit what one might call post-verdict correction, some of the case law on this and other topics would have been unnecessary.

The individual judge must be left with enough discretion to decide in the light of the circumstances everything that cannot be justly settled by general rule. It has been the difficult task of appellate judges to divide their province from his by deciding what ground should be cultivated and what should be left wild. It may well be that an excess of caution, justifiable when there was only a limited power of review, has resulted in too much land being tilled, fenced by appellate dicta, and signposted, too many notices about keeping off the grass, altogether too much planning. Undoubtedly

[1] *C.L.R.C. Eleventh Report*, Cmnd. 4991, para. 180; *Identification Report*, paras. 4.36 and 4.67.

where there is a complete power of review less formality is possible, but not a return to the desert.

'Safe and satisfactory' are words that can be put to good use, but they are also insidious words. They must be kept under control. The control will be lost unless appellate judges constantly remind themselves of two things. The first is that they are not words intended to transfer to the judge the power and function of the jury. These remain intact. The satisfaction of the judge is not a substitute for the satisfactory verdict, but a requirement added to it.

Let me look at this for a moment in a wider perspective. The administration of justice is a matter of balance and adjustment. We should like of course to have a system in which we could say that all the criminals are condemned and all the innocent acquitted, but we know that this is unattainable. We ought constantly to be overhauling the system to see that we have the balance as well adjusted as is humanly possible. It is notorious that the judges of the last century loaded trial procedure against the prosecution because of the excessive punishments that awaited conviction. Circumstances have changed, but the procedure has never been comprehensively reviewed. There is at present sitting a Royal Commission on Criminal Procedure, but its terms of reference direct its attention to the police investigation and the prosecution system rather than to procedure at the trial. There flourishes in the higher ranks of the police an opinion shared by some of the higher judiciary that at the trial the procedure is still too heavily loaded against the prosecution. There is much to be said for this opinion. But its acceptance would mark only the beginning of the real difficulty, which would be to reach agreement on specific measures to alter the balance.

There ought to be a comprehensive review, but it would be a mammoth undertaking. Why I call the 'safe and satisfactory' formula insidious is because it offers the lazy way out, the tempting solution. 'Do not worry *too* much,' the tempter will say, 'about the possibility of a wrong conviction, because unless it is safe the Court of Appeal will quash it. Where there is a wrong acquittal, the Court of Appeal can, alas, do nothing; so do not let us do anything to make conviction more difficult than it is.' This is the voice which says that juries need not be troubled with fresh evidence or exposed to the risk that they might fail to think things as safe and satisfactory as judges do; that if in adjusting the balance there is a choice between two tests, it is better to take the one that is less onerous for the prosecution. From the start that is made by using the formula to eliminate an excess of caution, there is an easy descent to the conclusion that all precautions and safeguards are unnecessary (and indeed unwise in that they may hinder a just conviction), since for the innocent everything will always be put right in the Court of Appeal.

The second thing to be remembered about the use of the formula is of the same sort. The satisfaction of a judge is not a substitute for law, but should be kept for use in circumstances in which there can be no rule. Those who live under the rule of law have as their entitlement the right to look first to the law for their protection and to the discretion of a judge only supplementarily in those recesses of justice into which the law is too solid to flow. This is our inheritance from ancestors who would not have understood Lord Justice Lawton when he talked of the tyranny of precedent (for indeed whose fault is it but that of the judges if precedents are allowed to tyrannize?)—but did understand the historian Gibbon when he made it the centrepiece of a famous passage that 'the discretion of the judge is the first engine of tyranny'.[1]

I believe in the jury and in case law for the same reason, that they are both restraints on judicial supremacy. I see the value of discretionary power, but where it is to be used widely, I would rather it was spread upon the diversity of the jury than concentrated in judges sitting singly or in like-minded groups; and where it is to be given to the judiciary I would rather it was used in accordance with the corporate wisdom and accounted for accordingly, than left to the individual judge to say yea or nay. I have admired immensely some individual judges, but my obedience has been not to the individual, but to a college of men working together under the discipline of the law. I have never felt the tyranny of precedent. It is a tie, certainly, but so is the rope that mountaineers use so that each gives strength and support to the others. The proper handling of precedent is part of judicial craftsmanship; the judge must learn how to use it and in particular how to identify the rare occasions when it is necessary to say that what judges have put together they can also put asunder.

So if tonight Mephistopheles were to visit me and offer me back my judicial youth in exchange for a promise to remain forever unfettered or unroped, I should refuse—even if he sweetened the offer with a pledge to consign to eternal oblivion all the speeches in *Stafford* v. *D.P.P.*

[1] The penultimate sentence in Chapter XLIV of *The Decline and Fall of the Roman Empire*, ed. Milman and Smith, John Murray, London, 1862, vol. V, p. 328.

Table of Cases

Index